D0989988

Southwest Virginia's Railroad

Kenneth W. Noe

University of Illinois Press   URBANA AND CHICAGO

Southwest Virginia's Railroad: Modernization and the Sectional Crisis

For Nancy

Publication of this work has been supported by a grant from the Oliver M. Dickerson Fund. The fund was established by Mr. Dickerson (Ph.D., Illinois, 1906) to enable the University of Illinois Press to publish selected works in American history, designated by the executive committee of the Department of History.

© 1994 by the Board of Trustees of the University of Illinois
Manufactured in the United States of America
C 5 4 3 2 1
This book is printed on acid-free paper.

Library of Congress Cataloging-in-Publication Data
Noe, Kenneth W., 1957–
Southwest Virginia's railroad : modernization and
the sectional crisis / Kenneth W. Noe.
p.   cm.
Includes bibliographical references and index.
ISBN 0-252-02070-7 (cloth : acid-free paper)
1. Railroads—Virginia—History—19th century. 2. Virginia
and Tennessee Railroad Company—History—19th
century. 3. Virginia—Economic conditions. 4. Virginia—History—
Civil War, 1861–1865.
I. Title.
HE2771.V8N64   1994
385'.09755'7—dc20   93-5632
                                                               CIP

Contents

Acknowledgments

ON A SNOWY DAY in December 1981, I found myself splitting firewood on my family's farm near Elliston, Montgomery County, Southwest Virginia. As a budding young British historian, I had given the history of my native region little thought before that day, but somehow that cold axe in my hands made me think of mountain farmers who had gone before me. Then, away in the distance, I heard a Norfolk and Western coal train rumbling toward Roanoke. How did the arrival of the trains change the lives of Southwest Virginia's farmers, I wondered. From such small beginnings a dozen years ago came this book.

In the months that followed, my friends Don Cole and Tim Thornton helped sharpen my interest in the antebellum history of Southwest Virginia. Their support has been a constant ever since. Eventually, however, it became apparent that any research beyond the cursory would require more in-depth graduate training in American history. Several of my professors and friends at Virginia Tech, notably Jay "Green" Peacock, strongly recommended study with Robert W. Johannsen of the University of Illinois. How right they were. Professor Johannsen proved the model dissertation director: exacting, learned, wise, and immeasurably kind. He is my *beau ideale* of the historian. I also owe much to Orville Vernon Burton, who took a fellow southerner under his wing and educated him in the ways of both southern history and statistics; Terry Finnegan, who took time out of his own writing to help me make sense of my crunched numbers; John Hoffmann, my employer and friend at the Illinois Historical Survey; Walter L. Arnstein; Robert M. McColley; and Winton U. Solberg, who cheerfully served on my dissertation committee; James Barrett, who first alerted me to Appalachian studies through his labor history class; and to Frederic C. Jaher, who asked me why I wasn't doing my seminar paper on Southwest Virginia when that's really what I wanted to study. I think a list so long speaks well of my second home among the cornfields.

Beyond the graduate environment, I also benefited greatly from a year spent as a temporary instructor at Berea College. Richard B. Drake, Loyal Jones, Gerald Roberts, and especially Shannon Wilson transformed that year into an informal seminar on Appalachian history. At

West Georgia College, Kenneth J. Bindas and John Ferling have provided critiques of my revisions as well as encouragement and friendship. Former department chair Steve Hanser also provided timely help in the form of release time that enabled me to complete my quantitative research. Vedat Gunay, Scott Hughes, and Stan Quinn were invaluable in helping me process census data. Michele Masucci created the excellent maps. Elmira Eidson helped in innumerable ways.

Many others also have lightened my load along the way. John C. Inscoe took an early interest in my work, supported me generously, read three versions of the manuscript, and offered a long list of suggestions that greatly improved this completed work. David Corbin read it as well and provided much-needed early encouragement and good sense. Todd Groce, David Hsiung, Gordon McKinney, and Altina Waller, all sharing my interest in the Appalachian region, thankfully compelled me to examine and sharpen various parts of my argument. Elizabeth Dunn, Joseph McCartin, and John McKivigan convinced me to examine more closely the idea of modernization, although I suspect that Elizabeth at least still will judge me too stubborn. Frank L. Klement graciously loaned me the original copy of his master's thesis on John B. Floyd when the library copy failed to surface. Mark Franklin of course was his usual self.

Archival research on this project was assisted greatly by many archivists and librarians, including Barbara Ritter Dailey and Lizz Frost of the Baker Library of Harvard Business School, William R. Erwin of Duke University, James J. Holmberg of the Filson Club of Kentucky, Stuart L. Butler of the Military Reference Branch, National Archives, Richard A. Shrader of the Southern Historical Collection, Michael Plunkett of the University of Virginia, Frances Pollard and E. Lee Shepard of the Virginia Historical Society, Glenn McMullen and Laura Katz Smith of Virginia Polytechnic Institute and State University, Conley L. Edwards of the Virginia State Library and Archives, and John A. Cuthbert of West Virginia University. Interlibrary loan librarians of Berea College, the University of Illinois, and West Georgia College, notably Nancy Farmer and Edith Hansen, were lifesavers. I am also grateful to the editors of the *North Carolina Historical Review* and *West Virginia History* for allowing me to borrow from previously published articles.

Research is an expensive as well as time-consuming activity. It was my good fortune that crucial financial assistance was provided at various points along the way by the Graduate School of the University of Illinois, Berea College's Appalachian Center, and West Georgia College's Learning Resources Committee.

Richard L. Wentworth of the University of Illinois Press expressed early interest in my topic and never wavered. Rita D. Disroe, Karen M. Hewitt, and Lisa Warne-Magro were invaluable in turning a flabby manuscript into a decent book.

Most of all I want to thank my family for putting up with me all these years. Special thanks are owed to my in-laws, Ray and Carole Wahlbrink; Emma Noe, the aunt who first encouraged my love of books; and Kenneth E. Noe, the fine man who is my father. My grandfather William Jesse Noe, union coal miner and Southwest Virginia farmer, remains as always my hero. His namesake, my son Jesse Benjamin Noe, helped me greatly by sometimes watching Sesame Street when his dad had to write, and by more often reminding me that being a father was my most important job. Two of the people most important to me, my uncle Benjamin Noe and my grandmother Thelma Noe, regrettably did not live to see this book finished. They are always in my thoughts.

Most of all, I want to thank my wife, Nancy, who first gave me the faith to return to graduate school, worked long hours while I sat at home reading my books, strained her eyes over poorly copied census returns, and put up with me generally. I have the best wife in the world, even if she *still* thinks my endnotes are too long.

Introduction

The MOUNTAINEERS left Richmond and retreated to the west quickly after the convention passed the secession ordinance. Reassembling days later in Clarksburg, Virginia's mountain unionist leaders reaffirmed their loyalty to the Union of their fathers and then called for the division of the commonwealth into two states. After Virginia voters overwhelmingly approved secession, the Second Wheeling Convention proclaimed itself the loyal "Restored" government of Virginia. Wheeling's "Virginia" legislature then promptly approved a dismemberment ordinance. After western Virginia's voters overwhelmingly approved the creation of a new state, a Third Wheeling Convention wrote a constitution. Having finally agreed with Congress to end slavery in the new state through the Willey Amendment, West Virginia entered the Union in June 1863.[1]

Almost immediately, the residents of the new state found themselves faced with an uncomfortable question: had the creation of West Virginia indeed been legal and justified? Over the years, a pro-dismemberment canon appeared to defend what had happened, an explanation that eventually was codified in Charles Henry Ambler's classic *Sectionalism in Virginia from 1776 to 1861.* A student of Frederick Jackson Turner at the University of Wisconsin, and later professor of history at West Virginia University, Ambler also added a Turnerian slant. Virginia's transmontane frontier experience, Ambler claimed, had created by 1800 an egalitarian society sharply at odds with the aristocratic east. Socially schizophrenic, Virginia lurched from one sectional crisis to another, struggles that largely concerned western Virginians reasonable demands for a more democratic state government. The events of 1861–63 thus comprised only the last phase of a lingering sickness, with dismemberment the healthy cure.[2]

Nearly a century old, Ambler's volume remains the standard discussion of pre–Civil War western Virginia. Yet it has not aged well. Beyond its Turnerian sweep, an interpretation largely superceeded or at least modified elsewhere, *Sectionalism in Virginia* all but ignores those areas of western Virginia that wanted to remain in the old state, the Panhandle and Southwest Virginia. It is in fact largely a history of *northwestern* Virginia, and while still useful in that respect, fails to adequately address sectionalism in the entire mountain west. Indeed, as historians Richard Orr Curry, Henry T. Shanks, and John Alexander Williams have noted, the antebellum and Civil War experience of Southwest Virginia calls the entire canon into question. Once allied with the Northwest, the two mountain regions clearly parted ways in the 1850s, demonstrating that there was no monolithic "West." The twenty-four counties south of Charleston largely supported Virginia's secession, sent thousands into Confederate service, and opposed their inclusion into West Virginia.[3]

What had happened to push apart the "western" regions on the eve of the Civil War? And if "East" and "West" were so incompatible, how could Southwest Virginia cast its lot with the former section? Although Ambler himself skirted the issue, his heroes, West Virginia's founding fathers, faced it head on as they grappled with the issue of drawing a southern border. At the Second Wheeling Convention, delegate Dennis B. Dorsey, to point to one example, opposed the addition of the southwestern counties into the new state as an "'unnatural connection.'" Southwest Virginia sympathized with eastern Virginia, "their interests are the same as hers. They lie along the line of Tennessee and Kentucky, connected with Eastern Virginia by railroads."[4] At the constitutional convention of the following November, Peter G. Van Winkle warned that "we go no further south . . . for obvious reasons. We leave all the counties in the valley through which runs the Virginia and Tennessee railroad."[5]

John S. Carlile, at that time the driving force behind the new state movement, also was the most vocal opponent of including Southwest Virginia, which he rightly saw as a tactic to derail the new state's creation. In June, at the Second Wheeling Convention, Carlile declared that: "in a political sense, there is no West, and never has been, save the Northwest. . . . look at the lines of improvement in Western Virginia outside the Northwest. Where do they lead? Where is the railroad that penetrates Monroe and Greenbrier and the whole Southwest? It is the road that runs from Richmond. . . . All the rest and residue of the State is bound by iron bands and commercial ties to the Eastern part of the State, and can never have any commercial interests or intercourse with us."[6]

He later added that "we never can have business relations with the rest of the State. The Southwestern part has its railroads, turnpikes, and canals penetrating through its valleys and mountains and leading to the capital of the State."[7] In the end, West Virginia's final southern boundary was decided less by geography or a sense of "the West" than by the occupation of soldiers in blue uniforms. Carlile's "iron bands and commercial ties"—the Virginia and Tennessee Railroad and the closer economic and ideological relations between Southwest Virginia and Richmond that followed in its wake—had in the view of the Wheeling delegates irrevocably divided the West and made the Southwest too much like the East.[8]

Since the 1950s, many social scientists and historians have used the term *modernization* to describe just such transformations. Richard D. Brown, perhaps the best known advocate of the concept of modernization among American historians, described it as the entire range of changes that produced "movement in the direction of the modern ideal type." More than just industrialization, technological advancement, urbanization, or "progress," although all of these factors were vital components, modernization also encompassed changing values and world views. Rural Americans suddenly connected to wider markets through transportation technology, eventually railroads, embraced not only the wider market but also the wider world. Cosmopolitanism, egalitarianism, and secularization—all were modernization's by-products. So was the Civil War, which Brown interpreted as a conflict between the modernizing North and a South where premodern traditions remained dominant.[9]

Brown, and modernization, had their critics, however. Indeed, by the late 1970s, criticism of modernization grew so vocal that historians openly wondered if the concept would, and should, survive at all. Opponents cited a litany of weaknesses: modernization was ethnocentrically Western, if not imperialistic or conservatively pro-American; it exaggerated change over continuity and played down the latter; it exaggerated consensus over conflict; it was teleological if not downright celebratory; definitions of modernization varied so greatly from scholar to scholar that one could hardly speak on any real theory at all; and in the end it added very little to scholarly discourse anyway. Yet, the concept did not disappear. As Raymond Grew, one of its most thoughtful critics, put it, "a kind of common sense makes one hesitate to throw the concept out. In the last two centuries, something similar happened to most of the world—in technology obviously, through economics clearly, but also in politics and social organization." "Modernization" ultimately described it better than anything else suggested. What Grew as well as Peter N. Stearns suggested was a narrower, more exact focus. Studies of modernization, they concluded, should concentrate only on discrete regions of Western society during the last two centuries, should be as specific as possible in demonstrating how people adapted—or refused to adapt—to catalysts for change, should utilize statistical comparisons when possible, and should strive for neutrality in presentation, noting that modernization did not translate automatically into benefits for all. In this more constricted, well-defined sense, modernization could function as a convenient shorthand for a plethora of related changes in recent Western society.[10]

Among American historians, scholars of the nineteenth-century South often have best followed this advice, and as a result modernization remains a topic for debate among the region's students. In so doing, historians such as William L. Barney, Bill Cecil-Fronsman, Paul D. Escott, Lacy K. Ford, Steven Hahn, James Oakes, John T. Schlotterbeck and Allen W. Trelease have firmly rejected much of Brown's model, including the assertion that the South and modernization were oxymorons. Instead, a consensus is emerging that in the crucial 1850s many parts of the South began to modernize rapidly, albeit in fits and starts and in the face of significant resistance. Construction of the southern railroad network particularly encouraged farmers to warily enter the market economy. Some benefited as a result, but this southern modernization ruined others, who lost their increasingly highly priced—and highly taxed—land and fell into tenancy or day labor, the latter often in the South's growing urban areas. Modernization sometimes also brought the expansion of slavery. While the peculiar institution hardly can be described as a "modern ideal type" or "progressive," the fact remains that market expansion in the South often meant increasing the labor force through slave labor. Barney also has linked southern modernization to the onset of war, arguing that the rising sectional crisis offered both a scapegoat for the bewildering, anxiety-producing changes—Yankees—and the only viable opportunity remaining for sons to prove their manhood to their demanding parents and neighbors.[11]

Southwest Virginia's experiences in the years 1848–65 support this growing consensus. All the factors described—a transportation revolution, the shift to a market economy, economic marginalization, the death and rebirth of communities, a challenge to traditional economic ideas, slavery expansion, support for secession—were also present in 1850s Southwest Virginia. Some may find this surprising, as Southwest Virginia was located in the one part of the South usually acknowledged as the antithesis of "modern," the southern mountains. That part of the South, known in the popular mind as "Appalachia," has been depicted until recently as the last bastion of traditional ways. The idea of antebellum Appalachian modernization certainly would have seemed ridiculous to shapers of the familiar mountain stereotype such as William Goodell Frost, who viewed southern mountaineers as living museum pieces, "our contemporary ancestors," or Horace Kephart, who saw mountain history from the American Revolution to the Civil War as a period of "deterioration" during which increasingly ignorant and isolated mountaineers steadily descending into shiftlessness and savagery.[12]

Recent scholarship, thankfully, has rejected and demolished the stereotypical "backward Appalachia" interpretation for good, but scholars have not agreed on what to bring in its stead. Ronald D Eller, who more than most helped shape the new "revisionist" interpretation of Appalachian history, was yet another scholar who utilized the concept of modernization. He identified it as a process that began only in the 1880s with the appearance of outsiders eager to exploit the land's coal and timber resources. In Eller's view, mountain society before 1860 was decidedly premodern, and the Virginia and Tennessee Railroad had "only marginal impact upon interior mountain counties."[13]

The problem with Eller's interpretation is that all the factors pointed to as post-1880 Appalachian modernization in sum—including the advent of outside corporate control, close alliances between the outsiders and local political leaders, industrialization, integration into the national market economy, urbanization, and the weakening of traditional, co-operative forms of living and working—were active in Southwest Virginia and other parts of the southern mountains well before the Civil War. As a result, a different interpretation of antebellum Appalachia has started to emerge. In general, that newer tendency has been to describe the region not as an isolated Jeffersonian paradise soon to be lost but rather to reaffirm its warts-and-all southerness, which included the South's antebellum modernization. Quite unique in many ways, all in all the region still provided only a variation of southern life. Durwood Dunn, John C. Inscoe, and Gene Wilhelm, Jr., for example, have demonstrated that despite the physical barriers mountains presented, real isolation was rare and contacts with the outside world many and regular. Along with Robert D. Mitchell and Paul Salstrom, Dunn, Inscoe, and Wilhelm also have located early commercial involvement in the market, although they still debate the degree of that involvement, and have shown how that involvement grew over time. While the gap between rich and poor was not as wide in the cotton South, class differences clearly existed and were growing more apparent. Inscoe, Frederick A. Bode, Donald E. Ginter, Ralph Mann, and Mary Beth Pudup have shown how the mountain south had its elites, landowning yeomen, tenants, laborers, and its desperately poor. It also had its slaves. While the mountains never contained the sheer numbers of slaves held in the deep South, Inscoe again as well as James B. Murphy have noted how the institution nonetheless was important to the region's economy and its psyche, and becoming more so in the decade before war. Finally, Dwight B. Billings, Kathleen M. Blee, David Corbin, Gordon B. McKinney, Louis Swanson, Altina Waller, and Paul J. Weingartner have shown how antebellum modernization helped shape the massive industrialization that began in the 1880s. Modernization did not strike a primitive culture in the 1880s, then; it began much earlier. The 1850s marked a period when modernization's pulse decidedly quickened.[14]

A discussion of Southwest Virginia in the 1850s, should not only reinforce the idea of antebellum southern modernization but also confirm the "southerness" of Appalachia, a characteristic missing in the popular mind since late nineteenth-century northern missionaries in the hills discovered that it hindered fund-raising. The scars left by the Civil War had not yet healed; few New England Yankees cared to send their money to former rebels. Thus, the solution was to sweep Appalachia's secessionists and Johnny Rebs under the rug.[15] Yet they too were part and parcel of the region's southerness, especially in Southwest Virginia, which surely was the part of Appalachia most devoted to the Confederacy. Rather than the unionist monolith many have depicted, the southern mountain region in reality was seriously and tragically divided between unionists and secessionists of varying degrees of loyalty. Awakened class conflict, rising opposition to the Confederacy, a bloody guerrilla war, and violent depredations were the result, as Martin Crawford, Paul D. Escott, W. Todd Groce, Mann, Phillip Shaw Paludan, and Waller have graphically proved. Southwest Virginia's antebellum and wartime experiences, then, generally little known despite the continuing avalanche of Civil War literature, promise to tell us more even more than the fact that the South, including the mountain South, modernized in the decade before the Civil War. They also help us to better understand the Civil War, and answer century-old questions about why there was secession and a war at all.[16]

Historians of course have debated these issues since Appomattox. Veterans and their children defended their causes as righteous and looked upon the enemy as evil, the so-called devil thesis. Secession thus was either a moral solution to a difficult problem or part of a satanic conspiracy. The twentieth century brought with it historians with less personal baggage who nonetheless blamed the South's craving for slavery, if only to maintain white supremacy. Others, notably Charles A. Beard, William E. Dodd, and Frank L. Owsley, interpreted secession as the perhaps understandable response of planters and yeomen farmers who saw control of the government and their livelihoods shifting to the industrial North. Only out of the union could they protect their economic interests. Then came the "repressible conflict" school, including Phillips to an extent, Avery O. Craven, and James G. Randall, who blamed the war on a "blundering generation" of demagogic politicians who stirred up passions best left cool. They were answered by "nationalists," such as John Hope Franklin, Samuel Eliot Morrison, and Arthur M. Schlesinger, Jr., who once again stressed the morality of the northern attack on slavery and the South's immoral refusal to give up the institution. W. J. Cash also blamed the South, particularly its tendencies toward fantasy, romanticism, and violence. In the 1950s and 1960s, gifted writers like Bruce Catton and Allan Nevins stressed slavery as the main cause, but also synthesized earlier interpretations into a popular whole. Also important in that period were Roland G. Osterweis's argument that the South's romantic cult of chivalry spurred southerners to make a defiant, romantic gesture, and Kenneth M. Stampp's contention that the slavery issue was a symbol for deeper political and economic motivations.[17]

Debate has not cooled in recent years. Many scholars, noting that fire eaters usually were in the minority and, in William W. Freehling's words, "at bay," have wondered how they came to set the argument during the secession winter. F. N. Boney saw secession as a panacea that after years of turmoil finally looked attractive. Daniel W. Crofts blamed the Lincoln Administration for at least the Upper South's secession. Patience and concessions might have allowed unionists time to bring their fellow citizens to their senses. Michael P. Johnson saw secession in Georgia as a tool of the elite used to maintain the hegemony of slaveholders, control threatened by Lincoln and the Free Soil ideology. Bertram Wyatt-Brown has interpreted secession as the "honorable" response to the perceived insults of the North by a people touchy to the point of violence about such things.[18]

Many others, however, have looked to modernization, a fact that again confirms that the concept has not lived beyond its usefulness. In addition to major syntheses such as James M. McPherson's *Battle Cry of Freedom* and Phillip Shaw Paludan's *"A People's Contest,"* which in many ways return to Brown's industrial North versus agrarian South model, historians of Virginia and the larger mountain South, notably David Goldfield, James M. Woods, Curry, Groce, Inscoe, and again Paludan all have noted that secession sentiments at least in part could be determined by the degree of commercial connection to the southern capitalist market. In a sense, both Northwest Virginia and Southwest Virginia, as well as the commercial minded of Arkansas, Western North Carolina, and East Tennessee, unloaded their ideology as well as their goods off the train. Not only did southern modernization and slavery go hand in hand, then, but the determination to defend slavery and the broader economic and social system it held on its back joined them. Linked to Richmond's markets, Southwest Virginians also were linked in 1861 to Richmond's cause.[19]

This is not to imply that modernization led to the Civil War in and of itself. Far from it. For an event as complicated as the American Civil War, there could be no one cause. Slavery in and of itself cannot be ignored as the burr under the nation's saddle, a constant source of sectional strife and hard feelings. Certainly from our vantage point it was an immoral practice as well that begged to be destroyed. Moreover, the South *was* more agrarian in orientation and did feel threatened by the much more industrial North's factories, labor unions, and tariffs. Having spent several years studying John B. Floyd and Henry A. Wise, among others, I question the quality of overall political leadership in the 1850s, figures such as Lincoln to the contrary. Honor too was a major factor; Southwest Virginians bristled at the North's insults throughout the secession crisis and feared that their reputations and, for some, their masculinity as well stood in the balance. And finally, one must note that the region only rushed to the Stars and Bars after Fort Sumter and Lincoln's subsequent call for volunteers. All of these factors will be discussed as part of the matrix. With all this said, however, the fact remains that the leading factor convincing most Southwest Virginians to don gray and most Northwest Virginians blue in 1861 was the divergence among western Virginians caused by their railroads: where they ran and what they carried, and how economic change caused by railroad building shaped ideology. The "iron bands and commercial ties" had created an iron road to secession.

The monograph that follows amplifies on all these points. Chapter 1 concerns the political as well as economic history of transportation in Southwest Virginia and the Virginia and Tennessee Railroad specifically from its origins to completion. One will note that while many Southwest Virginians expressed apathy toward the project, a handful of influential outsiders and eastern Virginia backed the road as a tool for their own economic expansion and a way to unite Virginia and the entire South in support of slavery and a southern Confederacy. Chapters 2, 3, and 4 deal respectively with the railroad's "modern" fruits: a shift toward market agriculture, the growth of industries, towns, and tourism, and a new commitment to slave labor. Chapter 5 begins in 1851 with Southwest Virginians ready to secede from Virginia and ends ten years later with them abandoning the United States. Economics, honor, slavery, and a political rapprochement between East and Southwest that paralleled the railroad figure as important reasons

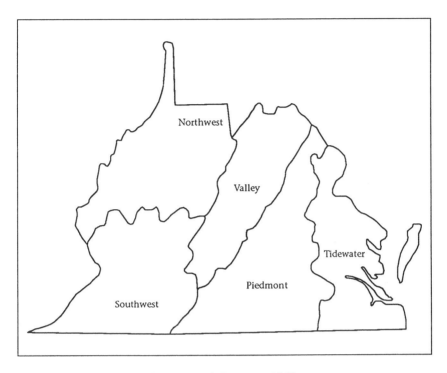

Map 1. The five grand divisions of Virginia, 1860.

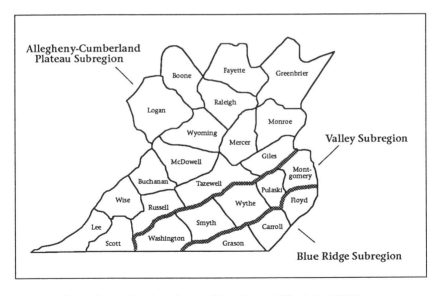

Map 2. Counties and subregions of Southwest Virginia, 1860.

for the change. Chapters 6 and 7 follow the region's war from the heady days of 1861 through the war-weariness and deprivation the war brought and on to the final collapse. A brief Epilogue ties up loose ends and sets the stage for Southwest Virginia's postwar history.

Two final points should be made. One is explaining my definition of Southwest Virginia, which may not satisfy everyone but is that devised by the state in 1860, when it divided the "Trans-Allegheny" administrative "Grand Division" in half. As Maps 1 and 2 illustrate, Southwest Virginia contained nine counties that now essentially form southern West Virginia: Boone, Fayette, Greenbrier, Logan, McDowell, Mercer, Monroe, Raleigh, and Wyoming. Conversely, it did *not* include five counties that modern Southwest Virginians, including myself, would be tempted to add: Botetourt, Craig, Franklin, Patrick, and Roanoke. These were placed just to the east in the "Piedmont" Grand Division. The Southwest Virginia counties not already named were Buchanan, Carroll, Floyd, Giles, Grayson, Lee, Montgomery, Pulaski, Russell, Scott, Smyth, Tazewell, Washington, Wise, and Wythe. I have used this definition throughout.[20]

One will also note that many conclusions are based on quantitative analyses of the 1850 and 1860 manuscript and published censuses. At times, samples taken from three counties, Floyd, Raleigh, and Washington, will stand in for the entire region, each representing one of Southwest Virginia's three geographic subregions. The reasons for choosing these counties are explained in the Methodology section.

1

"The Railroad Is Completed to Bristol"

ON OCTOBER 4, 1856, John E. Gilmer, a twenty-year-old Southwest Virginian, wrote his parents a letter. Gilmer was enrolled at Emory and Henry College near Abingdon, the region's first institution of higher learning, and like nearly every other student since he was out of money and homesick. "I never wanted to hear from home so bad since I have been here as I do now," he begged, "*wright. Wright, wright soon.*" Perhaps he exaggerated. He had after all waited a month to respond to his parents' last letter; his evenings were filled with preaching and social engagements, and only days before he had participated in an extraordinary event. "The railroad is completed to Bristol," he wrote, "and they had a great celebration at that place the day before yesterday. About fifty or sixty of the Students went to the celebration and I was one of the number."[1]

After decades of disappointment, Southwest Virginia finally had a railroad. The engine "J. Robin McDaniel," named for the line's president, pulled the first Virginia and Tennessee Railroad train to travel the 204 miles from Lynchburg to the twin towns of Goodson, Virginia, and Bristol, Tennessee, themselves creations of the railroad. It ran over two cows and derailed before arriving late in Goodson on the evening of October 1, where over a thousand well-wishers waited. Gilmer rode down the next morning, overwhelmed by the speed of the locomotive, which he estimated to be an incredible twenty-five miles per hour. When he arrived, cannons were roaring, and two bands added to the cacophony. Speakers assured the lively crowd, now swelled to eight thousand, that the completed V&T made Virginia's economic and political renaissance a certainty.[2] One, Carroll County planter William H. Cook, proclaimed the commonwealth awakened "like a *giant* from his sleep!"[3]

A world away in New York City, the celebrated northern travel writer Frederick Law Olmsted increasingly expressed skepticism. In *A Journey in the Seaboard States,* also completed in 1856, Olmsted hoped for the best. "Rail-roads and guano seem, just now, to give life and improvement to Virginia," he wrote. Activity, punctuality, and intelligence should follow, as would better prices for imported and exported goods.[4] *A Journey in the Backcountry in the Winter of 1853–54* painted a more pessimistic portrait. An account of a trip that had taken Olmsted through southwest Virginia, it appeared in 1860. Virginia's railroads, Olmsted now concluded, were nothing more than pathetic panaceas. "No one has any gumption," he complained. "In every neighborhood, I found hope to center in something to come from without. A railroad or canal . . . a copper or coal mine, or salt works." Virginia, he concluded, would never advance until it took a realistic look at itself and the institution that held it back: slavery.[5]

In retrospect, it is apparent that both railroad boosters like William H. Cook and northern critics like Olmsted saw a part of the picture, the portion they wanted to see, but not the whole. In many ways, the reality of the railroad exceeded its supporters' hopes. The V&T did hasten the commercialization of regional agriculture, contributed to industrialization and town development, and breathed new life into African American slavery, just as its boosters said it would. As a result, Southwest Virginia in 1860 was a very different place than it had been ten years before. Yet, as Olmsted predicted, it did not bring about paradise on earth. Indeed, the railroad forged the final links between the region and the wider South, including eastern Virginia, just in time to drag Southwest Virginia into a civil war fought to defend the institution Olmsted begged Virginians to confront. In that war, class cleavages, already extant but widened as a result of the railroad, would fester and ultimately explode. Southwest Virginia would confront the postwar world divided physically between two states, impoverished, embittered, and bereft of many of its sons, like John Gilmer, who died in the war's early months. All of that, however, was in the future on October 2, 1856, a day for celebrations.[6]

To comprehend Southwest Virginia, and its railroad, one must begin with geography. From the Atlantic Ocean roughly two hundred miles inland to the Blue Ridge Mountains, antebellum Virginia was well drained and relatively flat, rising gently above sea level from east to west. Past the fall line, which divided the coastal "Tidewater" from the central "Piedmont," the landscape grew more rolling but hardly mountainous. The Blue Ridge thus signaled an abrupt topographical change, the landscape suddenly transformed into a realm of high, wooded, hazy mountains divided by rich, deep valleys. This was "western Virginia." As Map 1 illustrates, Southwest Virginia, the southern half of the so-called "Trans-Allegheny Grand Division," stretched from the Blue Ridge westward to Kentucky, and northward from the North Carolina and Tennessee borders to the Kanawha River.

The geography of Southwest Virginia itself was not uniform. As Map 2 shows, three distinct geographical subregions comprised the whole. In the roughly triangular southeast corner of the region, the Blue Ridge Mountains at their most rugged passed through copper-rich Carroll, Floyd, and Grayson counties toward North Carolina. To the north and west of the Blue Ridge subregion, the "upper," or southern, section of the Valley of Virginia extended diagonally in a northeast-southwest direction to East Tennessee. More a series of interconnected valleys divided by high ridges, the valley subregion nonetheless offered fertile bottom land to farmers and easy transportation to travelers. The counties eventually located there, Montgomery, Pulaski, Wythe, Smyth, and Washington from east to west, were the first settled, the most populous, and the most commercially oriented, owing to their proximity to the region's main thoroughfare, the Valley Road. Finally, the Allegheny-Cumberland Plateau extended northward from the valley to the Kanawha and westward to the Cumberland Mountains and the Bluegrass State. In this, the largest of the three subregions, the mountains, generally, were steeper and sharper than those of the Blue Ridge, the valleys more narrow and irregularly oriented, and the soils thinner, with the exceptions the rich glades located at the heads of streams. As a result, the plateau was less conducive to agriculture and settlement. Indeed, as late as 1850, many sections of the plateau remained unoccupied. Two hallmarks of this subregion were its huge virgin forests, which supported an amazing array of hardwoods and softwoods, and its rich mineral deposits beneath the soil. Gypsum, iron ore, lead, manganese, salt, sandstone, and especially coal lay largely unexploited. In some locales, hot springs bubbled to the surface. By 1860, the plateau subregion contained sixteen counties.[7]

The first documented exploratory party encountered the New River in 1671, but settlement lagged until the 1730s and 1740s. The mountainous topography certainly was one reason, but it would be incorrect to regard this as paramount. As Gene Wilhelm, Jr. demonstrated, mountains did not lead invariably to isolation; they were not walls. Other factors were just as important. Southwest Virginia's rivers, for example, hindered the westward movement. With one exception, the region's rivers all flowed north or west into the Ohio-Mississippi River system. The exception, the Roanoke, crossed the southern

Piedmont and then dipped into North Carolina, finally entering the ocean at Albermarle Sound. Significant Native American opposition also delayed white settlement. While rarely establishing towns, the Cherokee, Iroquois, and Shawnee claimed the region for hunting and as a transportation corridor until roughly 1770, when a series of treaties lessened the Indian threat.[8]

Getting from place to place in early Southwest Virginia was a major undertaking. Buffalo paths and Indian trails formed the region's first roads. First the colonial and later the early state governments left road improvement matters to county courts and profit-seeking entrepreneurs. The end result was a hodgepodge of badly constructed and poorly maintained roads. Many Virginians, notably Thomas Jefferson, John Marshall, and George Washington, understood the system's deficiencies, but the state did little to correct the situation until after the War of 1812. In the first flush of perceived victory, Virginia legislators, like their fellows in Washington, reconsidered their attitudes toward internal improvements. The financial promise of western trade, coupled with a fear of losing that trade to other states, finally convinced the General Assembly to act.[9]

In February 1816, the legislature created the Fund for Internal Improvements and, to supervise the fund, the Board of Public Works. The act also empowered the board to employ an engineer, conduct surveys, and recommend projects for state aid, to be two-fifths of the total funds necessary. Later, the state's percentage grew to three-fifths. Internal improvement companies, chartered by the legislature, were expected to raise the difference through private investment. The act further divided the state officially into four "grand divisions," Tidewater, Piedmont, Valley, and Trans-Allegheny. The last named was divided into Northwest and Southwest only in 1860.[10]

Fiscally conservative, the potentially powerful board nonetheless drew fire from the first in the Tidewater and Piedmont, especially after the Panic of 1819. The sole improvement with any widespread support in the east was the James River and Kanawha Canal, designed to connect eastern Virginia with the Ohio Valley. It did have supporters in the plateau subregion of Southwest Virginia, particularly in the Greenbrier Valley. That area benefited greatly from roads built to connect the Kanawha River to the James. A notable example was the Kanawha Turnpike, which ran from the Valley town of Covington to the mouth of the Big Sandy River.[11]

Aside from the Greenbrier region, the board soon lost its western support as well, but for vastly different reasons. Viewed as a bureaucratic monster in the conservative east, the board seemed painfully inadequate west of the mountains. Higher construction costs, the result of the rugged mountain terrain, as well as a shortage of banks and capital, stymied transmontane construction projects. Western Virginians asked the board to make exceptions to the two-fifths rule and either increase the state's subscription or make projects entirely public works. The board refused, and continued to concentrate on the canal. The board's favoritism made the "ditch" an unpopular symbol of what the western counties perceived as their second-class status within the commonwealth. A public work from 1820 until 1835, the canal nearly bankrupted the state.[12]

By then, mountain internal improvements had acquired critical symbolic overtones. The 1829–30 Constitutional Convention was the climax of nearly fifty years of campaigning for reforms in representation and suffrage. Representation in Virginia since the 1630s had been based on the county, each receiving two delegates. As eastern counties were smaller and more numerous, that area controlled the majority of seats. Reformers wanted to change this system to a more equitable one based on white population, the so-called white basis. Likewise, they wanted to broaden the electorate from the minority eligible under a freehold system to universal white manhood suffrage. At first, the controversy was hardly the sectional struggle Charles Henry Ambler later depicted. Reformers campaigned in the upper Potomac counties of the Tidewater, the southwestern Piedmont, the eastern shore, and among the artisans and mechanics of the eastern cities as well as in the west.[13]

When the convention began in October 1829, however, it quickly degenerated into an sectional shouting match. Many of the state's fears and prejudices swept to the fore, as the debates ultimately concerned the future of slavery as much as they did constitutional questions. Who would rule Virginia, slaveholders or nonslaveowners? During the debates, mountain internal improvements came to be equated with opposition to slavery.[14] Eastern conservatives branded their opponents as Yankeefied abolitionists and would-be tyrants, who would destroy slavery in their obsession with state-financed internal improvements. John W. Green of the Piedmont's Culpeper County, for example, proclaimed that the western delegates had "one great object of desire, and the whole history of our State Legislature will prove it, and that is the construction of roads and canals." Once in power, mountain Virginians would "tax the lowlands for the benefit of western interests." That heavy taxation, Green claimed, threatened the financial survival of planters already beset with soil depletion and a collapsing tobacco market. Bankrupt planters would mean the end of the entire slavery system.[15]

In the end, the convention concluded infelicitously. With the votes of wavering Piedmont delegates, the majority approved a plan that reapportioned seats on the basis of the 1820 census. Transmontane Virginia gained thirteen legislative seats, but all but two went to Valley counties. To add insult to injury, the new constitution prohibited reapportionment at a later date. Reformers faced similar disappointments in regard to universal suffrage. Indeed, little of substance separated the new document from its predecessor. The convention approved the constitution by a vote of 55 to 40, with only one Valley delegate and no Trans-Allegheny representatives voting in the affirmative. While the electorate ratified the new constitution with a vote of 26,005 to 15,666, Southwest Virginians rejected it 4,792 to 832.[16]

The Trans-Allegheny division as a whole reacted to ratification with bitterness. The angry and resentful mountaineers demanded redress. Some called for a new state of their own, and a few Virginians spoke openly of civil war, one that might spread into the backcountries of the Carolinas and Georgia. Prodded by western politicians like the new governor, John Floyd of Montgomery County, the legislature desperately turned to internal improvement legislation as a means of placating at least Southwest Virginia.[17] "A crisis is approaching," advised the *Winchester Republican.* "The northern counties demand to be separated from the state . . . the southwest counties go for a division of the state into two commonwealths. . . . prosecute the improvements called for in the southwest, and that portion of our state . . . would give up its desire for separation."[18]

The legislature listened and responded. In April 1831, the General Assembly chartered both a "South-Western Turnpike Company" and a railroad to penetrate Southwest Virginia, the Lynchburg and New River Railroad. The railroad project, however, came to nothing, collapsing abruptly the next year. Nat Turner's slave rebellion convinced slaveowner Governor Floyd that only gradual abolition could prevent additional outbreaks. Floyd also believed that emancipation would revitalize the state's stagnant economy. Careful to conceal his true feelings, Floyd called on the legislature to reconsider slavery. In January 1832, debate began. Like the recent convention, the two-month-long debate rapidly developed along sectional lines. Mountain delegates endorsed gradual, compensated emancipation while easterners espoused the status quo. Among the West's leaders was the governor's nephew, twenty-six-year-old William Ballard Preston of Montgomery County. The West's support of even a weak plan of emancipation reinforced eastern stereotypes of mountaineers as traitorous abolitionists. After beating back the challenge to slavery, eastern delegates punished their opponents by denying necessary aid to the railroad and defeating a bill generally providing state loans for railroad construction. Without state aid, the railroad project quickly collapsed.[19]

Eastern retaliation proved to be only temporary. Once tempers cooled, the legislature's cismontane majority revived its reluctant policy of purchasing Southwest Virginia's fidelity with internal improvements. Half-heartedness, however, prevented real success. Eastern legislators approached the topic grudgingly, and the results always fell short of hopes in the mountains.

One notable example was the Cumberland Gap Road. Authorized by the General Assembly of 1833–34, the completed road ran over 260 miles, from Fincastle to the Cumberland Gap. The financing derived from a combination of private and public sources, and it was an instant success, with stock drovers especially favoring the route. Not long after, however, the triumph began to sour. Squabbles between Richmond and Southwest Virginia counties over jurisdiction and maintenance, as well as outright fraud, eventually convinced the legislature that the road's benefits did not outweigh the headaches it created. In the mid-1840s, the General Assembly abandoned the road entirely to the counties. By that time, disrepair made it nearly useless.[20]

More disheartening to Southwest Virginia was the failure of a second railroad project. The 1835–36 General Assembly chartered the Lynchburg and Tennessee Railroad Company. Securing the charter was only part of the battle, as state aid was crucial if the railroad were to be built. In December 1836, Whig Governor Wyndham Robertson championed the cause of internal improvements. Robertson singled out the railroad as the state's most needed improvement, as it would connect Virginia to her sister southern states. Robertson feared also that a proposed Charleston, South Carolina, to Cincinnati railroad would siphon off the western trade he wanted to steer toward Virginia's ports. Thus, the governor called upon the legislature to construct the railroad completely from public funds. The General Assembly rejected so radical a proposal, but did vote the company two hundred thousand dollars.[21]

Despite its hopeful start, the railroad never materialized. Hardly had the ink dried on the state's subscription when the Panic of 1837 struck. New Governor David Campbell of Washington County called for a moratorium on new projects in the hope that enough state money would remain to finance existing ones. It was to no avail; the squeeze killed the railroad. Investors proved unwilling to risk private investments despite Campbell's constant urgings.[22]

Here matters stood for nearly a decade. While internal improvements for Southwest Virginia were broached from time to time, the legislature stood pat. Southwest Virginia's main connections to the outside world remained the collapsing Cumberland Gap, Kanawha, and Valley roads, the last little more than a series of independent turnpike and bridge companies of varying competence. The idea of the legislature ever authorizing a railroad for the region, according to the *Richmond Enquirer,* was "a chimerical phantasy," its few supporters drawing only ridicule.[23]

The year 1845 marked a major change in direction, with Virginia moving in the context of greater transformations across the South. Better agricultural yields and market prices stimulated a general return to prosperity. Many southerners, echoing northern counterparts, began to champion railroads as the sure way to maintain flush times. Such sentiments crystallized into a new phase of the Southern Commercial Convention movement. Originally, the movement had developed in Atlantic port cities as a result of the panic, with direct trade with Europe supported as the cure for hard times. It made only a marginal impact in Virginia. In 1845, however, the center of the convention movement shifted westward to inland cities like Memphis and New Orleans. With the shift, railroad connections between the South and West, heretofore a minor plank in convention platforms, moved to the forefront. Supporters such as J. D. B. DeBow of *DeBow's Review* envisioned railroad connections creating an economically and politically stronger south.[24]

Prosperity and the revitalized convention movement galvanized supporters of Southwest Virginia internal improvements. Residents of the region renewed their agitation for better trade outlets. Lynchburg, Norfolk, and Richmond boosters advocated routes westward as necessary for the growth and prosperity of their communities. William M. Burwell, a Valley Whig from Bedford County and Virginia's most active participant in the southern conventions, asserted the necessity of a Southwest Virginia railroad for the entire South. So did Tidewater Democrat Henry A. Wise, who argued that large-scale internal improvements, as well as educational and political reforms, would reverse Virginia's decline in status among the states and unify it in a time of increasing northern hostility.[25]

Changing opinion swept resistance aside in the General Assembly. As the 1844–45 session began, Governor James McDowell highlighted internal improvements as the best way to tighten Virginia's internal bonds. His successor, William "Extra Billy" Smith, advocated in December 1846, a railroad through Southwest Virginia and a second line to the Kanawha River as the state's most vital concerns. Smith pressed for complete state funding of these projects.[26]

The legislature responded with both turnpike and railroad initiatives. With regard to the former, it chartered and funded the South Western Turnpike to supersede the Valley and Cumberland Gap roads. The act envisioned a macadamized road running from Salem, in Roanoke County, to Tennessee, roughly along the path of the Valley Road. The legislature chose Salem as the eastern terminus in order to protect the road from the growing rivalry between canal towns Lynchburg and Buchanan, the former championed in the Piedmont and the latter in the Valley. One of the communities eventually would win the eastern terminus.[27]

At the same time, the General Assembly chartered the Richmond and Ohio Railroad Company to penetrate Southwest Virginia. While it too was stillborn—investors failed to put up enough money to get the company off the ground—failure did not deter the region's railroad boosters. In November 1847, a statewide convention gathered in Wytheville to support regional railroad construction. The majority resolutions, reported by former Governor Campbell, called for a renewed effort to breathe life into the moribund Richmond and Ohio Company, which was to be extended eventually to the Tennessee line, and for a branch line from the New River to the Ohio River. Finally, the delegates reaffirmed support for the South Western Turnpike, which they saw as a complementary improvement. Eastern rumblings to the effect that a railroad negated the need for the turnpike worried the convention. The resolutions of course did not please all those involved. Benjamin R. Floyd, a son of John Floyd, supported instead extending the proposed Richmond and Danville Railroad to Wytheville. Carroll, Floyd, Grayson and Wythe county delegates, who would benefit directly from Floyd's scheme, backed the minority report.[28]

When the legislature convened in December 1847, national affairs dominated the political horizon. The Wilmot Proviso, introduced in Congress to prohibit slavery in lands conquered from Mexico, electrified the south. Southerners considered the proviso unconstitutional and insulting.[29] The General Assembly, noted the *Richmond Enquirer,* had determined to confront the "one vital question" by upholding "the constitutional rights of the south." Internal improvements, however, appeared as important, as the newspaper noted that the subject promised to present "some knotty and interesting points. A very large portion of the State seems to feel the excitement on the subject."[30]

Governor Smith opened the assembly with an impassioned plea for western internal improvements. Fear of debt, he argued, must not stand in the way of the commonwealth's needs. As a leading priority, Smith singled out a route to the falls of the Kanawha, and hence to the Ohio River, as the state's paramount concern. Instead of accomplishing this with an extension of the canal, he proposed a railroad running northward through the Valley. The second priority, he continued, was a railroad from Buchanan, in the Valley, into Southwest Virginia.[31]

Southwest Virginia legislators remained skeptical. Whig State Senator Allen Caperton of Monroe County, a member of the Senate's Committee on Internal Improvements, complained that "the various internal improvement schemes have not yet been developed—My impression is that very few appropriations will be asked for owing to general distrust of the temper of the legislature in regard to those subjects."[32]

Freshman delegate John Buchanan Floyd of Washington County, the former governor's second son, agreed, but nevertheless had determined to make the effort. He wrote Leonidas Baugh, editor of the *Abingdon Democrat,* with expressions of disappointment in regard to the "lazy" legislature he had just joined. "Everybody says my notions are antiquated unfashionable & vulgar!" Floyd exclaimed. Nonetheless, he was determined to at least secure the future of the South Western Turnpike.[33] The road's opponents had united in early January to cut off new appropriations, especially if a railroad bill negotiated its way through the General Assembly. Floyd rallied its supporters, citing in debate Washington County's desire for both. He demanded that the state fulfill its pledge to complete the road from Salem to Tennessee, and to construct the eastern branch from Salem to Buchanan as well.[34]

The discussion remained moot until a railroad bill actually passed. Events came to a head when Burwell's bill incorporating a Southwest Virginia railroad, also to be styled the Lynchburg and Tennessee Railroad, came up for debate. The author's vision was grandiose. With an eye toward "an extension . . . to a point at or near the town of Memphis," the legislature sought to "establish a communication between the Atlantic ocean and the Mississippi river, promotive of great purposes of international intercourse and of national defence."[35]

John B. Floyd, like his brother, was on record favoring an extension of the Richmond and Danville line into the region. Nevertheless, he offered full support to Burwell's bill, providing Southwest Virginia passengers and goods would be able to continue on to Richmond via railroad, rather than on canal boats.[36]

The bill came up for a vote on March 15 and the House of Delegates rejected it. Supporters succeeded, however, in winning a reconsideration, and the House scheduled a second vote for March 23. Partisans raced to come up with the needed votes, but as the moment approached, Burwell realized he still was short of victory. Quickly, he persuaded delegate Thomas M. Tate of Smyth County to "faint," in order to buy time. Several doctors who were present rushed onto the floor and proceeded to bleed the convincing if unlucky Tate. The House adjourned in confusion. The evening gave the bill's supporters enough time to enlist extra support. The next day, the House incorporated the Lynchburg and Tennessee Railroad. Tate's blood sacrifice had won Southwest Virginia a railroad.[37]

Previous experience dampened enthusiasm, however. While chartering the railroad, the legislature neglected to vote the railroad state aid before April's adjournment. Without public funds, the railroad would end up as much a dead letter as its unfortunate predecessors. Lynchburg and Southwest Virginia investors promptly showed their support for the line by investing $766,200 in the company by the end of the year.[38]

National affairs remained uppermost when the General Assembly returned to Richmond in December. Whig Zachary Taylor had been elected president weeks before, and had done well even in Southwest Virginia, usually a Democratic stronghold. The national crisis regarding the land won from Mexico showed no sign of abating, however. Opening the legislature, Governor Smith attacked the Wilmot Proviso as dangerous to the union. If the hated proviso passed, Smith warned, the southern states had no recourse but secession. To demonstrate Virginia's unequivocal stand, Smith called on the legislature to pass strong anti-Wilmot resolutions, deport the state's free blacks, and build railroads that would further unite the south. He praised the Lynchburg and Tennessee as just such a unifying force, and urged the General Assembly to fund it generously. To meet the costs, he advised canceling the South Western Turnpike.[39]

Before it could confront either the railroad question or the North, the General Assembly had to elect a new governor. Under the 1830 Constitution, the combined houses of the legislature chose the chief executive. Since the turmoil surrounding the ratification of that document, the assembly had followed an informal policy of electing the governor alternately from the East and West. 1848 was the West's turn. From the Piedmont came vehement cries that at such a critical moment in the history of the republic, the practice must be scrapped. A westerner could not be trusted to protect the slave interests of Virginia. Mountain Virginians, in the meantime, were advocating a host of possible candidates. One was John B. Floyd, whose southwestern friends promoted their man despite his professed unwillingness. Although inexperienced, they argued, Floyd possessed strong credentials. His known states rights, pro-slavery stance made him palatable to eastern planters. Educated at South Carolina College, Floyd had learned the doctrine of nullification at the feet of the institution's president, Thomas Cooper. Family ties also made for close contacts with the state's elite. Floyd also benefited from the continued popularity of his father. In his native Southwest, his uncompromising stand for internal improvements had endeared him even more to his constituents.[40] "South-West" praised Floyd in the *Richmond Enquirer* as a loyal Democrat "with no stain upon his escutcheons as a man and a citizen." "A Voice from the East" singled out Floyd as the front-runner most acceptable in the east.[41]

Two groups opposed Floyd's trial balloon. Bowing to eastern pressure, the regular Democratic caucus selected eastern Judge William Daniel, breaking the unofficial sectional accord. Angry Floyd backers, primarily Southwest Virginians, staged a walkout when the caucus chose the easterner. They vowed to continue to support Floyd, and aimed for Whig votes. At the same time, the Floyd campaign faced northwestern opposition. The residents of the northwestern counties did not believe in the existence of a monolithic "west." They strongly reminded the General Assembly that Virginia's "western" governors, men such as David Campbell and John Floyd, were in fact all *Southwest* Virginians. The election of 1848, they asserted, should honor the Northwest. "Brooke" argued that Northwest Virginia produced men as able as the Southwest's and deserved to have a native son in the governor's chair. Likewise, "Justice" charged that "the North West is to be neglected as usual." The region's hopes soon centered around George W. Thompson of Wheeling.[42]

The legislature gathered to vote on December 12. Southwest Virginia's delegates, other anticaucus Democrats, and many Whigs supported Floyd. The legislature voted three times. Each time, Floyd led but only on the third ballot did he receive the necessary majority, polling 96 of the possible 162 votes. Thompson finished second with Daniel a distant third.[43]

The immediate aftermath was confusion. Regular Democrats prepared to accept Floyd, but worried that the party's organization had suffered "a deadly wound." Whigs enjoyed their opponents' divisions immensely, but still found themselves saddled with a Democratic governor. Most were content if unenthusiastic with the result their votes had wrought, although the Lexington *Valley Star* worried about Floyd's nullifier past. Northwest Virginians were disappointed, although they hoped that Thompson's strong showing was a precursor of things to come. Only in Southwest Virginia did real jubilation occur.[44] Floyd himself viewed his election as both a personal triumph and a golden opportunity for his native region. "I cannot help regarding it," he told the legislature," rather as an honor due the west and conferred upon my constituency, than one to which I myself am entitled from any merit of my own."[45]

Controversy over the Wilmot Proviso was increasing nationally and in Virginia as Floyd took office. Only the topic of internal improvements seemed as important to Virginians, and in that respect, Floyd took office at a critical juncture. On January 10, 1849, acting on a resolution of Burwell, the House Committee on Roads and Internal Navigation presented a bill empowering the state to subscribe to Lynchburg and Tennessee Railroad stock.[46]

Supporters feared that passage of the bill was unlikely. The *Lynchburg Patriot* blamed the jealous machinations of rival corporations, the everpresent eastern opposition to internal improvements, and blind devotion to the Union. The last consideration especially concerned the *Patriot*. Virginians were fools not to see the railroad as a necessary military measure, argued the newspaper. With northern abolitionist pressure growing and the Wilmot threat on everyone's lips, dissolution of the union seemed likely and civil war a possibility. Virginia possessed in its southwest counties "mineral treasures" sufficient to render a southern confederacy "invincible." If the General Assembly funded the railroad, the *Patriot* predicted, "saltpetre, iron, and lead sufficient to supply the wars of Napoleon himself, would be at our command." The railroad also would facilitate the transportation of troops into Virginia, making the state "ten fold stronger" in the event of northern attack.[47]

Both the *Richmond Enquirer* and its great rival, the *Whig*, agreed, albeit with less overt militancy. To the *Whig*, especially, the railroad seemed the means to reverse Virginia's economic and political decline. Southwest Virginia's great agricultural and mineral wealth would revitalize Piedmont markets and Tidewater ports. Virginia would grow as strong as a European "empire of at least second rate importance," and the state's "humiliation" would end. Overall, the railroad, promised the *Whig*, would "restore our State to the position which nature seems to have designed for it; to make it first in wealth, first in population, and as a consequence of these two, first likewise in political power and importance." The newspaper warned readers that the "great and holy work" was Virginia's last chance.[48]

The *Whig* also saw the Lynchburg and Tennessee Railroad as a way to unite Virginia and then link it to the Deep South in the event of secession. The newspaper editorialized: "To all those who are sensitive upon the sublect of our domestic institutions, the scheme of uniting the Southwest should present itself with peculiar force. . . . In union there is strength. The improvements which proceed in a Southwestern direction, have for their ultimate object, the formation of a more intimate union with the great slaveholding state of Tennessee, and through her, with the entire slave holding interest of the lower Mississippi."[49] In other words, the railroad would be the medium by which slavery would take a firm hold in Southwest Virginia, uniting the region to the Piedmont and Virginia to the cotton states on the basis of black bondage.

Opponents of funding were not easily persuaded. Many eastern planters, their fears increasing in response to the national crisis, dug in their heels and refused to budge. Other opponents acted out of local interest. The ongoing Lynchburg-Buchanan feud led many Buchanan supporters to either oppose the railroad entirely, or to demand an expensive branch from Buchanan to the Southwest. They saw the road, rightly, as an attempt of Lynchburg, Richmond, and the Piedmont to expand their hinterlands at the expense of Buchanan and the Valley. Supporters of rival railroads, notably the Richmond and Danville line once trumpeted by the Floyds, craved Southwest Virginia's resources for themselves. Finally, the ever-present canal backers opposed state aid, fearing that less money would be forthcoming for that improvement.[50]

With Floyd squarely behind funding, debate on the bill began in mid-February. Legislators offered a plethora of amendments designed to aid or kill the measure. To help it past wary eastern planters, Thomas J. Boyd of Wythe and Pulaski counties offered an amendment that would limit funding to $150,000 in fiscal year 1849, $300,000 in 1850, and no more than $400,000 per year thereafter. It also opened Lynchburg and Tennessee rails to the rolling stock of the rival Richmond and Danville Railroad. Meanwhile, the Lynchburg-Buchanan feud threatened to sink the bill. Buchanan interests demanded a branch from that town to a point in Roanoke County, where it would meet a comparable branch out of Lynchburg as well as the Richmond and Danville line. The continued rivalry led one exasperated Tidewater delegate to suggest a name change. Perhaps the Buchanan-Valley contingent would be mollified, he reasoned, if the railroad were renamed the *Virginia* and Tennessee Railroad.[51]

The House voted on the bill on February 26, defeating it by a close vote of 65 to 60. As before, however, its supporters succeeded in winning a reconsideration. On March 1 and 2, the House again took up the measure. Opponents again attempted to attach crippling riders to the bill, but to no avail. Late in the day on March 2, the delegates again voted on funding. This time, the bill's supporters won a vote of 76 to 54. In the new act, the restrictions of Boyd's amendment were incorporated and the name of the line became the Virginia and Tennessee Railroad. The act authorized the Board of Public Works to subscribe immediately to nine thousand shares of stock.[52]

Governor Floyd was jubilant. He wrote political rival but fellow Southwest Virginian William Ballard Preston, Zachary Taylor's Secretary of the Navy, "We passed the rail road bill in the house to day and I presume it will pass the senate without doubt. So Virginia is at last about to rise up renewed and glorious from the torpor and decay which long long years of inactivity & folly have brought upon her." On March 12, after the Senate acted, Floyd wrote Preston again. "We are fighting most gloriously for the improvement of the venerable old commonwealth," Floyd exclaimed.[53]

In Southwest Virginia, meetings occurred in Abingdon, Christiansburg, and Giles County to thank the General Assembly and more importantly to encourage local stock purchases. In the legislature's autumn session, Burwell as well as Floyd's replacement in the House, railroad booster Samuel E. Goodson, fought off challenges to the bill. Floyd himself conducted a well-publicized promotional tour of the state's internal improvements in September and October. The railroad itself conspicuously geared up for construction. In June, the directors appointed a chief engineer, Charles F. M. Garnett, an experienced southern railroad builder and the former chief engineer of Georgia, and began purchasing land for the initial Lynchburg-to-Salem stretch.[54]

The General Assembly reconvened in December to receive Floyd's first gubernatorial message. On the national scene, events in Washington were coming to a head. Congress prepared to deal with the potentially divisive issues of California and New Mexico, the Texas boundary, fugitive slaves, and the slave trade in the District of Columbia. Above all, the "fearful question" of the Wilmot Proviso galled the South.[55]

Floyd condemned supporters of the proviso as disunionists and fanatics. Their goal, he claimed, was to destroy slavery everywhere it existed. Virginia, he vowed, would not "submit to this usurpation of authority, this violation of her rights, this wanton degradation." It was time to settle the issue "now and forever. . . . If a conflict must come, let it come now."[56]

Internal improvements were to be a source of unity in its dark hour, and Floyd consequently devoted much of his militant message to them. He championed three improvements as connectors to the South and

West. Eager to obtain Piedmont support, Floyd dismayed his old constituents and supported continued work on the James River and Kanawha Canal. After noting briefly the Southwest's "great work," the governor went on to introduce a new project, a railroad from Covington, in the Valley, through Monroe or Tazewell counties, to Louisville, Kentucky. "It is," said Floyd, "of no moment whether this road be a branch of the Virginia and Tennessee railroad. . . . the advantages of a connection at Louisville are numerous and very striking." Such a railroad eventually would form part of a trans-continental railroad that would bring the riches of Europe and Asia to Norfolk's wharves.[57]

Floyd then plunged ahead to instigate more controversy. Unexpectedly, he called upon the General Assembly to authorize a plebiscite on a new constitutional convention. Attacking the state's "repugnant" county court system, "arbitrary" suffrage, and allegedly corrupt judiciary, Floyd called on the people to overturn the 1830 Constitution.[58]

Floyd's message ignited firestorms on several fronts. His sudden pronouncement on a new constitution, as discussed in a later chapter, sent the state's body politic into convulsions. His militant anti–Wilmot Proviso stand frightened Whigs, who attacked the governor as a disunionist. Floyd's advocacy of internal improvements found the best response statewide, but even then, he had made trouble for himself.[59]

The problem was Southwest Virginia, especially in the counties of the valley subregion. Many residents there reacted with dismay to the governor's pro-canal statements and especially to the Covington-to-Louisville railroad proposal. The Whig *Abingdon Virginian* condemned the latter scheme as "absurd and impracticable." Such a line, the newspaper charged, would function as a dangerous rival to the V&T. Floyd, the *Virginian* concluded, had betrayed Southwest Virginia.[60]

Partisan condemnation was one thing, but reproach from friends was something else again. The *Abingdon Democrat* matched its rival in criticism of the hometown governor. Editor Leonidas Baugh also charged betrayal, opening a breach with Floyd that widened in the next two years. Floyd's supporters rushed to his defense. "A Southwestern Man" expressed amazement at the charges. Floyd's proposal, he assured the *Richmond Enquirer,* in no way harmed the Virginia and Tennessee Railroad. Floyd had been "the ardent, consistent, resolute champion of the great Southwestern enterprise," and it was ridiculous to accuse him of selling out the line. "A Southwestern Man" further warned that the controversy could divide Southwest Virginia just at its hour of victory. The proposal promised to benefit the counties of the plateau subregion. "Washington County is not the whole Southwest," he warned.[61]

"A Southwestern Man" was right; subregional bickering immediately followed Floyd's message. John Carroll, delegate from Grayson and Carroll counties of the Blue Ridge subregion, offered a resolution in the House of Delegates on January 21, 1850, calling for the discontinuation of the South Western Turnpike, freeing the funds for the railroad. The plateau subregion counties launched salvoes as well. In October, two hundred mountaineers met in Tazewell to condemn what they saw as favoritism in the General Assembly for the valley subregion. Already, delegates charged, pro-valley bias had placed the South Western Turnpike there, when a route from the New River through Tazewell County would have been cheaper, shorter, and more practical. Now that Wythe and Washington counties had the turnpike, let them use it. Put the railroad through Tazewell and the plateau, the delegates demanded, as the "northern route" possessed better features than a route along the turnpike.[62]

The subregional bickering over the line's route was in reality only the tip of a more treacherous iceburg. Simply put, the railroad was attracting little financial support outside of the valley subregion. To be sure, there was little of the violent resistance to railroad construction that existed elsewhere. The railroad recorded only three acts of vandalism directed against it during construction. All three occurred at the same spot in Montgomery County in late 1855 and early 1856. The vandals attempted—and finally succeeded—to derail a train. Such violent opposition, however, concerned the railroad's management much less than the greater threat of bad weather and mudslides.[63]

Opposition, however, need not be violent. Nonviolent resistance to railroads and what they meant to the survival of locally oriented economies ran the gamut in the nineteenth century from apathy to suspicion to actually moving away from the new railroad for less-populated areas. This sort of resistance clearly was present in the Blue Ridge and the plateau during the V&T's early days. Abingdon and Richmond newspapers condemned "apathy" for the project in the plateau, especially in Lee, Russell, and Scott counties, and even attacked Wythe. Moreover, few residents of those areas risked investments in the company. Of the 2,558 shares sold in Southwest Virginia by 1860, only 39 belonged to Blue Ridge or plateau mountaineers. Conversely, more than half were purchased by Washington Countians. Southwestern stockholders as a whole lived in the valley subregion.[64]

Stockholder statistics also reveal something else. The 2,558 shares owned by Southwest Virginians comprised only 7.2 percent of the 35,402 total shares sold. Whose railroad was it? The state government, with 23,000 shares, was the leading partner. Next in importance were the cities of the Piedmont, especially Lynchburg and Richmond, whose residents owned 7,673 shares of stock, nearly 22 percent of the total. Clearly, like Virginia and West Virginia's postwar mountain railroads, the V&T was financed and built by a combination of a handful of well-placed mountain speculators and wealthy outside capitalists, with the power and the profits ultimately found outside Southwest Virginia. What Eller termed "the selling of the mountains" clearly was underway already in 1850.[65]

What differentiates the antebellum supporters from the New South builders was that the politics of slavery often were just as important as profit. Certainly a handful of boosters were also unionists who hopefully viewed the Virginia and Tennessee Railroad as a rail line that would cement national bonds and prevent disunionism. William Burwell for example counseled President Millard Fillmore that the railroad really was the linchpin of a projected southwestern railroad route from New York to New Orleans, a project bound to weaken secession sentiments.[66]

Most of the boosters, however, occupied the opposite end of the spectrum. William Barney has described how southern proslavery politicians viewed the institution's expansion into the West as vital to its survival. What Barney missed was their equal determination to spread it into the white belt sections of the existing South as well, in order to make the South solidly pro-slavery. As "A Son of Virginia" put it, the railroad's purpose was to link Virginia to a southern confederacy and to make Richmond its most important city.[67]

The best example of this expansionist sentiment was Henry A. Wise. Wise had been a supporter of internal improvements in the West for several years. The Wilmot crisis spurred him, however, to increase his advocacy of improvements. He presented the railroad as a tool that would unite Virginia and secure its continued devotion to slavery before the sectional showdown he foresaw. In a January 1850, speech, for example, Wise pleaded with Richmonders to help Virginia and the South present a united front as the North had done. In Virginia, the largest roadblock remained the western counties' incomplete devotion to slavery and southern rights. Internal improvements, Wise argued, would change the situation. "The East should assist the west in opening a market for its products," he asserted. "Those products would flow down in golden streams to enrich the East. . . . Meanwhile the slaves of the East would find labor in the fertile valleys of the West. The whole state would be cemented together."[68]

Through the summer, Wise continued his campaign. In May, he wrote his Accomac County constituents that, "The Western people are our natural allies, and they want what we want." Aiding the West in the struggle for internal improvements, as well as in the struggle for constitutional reform, would benefit the Tidewater as well. The Chesapeake would come alive with western goods. Moreover, railroads would create opportunities for agricultural and industrial expansion in the West that invariably would lead to the expansion of slavery. Virginia, according to Wise, "would be no longer like Nebuchadnezzar's image, part brass and part clay. Western Virginia as well as Eastern would have slaves, slavery would become more diffused, our interests would be at once more homogeneous and they *could* not tax us without equally taxing themselves."[69]

In the meantime, Virginia and Tennessee Railroad construction crews went to work. On January 16, 1850, Floyd presided over groundbreaking ceremonies in Lynchburg. Amid the strangely prophetic sounds of martial music, marching militiamen, and artillery salutes, the governor turned the first spadeful of dirt. Gangs of hired slaves and Irish laborers began working on the Lynchburg-to-Salem division, the first of three, with the completion of grading anticipated by the end of the year. Workers also began digging a tunnel through the Blue Ridge west of Lynchburg. Thirty-five months later, the first engine steamed into Salem. The railroad was poised to enter Southwest Virginia.[70]

To the west, crews were already at work. By the end of 1852, four-fifths of the second division, between Salem and Wytheville, was complete. The imposing face of the Allegheny Mountains between Salem and Christiansburg still defied workmen, however. Undaunted, Chief Engineer Garnett went to the legislature for more help. The General Assembly responded with a $1 million loan and more stock purchases. Fortified with the new funds, Garnett attacked the mountain grade. In September 1853, trains reached Big Spring, situated in eastern Montgomery County. Once workmen laid tracks between Big Spring and Cambria, the latter Christiansburg's new depot, construction proceeded apace. Engines reached Newbern, Pulaski County, in June 1854; Max Meadows, Wythe County, in October; and Wytheville itself on December 14. Only the last stretch, from Wytheville to Tennessee, remained, and construction there proceedeed quickly. In less than two years, with John Gilmer in attendance, the work was done.[71]

Success bred visions of expansion. As the railroad surged westward, supporters threw their support to a variety of proposed branches, such as a connector from Abingdon to the Cumberland Gap or from Christiansburg northward to the projected Chesapeake and Ohio Railroad. The Southside Railroad unveiled its own plans for a branch from Danville to the V&T. In the end, the railroad built only one, short branch. It was an important one, however. Completed in 1856, the 9 1/2 miles long Saltworks Branch linked the railroad's Glade Spring depot to Saltville's burgeoning saltworks and pumped welcome capital into the line's coffers.[72]

The Virginia and Tennessee at completion marked the pinnacle of antebellum railroad engineering. In seven years, its workers had graded and laid track over a rugged route 213 miles in length, including the Saltworks Branch. They had blasted five tunnels, erected 233 bridges, and constructed nineteen depots. At $84,000 per mile, it had been one of the nation's costliest railroads to build.[73]

Yet an engineering marvel alone does not necessarily guarantee success. Much would depend upon the reactions of Southwest Virginians. Would they ignore it, or even actively oppose it, now that it was complete? Would the apathy continue? Or would they (like the North Carolinians living along the new North Carolina Railroad as well as many of their fellow Virginians in Orange and Greene counties) eventually overcome initial anxieties and embrace it? The quickened pace of commercial agriculture in Southwest Virginia between 1850 and 1860, particularly in regard to market strategies and transportation, was one indication that some mountaineers in every subregion—but not all—chose the latter course.[74]

2

"The Most Favored Region for Agriculture": White Mountaineers and Commercial Farming

"MUCH OF WESTERN VIRGINIA is yet a new country . . . and in some of the more remote and inaccessible counties, the manner of living and the habits of the people quite primitive." So wrote pioneer American historian Henry Howe in the early 1840s as he endeavored to describe life in the commonwealth's mountains. To be sure, Howe largely avoided the harshness that typified contemporary and especially later writings on Appalachia. Independent, industrious, honest, and hospitable, Howe's mountaineer "leads a manly life, and breathes the pure air of the hills with the contented spirit of a freeman." The mountaineer's wife, "as rosy and blooming as 'flowers by the way-side,'" served as a model of domesticity for women elsewhere, especially in her disregard for fashion. Still, mountain isolation shaped and ultimately stunted their lives, Howe concluded. With "the country . . . too thinly settled to carry out a system of common schools," the mountaineers were both innocent of the world and ignorant of its knowledge. Moreover, his mountain environment prevented commercial development. Howe's mountaineer was a subsistence farmer who supplemented his corn crop with wild game and "an immense drove of hogs." In order to acquire a few luxuries from the outside world, such as coffee or sugar, he bartered animal skins or supplied drovers on route to distant markets.[1]

What Howe termed "primitive" has been called "precapitalist," "preindustrial," "premodern," or "traditional" by modern scholars. Ronald D Eller, in seeking to erase a century of crudely negative misinformation about preindustrial mountain life, presented a world much akin to that described by Howe in the first chapter of his justly celebrated monograph on modernization in Appalachia. Eller described an area that "more closely exemplified Thomas Jefferson's vision of a democratic society" than any other in the nation. While never completely isolated from the rest of America, preindustrial Appalachia largely ignored it. Mountain people instead created their own world, which was based on egalitarian values, noneconomic status distinctions, rather than economic class, and a diversified, noncommercial economy that maximized independence. Economics, politics, and religion all flowed from the basic building block of the family. The appearance of industrialization after the Civil War, Eller concluded, destroyed this nearly ideal society.[2]

Much of what both Howe and Eller said about antebellum southern mountain life was true in Southwest Virginia, especially away from the valley subregion. Two elements, however, are problematic. First, as several historians have found elsewhere, mountain agriculture was commercialized quite early and to a surprisingly high degree. Many immigrants came to the region with commercial activities in mind, and, like Western North Carolinians and the East Tennesseans of Cades Cove, began producing for outside markets quite early. What Steven Hahn called "capitalist transformation"—the transition from subsistence to cash economies—was well in place before 1850. The railroad did not create a capitalist economy, then, but hastened a transformation already in operation, albeit with the throttle wide open.[3]

Moreover, class distinctions were important in Southwest Virginia. Far from being a Jeffersonian paradise of sturdy landowning yeomen, the region was one in which tenantry was common and the gap between rich and poor wide. Again, while not creating classes, the railroad increased economic marginalization and gave it subregional shadings. Just how important the political economy of rich and poor was would become apparent only under the strains of civil war.

By 1850, several factors had combined to produce in Southwest Virginia what John Schlotterbeck has called a "social economy," a common mountain culture that to a great degree unified its residents. One important factor was Protestant evangelical religion, generally expressed in Primitive Baptist, Southern Baptist or Methodist Episcopal Church (South) congregations.[4] Even more important were kinship networks. Intermarriage among neighbors created closely-knit communities in which members freely exchanged both goods and labor.[5] Finally, there was mountain agriculture. While actual practices differed from individual farm to farm, Southwest Virginia's landowners, tenants, and laborers all acted within common bounds and held similar expectations. Whatever their status, all but the region's wealthiest

Table 1. Cereal Production in Southwest Virginia, 1850

County	Wheat (bu.)	Corn (bu.)	Oats (bu.)
Boone	3,215	134,040	19,185
Carroll	11,578	132,189	82,847
Fayette	8,414	111,064	56,037
Floyd	23,992	104,630	92,654
Giles	38,565	204,720	68,494
Grayson	17,127	177,266	110,770
Greenbrier	47,778	182,119	124,158
Lee	20,243	485,625	107,030
Logan	1,588	154,943	20,014
Mercer	12,284	105,949	35,289
Monroe	51,436	250,456	97,460
Montgomery	51,827	266,616	106,120
Pulaski	35,284	175,510	63,367
Raleigh	2,893	49,511	19,253
Russell	25,604	378,919	154,305
Scott	15,722	319,240	106,342
Smyth	34,742	201,222	139,580
Tazewell	21,327	235,126	125,214
Washington	69,264	438,900	249,674
Wyoming	1,552	47,506	8,765
Wythe	72,738	280,652	155,207
Total	567,173	4,436,200	1,941,765

Source: *Seventh Census,* 275–76.

farmers had one goal, economic independence. In order to maintain or achieve economic liberty, they strove for self-sufficiency. Mixed farming, the production of a wide variety of crops, rather than reliance on a staple, insured independence by limiting the farmer's dependence on the local merchant or the national marketplace. The mountaineer generally worked an average of one hundred acres, clearing about forty acres of bottomland and leaving the rest forested. Mountainsides, sometimes partially cleared, supported livestock and wild game, and provided lumber and other necessary products.[6]

Virginia was best known as a tobacco producing state, but very little tobacco grew in Southwest Virginia before 1850. As demonstrated in tables 1 through 3, the mountain farmer principally raised cereals,

Table 2. Selected Non-cereal Production in Southwest Virginia, 1850

County	Tobacco (lbs.)	Flax (lbs.)	Hay (tons)
Boone	8,019	16,299	110
Carroll	5,526	15,285	2,715
Fayette	170	3,392	950
Floyd	14,624	16,348	3,326
Giles	1,022	19,997	1,960
Grayson	0	20,980	3,522
Greenbrier	0	10,931	6,359
Lee	5,131	28,501	1,407
Logan	8,353	2,936	129
Mercer	0	11,559	1,375
Monroe	4,017	11,547	6,073
Montgomery	46,100	10,055	4,453
Pulaski	0	14,141	2,639
Raleigh	0	3,790	279
Russell	7,577	50,589	2,528
Scott	4,440	20,528	924
Smyth	0	12,849	3,952
Tazewell	300	23,117	72
Washington	0	23,197	4,238
Wyoming	2,441	5,260	286
Wythe	0	22,210	7,193
Total	107,720	343,511	54,490

Source: *Seventh Census*, 277–82.

especially corn and oats, but also buckwheat, rye, and wheat. Most of the total crop ended up on the family's table. Mountaineers ate corn bread at every meal, and frequently ate corn in other forms, such as creamed or roasted on the cob. Whiskey distilled from corn provided a potent beverage. To complement the fare, the women of the family kept orchards and raised vegetable gardens that furnished beans, potatoes, and other foodstuffs. Many kept bees for honey and wax, and boiled syrup from nearby maple trees. In addition to these edible crops, mountain yeomen raised a prodigious amount of flax. Over 34 percent of the state's flax grew in Southwest Virginia. The region's women transformed most of it into homespun cloth.[7]

Of even greater importance to the regional economy was the rais-

Table 3. Selected Virginia Agricultural Products Produced in Southwest Virginia, 1850

Agricultural Product	Southwest Virginia Total	Virginia Total	Percentage
Beeswax/honey (lbs.)	248,138	880,767	28.2
Butter (lbs.)	1,859,077	11,089,359	16.2
Cattle	201,698	669,137	30.1
Corn (bu.)	4,436,200	35,254,319	12.6
Flax (lbs.)	343,511	1,000,450	34.3
Hay (tons)	54,490	369,098	14.8
Horses	45,697	272,403	16.8
Oats (bu.)	1,941,765	10,179,144	19.1
Sheep	248,040	1,310,004	18.9
Swine	292,780	1,829,843	16.0
Tobacco (lbs.)	107,720	56,804,227	0.2
Wheat (bu.)	567,173	11,212,616	5.1
Wool (lbs.)	487,458	2,860,765	17.0

Source: *Seventh Census,* 272–82.

ing of livestock. Land too hilly to cultivate still provided excellent grazing. Indeed, travelers found themselves enthralled by the richness of Southwest Virginia pastures. The English writer and temperance reformer James Silk Buckingham pronounced the valley counties "the most favored region for agriculture, pasture, and climate in all the United States." His fellow Englishman George W. Featherstonhaugh agreed. In Pulaski County, Featherstonhaugh declared "finer pastures I have never seen, nor a more promising-looking district for grazing."[8]

Southwest Virginians raised cattle, hogs, horses, and sheep. Greenbrier County's horses were nationally famous for their size and beauty, and by 1850, Southwest Virginia furnished 17 percent of the state's wool. Swine and cattle were paramount, however, as shown in table 4. In large part, this was because pork was the staple in the mountaineer's diet. To paraphrase Sam Bowers Hilliard, if cotton was king, pork was queen. Wealthy planters, yeomen, tenants, and even townspeople raised swine and cattle as an adjunct to growing crops.[9]

While they most fully engaged in the local economy, which often was based on barter or exchanged obligations rather than cash, Southwest Virginians also participated to a limited degree in the larger mar-

Table 4. Selected Livestock Holdings in Southwest Virginia, 1850

County	Horses	Cattle	Sheep	Swine
Boone	720	4,123	3,808	7,116
Carroll	1,339	7,170	9,666	12,423
Fayette	999	4,560	6,529	7,269
Floyd	1,240	5,428	7,248	9,500
Giles	2,126	8,147	10,762	11,589
Grayson	2,135	9,287	13,322	12,843
Greenbrier	4,088	15,713	20,971	13,161
Lee	2,720	10,611	12,181	25,114
Logan	983	8,631	4,793	11,186
Mercer	1,127	5,587	6,210	9,138
Monroe	3,354	14,181	21,789	14,307
Montgomery	2,235	8,647	10,426	15,160
Pulaski	1,467	7,423	9,159	10,384
Raleigh	447	2,018	2,845	4,416
Russell	3,427	19,967	21,442	24,645
Scott	2,203	9,215	12,187	18,697
Smyth	2,697	10,296	13,207	11,792
Tazewell	3,604	16,625	17,372	27,291
Washington	4,666	15,424	22,170	26,248
Wyoming	427	3,206	1,789	4,092
Wythe	3,696	15,439	20,164	16,509
Total	45,697	201,698	248,040	292,780

Source: *Seventh Census*, 273–76.

ket. No more impressive evidence can be offered than the breadth of commercial droving activities. Southwest Virginians not only drove herds across the state, beginning as early as 1750, but also to points as distant as Baltimore, Philadelphia, and New Orleans. Large-scale droving remained predominantly, though not exclusively, the business of wealthier planters before 1850, although the trend moved toward more yeoman enterprises. Small farmers still participated in other ways, supplying drovers en route to market with corn, or selling stock to farmer-middlemen assembling large herds for sale.[10] James Silk Buckingham left a vivid description of one herd of cattle in preparation for the drive near Newbern, Pulaski County: "Vast herds of cattle are driven up here from the southern and western parts of the State—we saw as many as 600 at least in one drove—to be pastured and fattened for the eastern markets; and it is thought to be more profitable even than planting, though capital invested in that yields 25 to 30 per cent; but in grazing it is said to realize 50 to 60 per cent, on the average of many years running."[11]

Such returns, of course, required a sizable initial investment. In 1850, the average beef price at Virginia stock markets was a low 2.7 cents per pound. Bacon and ham during the same month paid 7 cents per pound. Such low prices, coupled with the investment, time, and distance involved, discouraged small producers from entering the market.[12]

Historians have noted the crucial role stock droving played in the southern mountain economy, but often they have not paid the same attention to the equally important transportation and sale of other agricultural goods. In fact, this too was a major part of Southwest Virginia's commercial economy. Early in the antebellum period, wagons creaking with goods followed the same routes as the drovers. John D. Imboden, later a Confederate general and New South booster, remembered "caravans of 'Knox teams'" passing through the lower valley bound for Winchester, Virginia, and Baltimore in the 1830s. Imboden described "wagons . . . large and heavily laden with hides, beeswax, furs, feathers, ginseng, canes for fishing-rods, maple sugar, and other products of a mountain region."[13]

After the James River and Kanawha Canal reached the Piedmont city of Lynchburg in December 1840, that city became the focal point of Southwest Virginia's trade. Wagons from Western North Carolina and East Tennessee rolled through Southwest Virginia to Lynchburg as well. In addition to the goods enumerated by Imboden, Southwest Virginia apples, butter, cheese, hemp, and whiskey also were transported to Lynchburg. When the canal was extended further to Buchanan, Virginia, its eventual western terminus, Southwest Virginians routed produce there as well.[14]

Commercialism, in short, was active in Southwest Virginia well before the construction of the Virginia and Tennessee Railroad. The railroad's role in Southwest Virginia as elsewhere in the South was to quicken the transition to marketable crops. The most dramatic result was the annexation of Southwest Virginia into the tobacco kingdom.

This change is revealed in tables 5 and 6. In 1860, Southwest Virginia produced 2,284,167 pounds of tobacco, a remarkable 2020.5 percent increase since 1850. Seven individual counties—Fayette, Floyd, Mercer, Monroe, Montgomery, Pulaski, and Wythe—grew more tobacco individually than had the entire region in 1850. Nine produced over 137 pounds of tobacco per white resident, enough to generate an av-

Table 5. Selected Agricultural Products of Southwest Virginia, 1860

County	Wheat (bu.)	Corn (bu.)	Tobacco (lbs.)
Boone	15,278	143,808	18,729
Buchanan	5,164	57,975	2,365
Carroll	30,804	130,231	24,542
Fayette	25,693	131,425	127,713
Floyd	39,847	121,510	375,065
Giles	54,874	184,785	99,952
Grayson	46,742	177,144	50,842
Greenbrier	52,017	231,479	3,000
Lee	49,993	582,648	38,162
Logan	11,025	199,385	13,545
McDowell	1,041	20,445	1,275
Mercer	43,131	131,654	182,554
Monroe	84,805	216,513	132,019
Montgomery	118,271	256,735	727,995
Pulaski	69,676	202,910	141,662
Raleigh	6,700	39,301	34,827
Russell	56,058	327,197	7,805
Scott	62,337	512,829	16,773
Smyth	92,782	234,904	24,020
Tazewell	44,619	206,320	12,470
Washington	119,368	664,566	198,490
Wise	11,108	115,925	2,300
Wyoming	5,601	62,420	4,778
Wythe	90,485	301,368	43,644
Total	1,137,419	5,253,477	2,284,167

Source: *Eighth Census: Agriculture.*

erage annual profit of ten dollars for each white farmer—Bill Cecil-Fronsman's standard for a "market county." None fit the bill ten years before. Moreover, tobacco farming had spread into every county in Southwest Virginia. In 1850, eight counties, including Mercer, Pulaski, and Washington, produced no tobacco at all. Ten years later, every county yielded at least one thousand pounds. In their zeal to raise even more tobacco, Southwest Virginians plowed up grazing land and cut down forests.[15]

Who raised tobacco in Southwest Virginia in 1860? Involvement in

Table 6. Selected Virginia Agricultural Products Produced in Southwest Virginia, 1850–60

Agricultural Product	Southwest Virginia Total	Virginia Total	Percentage	Percentage Change[1]
Beeswax/ honey (lbs.)	459,930	1,526,451	30.1	+46.0
Butter (lbs.)	1,991,591	13,464,722	14.8	7.5
Cattle	180,205	1,044,467	17.3	-10.7
Corn (bu.)	5,253,477	38,319,999	13.7	18.4
Flax (lbs.)	190,185	487,808	39.0	-44.6
Hay (tons)	55,443	445,133	12.5	1.7
Horses	45,947	287,579	16.0	0.5
Oats (bu.)	1,518,216	10,186,720	14.9	-21.8
Sheep	199,161	1,043,269	18.3	-0.3
Tobacco (lbs.)	2,284,167	123,968,312	1.8	2,020.5
Wheat (bu.)	1,137,419	13,130,977	8.6	100.5
Wool (lbs.)	414,291	2,510,019	16.6	-17.7

1. Defined as (1860 total - 1850 total) ÷ 1850 total.

Source: Table 3; *Eighth Census: Agriculture*, 154–65.

tobacco production varied from subregion to subregion. In Washington County, tobacco farming was the enclave of a few landowners. Only 61 of the 1,004 householders listed on the manuscript agricultural census produced tobacco during the year. Of those who also appeared in the Washington County sample, all were landowners. Production ranged from farmer Hardy Lilly's 20 pounds to Francis Preston's 26,000 pounds, with a mean of 3,254 pounds.[16]

Elsewhere, tobacco farming was more of an egalitarian pursuit. In Floyd and Raleigh counties, roughly one-third of householders appearing on the manuscript agricultural schedules listed tobacco yields. While landowners comprised a majority in these counties as well, twenty-one percent of Floyd County tobacco producers sampled and thirty-eight percent of Raleigh's sampled tobacco growers were tenants.[17]

Simultaneously, Southwest Virginians embraced the state's other major cash crop: wheat. "The excitement in the wheat trade continues," James M. Johnston wrote from Bristol in 1858, "and gives a business appearance here not to be seen, I am told, anywhere else between

Table 7. Selected Livestock Holdings in Southwest Virginia, 1860

County	Horses	Cattle	Sheep	Swine
Boone	787	4,950	3,248	7,663
Buchanan	406	2,923	1,983	4,463
Carroll	1,137	5,293	8,442	10,022
Fayette	1,266	4,705	6,998	7,723
Floyd	1,496	5,607	7,101	10,280
Giles	1,517	5,497	5,755	9,316
Grayson	2,304	8,302	13,680	16,622
Greenbrier	3,714	12,833	16,067	10,971
Lee	3,167	9,149	10,422	29,688
Logan	855	5,935	6,546	9,917
McDowell	222	1,383	866	2,463
Mercer	1,552	6,545	10,225	11,308
Monroe	3,216	12,646	12,288	10,172
Montgomery	2,161	8,266	8,152	14,224
Pulaski	1,430	5,809	4,647	8,878
Raleigh	486	2,183	3,569	3,663
Russell	2,726	13,209	13,357	17,989
Scott	3,335	9,513	12,854	27,450
Smyth	2,459	8,960	9,632	11,385
Tazewell	2,976	15,653	11,138	13,962
Washington	4,207	11,561	14,866	22,762
Wise	825	3,955	4,268	10,847
Wyoming	414	3,332	1,233	4,733
Wythe	3,205	11,966	11,824	16,198
Total	45,947	180,205	199,161	261,969

Source: *Eighth Census: Agriculture,* 154–55, 158–59, 162–63.

Lynchburg and Knoxville. . . . The depots are full."[18] In 1850, Southwest Virginia had produced 567,173 bushels of wheat, about 5 percent of the state's total yield. Greenbrier, Monroe, Montgomery, Washington, and Wythe counties led the region. By 1860, as shown in tables 6 and 7, Southwest Virginia had doubled its production to 1,137,419 bushels, 8.6 percent of the state total. High prices stimulated production. Because of European demand caused by the Crimean War, wheat prices rose from a low of eighty-three cents per bushel on the Richmond market in November, 1851, to a high of two dollars per bushel in November, 1855. Prices fell somewhat when the demand created by the war coupled with overproduction saturated the market, but they never returned to the 1850 levels. According to economist Arthur G. Peterson, the Virginia and Tennessee Railroad was responsible for keeping the prices high.[19]

In addition to tobacco and wheat, Southwest Virginians increased the production of several other marketable farm goods. They produced nearly three times the amount of beeswax and honey in 1860 as in 1850, for example. Fruits and vegetables proved another successful commodity.[20] On the whole, cash crop cultivation and generally higher prices across the state created a boom economy in Southwest Virginia. A sizable minority of mountaineers now devoted themselves to tobacco and wheat cultivation. In so doing, they neglected the subsistence goods that had formed the basis of the mountain, mixed farming economy.

Grazing, for example, suffered. Mountaineers plowed up prime grazing land to put in tobacco and wheat, consigning livestock to less-productive lands. "The herds and flocks take the mountains and hills," William Ballard Preston remarked to the Virginia State Agricultural Society in 1854, "the valleys & plains are devoted to the labor of man; in the *diversified* crops of tobacco, wheat, corn, and vegetables."[21]

Livestock production, though, failed to keep pace with the region's growing population (tables 6 and 7). While Southwest Virginia's population grew 22.6 percent during the decade, hogs remained at 1850 levels and the numbers of cattle declined 10 percent. The population increase itself would have meant less meat in the mountaineer's diet on the average. Increased marketing of livestock due to higher available prices, however, further depleted the supply for home use. Again, the railroad made the difference. In negating the necessity for costly and time-consuming stock drives, the railroad encouraged more mountaineers to enter the marketplace.[22]

By following the routes chosen by drovers as the railroad pressed into Southwest Virginia, scholars can actually chart the shift in market production. The nearest depot, rather than the actual market, became the goal of the region's stockmen. Tazewell County drovers, for example, principally had driven their stock eastward to market on the Cumberland Gap and Fincastle Turnpike. As the railroad advanced, however, the drovers abandoned the old route in favor of the South Western Turnpike, driving their stock down the macadamized road to the nearest railhead. When the railroad opened as far as Wytheville, Tazewell's stockmen promptly abandoned the turnpike and made directly for Wytheville's new depot. Observers noted overall that the volume of traffic on all regional roads had increased sharply.[23]

Indeed, the sheer volume of goods farmers brought to the railroad for shipment astonished and nearly swamped the V&T itself as it progressed southward. In January 1855, General Superintendent Edward H. Gill wrote that Christiansburg's Cambria depot "is now the most important one on the road, except those at the termini, and does by far the largest amount of business."[24] As the year wore on, Gill warned his superiors that business was increasing, taxing his abilities to keep up. He reported in November that "the freight business has been greater than in any preceding month and one extra train has been kept constantly at work and an additional was required but could not be placed on the road." Gill needed the additional locomotive, he said, by the spring of 1856 "to keep pace with the increased business of the coming year."[25]

The completion of the line in 1856 led in turn to another increase in volume that nearly overwhelmed Gill. As farm products, especially hogs, poured out of far southwestern counties into Abingdon and Goodson, Gill pleaded with the railroad board for help. On December 1, 1856, he reported that

> there has been more freight brought to the western depots for transportation than our locomotive engines could possibly transport, and consequently there has been some considerable complaint and disappointment on the part of some of the customers of the road, every engine that was fit for use has been kept constantly running during the month, but many of the depots are still crowded with freight.
> This sudden press of business was unexpected.[26]

Gill begged for two new engines to take up the slack. In January 1857, with eighty-one carloads of freight sitting idle, waiting for engines to haul them to Lynchburg, Gill upped his demands to three freight engines, one passenger engine, and fifty new boxcars. He got them.[27]

Hog traders continued to prosper well into the war. In October 1858, Bristol's James M. Johnston admitted considering going into the business himself. He expected the price to rise shortly as shortages had occurred. The reason was not the availability of marketable hogs per se, but instead a shortage of corn to feed hogs driven in from outlying areas. Only towns and cities on the railroad, he wrote, contained adequate supplies of corn.[28]

The corn shortage Johnston described was not primarily the result of less cultivation. In the 1850s, corn yields in Southwest Virginia increased 18.4 percent, totaling 5,253,477 bushels in 1860. Admittedly,

in three of the counties most affected by the developing cash-crop economy—Monroe, Montgomery, and Raleigh—corn production declined.
In those counties, farmers clearly had given over fields reserved for corn
to tobacco and wheat. Other leading tobacco producing counties, however, also had increased corn production by 1860. Thus, one cannot argue simply that cash crop cultivation led directly to corn shortages. The
answer lay more in how mountaineers utilized corn. As Paul Salstrom
demonstrated in his study of the southern mountain region, decreases
in livestock earmarked for home consumption due to marketing meant
a greater need for corn in the diet. Farmers made less corn available for
stock drovers because having sold their animals to the drovers, they
needed to keep the corn to eat. Salstrom found this true especially in
the Allegheny Plateau, where population growth cut even further into
available supplies. The result there, he concluded, could not be called
poverty but did involve definite "belt-tightening."[29]

In sum, the Virginia and Tennessee Railroad had hastened the development of capitalistic, slave-based, cash-crop agriculture in Southwest Virginia. Many farmers in the region increasingly involved themselves deeply in goods bringing high profits on the Richmond markets.
In the process, however, wealthier farmers pushed aside many of their
landless counterparts and marginal yeomen, driving them into tenancy if not day labor. The end result was an intensified regional class
structure.

Class had not always been Southwest Virginia's most divisive element. Early in the region's history, ethnicity had been just as important. When white mountaineers first entered Southwest Virginia in significant numbers in the 1740s they generally came from the north,
from western Pennsylvania and its satellite settlements in the Shenandoah Valley. Unlike the largely English stock east of the Blue Ridge
Mountains, the Southwest's settlers were predominantly Scotch-Irish
and, to a lesser extent, German. Relations between the British and
German groups were strained from the start, and remained rocky for
decades as ethnicity grew entangled with politics. A handful of Scotch-
Irish families, as fluent in English as they were familiar with British
law, quickly monopolized local politics. Intermarried families—including the Breckinridges, Campbells, Christians, Floyds, Prestons, and
Triggs—most of them connected to the locally influential Loyal Land
Company, climbed to the top of the social order soon after their arrival from the Shenandoah Valley around 1760. This backcountry elite
quickly cemented its political control through connections with prom-

inent eastern Virginians such as the Byrd family and the Scotch-Irish Patrick Henry, and ultimately through a close identification with the ideals of the American Revolution. With control of the courthouses and friends in the state capitol, the elite profitably tied up vast tracts of land, much to the resentment of the German settlers as well as minority English and Welsh groups.[30]

The reluctance of German ethnics to assimilate heightened antagonisms. The earliest Germans refused to abandon their language and heritage. Periodic waves of new immigrants reinforced the tenacity of German ethnic customs. As late as 1850, the German language still could be heard in the church and in the home. Most Germans by then were bilingual, but isolated pockets persisted where solely German was spoken. The German presence remained especially strong in the valley subregion.[31] Anne Royall, the acerbic travel writer and northern-born widow of an eastern Virginia squire, wrote in 1826 that "as soon as you are in Washington county, Va. you have Dutch (as they are called) drivers, Dutch inns, and Dutch everything."[32]

The German presence was noticeable down the valley in Montgomery County as well. John Hammet, John Preston's Irish overseer, wrote that his neighbors "are in general dutch and far from being like the real Virginians" he had known in the Piedmont. He considered the "dutch" social inferiors, and contemplated leaving Southwest Virginia in order to find more suitable companions.[33]

As these comments suggest, the Germans' failure to assimilate, coupled with a greater likelihood of Tory sympathies during the revolution, stimulated an already pronounced xenophobia among the mountaineers of British origin. Royall, reflecting the prejudices of her hosts, pronounced the "Dutch" of Southwest Virginia "grossly ignorant and immoral, particularly the females." Germans, she declared, resisted education and "polish." Sexual liaisons with blacks and an alleged penchant for producing illegitimate children naturally resulted, she claimed, from the refusal to mimic accepted British-American ways.[34]

As the nineteenth-century passed, however, sentiments such as these appeared less frequently. In their place increasingly reared the specter of class conflict. On the most basic level, class conflict involved developing tensions between slaveowners and nonslaveowners. The latter often harbored resentments toward the slaveholders who held local control as well as those east of the Blue Ridge who kept a tight grip on state government. Former governor David Campbell warned fellow slaveholders of the untrustworthiness of his neighbors. Most Virginians west of the Blue Ridge, he wrote, owned no slaves and "never expect or intend to own any." Elaborate defenses of the institution did not stir them, Campbell believed. "I know the fact," he wrote, "that they are not at all interested—So far from it many of them feel exactly like the men of Indiana or Illinois or any of the northwestern states do." Moreover, the former governor feared that ardent pro-slavery rhetoric might stir up latent class discord. So far, he agreed, white supremacy tentatively bound the region's slaveowners and nonslaveholders. Northern abolitionists, who seemed to want to put blacks and whites on an equal footing, recently had forged the bond of supremacy even stronger. If these fears proved unfounded, however, cracks could appear in the united white front. Thus, Campbell counseled large slaveowners eager to defend slavery to tone down their increasingly fiery language.[35]

It would be too simplistic to rely on slaveownership alone as a delineating factor, however. The actual situation was far more complex. Wealth, particularly real wealth, divided white Southwest Virginia mountaineers into several fluid class groupings. Southwest Virginia already was seriously stratified.

Washington County of the valley subregion offers one example. Approximately 72 percent of the sampled householders identified themselves as either a "farmer" or "laborer." Moreover, many of the 11.8 percent of the sample who listed no occupation were involved in agriculture in some fashion. This latter group included the 10.7 percent of householders who were women as well as several men such as John D. Mitchell, who owned twenty thousand dollars worth of real estate and six slaves but listed no occupation. Thus, perhaps as many as eight out of ten Washington County householders were agriculturalists in 1850.[36]

A closer examination of the census, however, presents a different picture. The word *farmer* apparently had many definitions. Only 18.9 of the county's sampled population owned real estate and also appeared on the agricultural schedules as farm producers. An additional 11 percent of "farmers" appeared on the population schedules as real estate owners but did not show up on the agricultural schedules. In their study of tenantry in Georgia, Frederick A. Bode and Donald E. Ginter suggested that at least some of these latter "farmers" were tenants, although the group probably also included first year landowners and the retired. Even if one generously assumes that all of them were landowning farmers, however, and includes as well those residents who listed no occupation but owned property, one still must conclude that *at most* only 34.6 percent of Washington Countians were classic landowning "yeomen" or better, as shown in table 8. This left at least 40 percent of the sampled heads of householders, and 55.5 percent of

Table 8. Percentage of Farmers in Counties
Sampled, 1850

County	Floyd	Raleigh	Washington
Yeomen	51.7	39.0	34.6
Tenants	27.2	48.0	40.0
Laborers	4.6	4.7	8.4
Total	83.5	91.7	83.0

Source: Federal Manuscript Census Sample

Table 9. Percentage of Yeomen and Tenants
among Self-described "Farmers" in Counties
Sampled, 1850

	Floyd	Raleigh	Washington
Yeomen	69.1	45.6	44.5
Tenants	30.9	54.4	55.5

Source: Federal Manuscript Census Sample

the self-described "farmers" in the sample, almost certainly tenants. In short, farmers working someone else's land outnumbered the landed in Washington County.[37]

Washington County's landowners were more prosperous overall. Expressed rather broadly in means, the "average" yeoman was a forty-six-year-old man who owned 201 acres of land, 46 percent of which was improved acreage, 5 horses, 15 cattle, 22 sheep, and 25 swine. He produced 393 bushels of corn in 1850. In contrast, the "average" tenant was a thirty-nine-year-old man who worked 94 acres, 61 percent of which was improved. He owned 3 horses, 10 cattle, 14 sheep, and 18 swine. The mean tenant produced 355 bushels of corn in 1850, and even this set of figures is undoubtedly skewed toward the more prosperous tenants since 24.5 percent of tenants did not appear at all on the agricultural census.[38]

With local variations, the pattern repeated itself throughout Southwest Virginia in 1850 (tables 8–10). In the plateau subregion's Raleigh

Table 10. Improved (I) and Unimproved (U) Acreage Owned, by Bode and Ginter Farming Categories, in Counties Sampled, 1850

Category	Acreage Owned	Floyd	Raleigh	Washington
Landowner	I	74.30	38.76	91.88
	U	167.19	195.93	108.79
Category 3 Farmer	I	36.43	28.27	57.28
	U	51.7	208.37	37.23
Category 5 Farmer	I	0	5.48	0.50
	U	0	0.14	0
Laborer	I	0	2.50	4.78
	U	0	5.00	1.07
No occupation	I	11.70	11.58	29.68
	U	24.02	74.69	31.68

Source: Federal Manuscript Census Sample

County, tenantry involved at least 48 percent of all heads of households, and 54.4 percent of "farmers." In Raleigh, tenants who headed households were younger than their landowning counterparts, but elsewhere age varied little, negating to an extent the argument that tenancy was little more than a young man's stepping stone to landownership. Property disparities between yeomen and tenants, however, were not as wide as in Washington. An additional noticeable difference was the percentage of unimproved land. While tenants elsewhere usually worked older tracts with a relatively high proportion of improved land, Raleigh's tenants possessed more unimproved land. This resulted from the practice of having tenants clear newly acquired properties. In these cases, the landlord received improved land as payment rather than cash or a share of the crop. This practice was prevalent in the Blue Ridge subregion as well. In Floyd County, the proportion of probable tenants was smaller, 27.2 percent of sampled householders and 30.9 percent of "farmers," but disparities in real holdings and property were wider.[39]

Yeomen farmers, in short, comprised only about half of the population. This left anywhere from a third to a half of the population landless, a people who ranged in circumstance from tenants who owned their own tools and animals, to tenants who appear to have owned little or no property, to hired laborers paid in cash wages or shares of the crop—sharecroppers. Their distress mitigated somewhat by kin networks and mutual obligation, their lives nonetheless hardly matched the Jeffersonian ideal. Trapped in poverty and often required to act deferentially toward landowning patrons, laborers had little control of their lives. As Olmsted and others noted, other Southwest Virginians regarded laborers as the absolute dregs of white society, hardly better than African American slaves.[40]

Ten years later, the railroad, coupled with the more usual factors, had occasioned dramatic changes in regional white population. First of all, it increased. From 1850 to 1860 (table 11), the white population of Southwest Virginia increased by 32,173, a rate of 23.5 percent. The trend was especially strong in Carroll County, where a local copper mining rush created a 52.7 percent increase in white population, and in the counties of the Allegheny Plateau subregion. In the latter area, Boone, Fayette, Mercer, Raleigh, and Wyoming counties all saw their white populations leap by more than 50 percent. Raleigh County's white population nearly doubled.[41]

William Ballard Preston credited the incomplete Virginia and Tennessee Railroad with the population increase. In making eastern markets more accessible, the V&T first had encouraged Tidewater and Piedmont Virginia planters to relocate in Southwest Virginia's fertile valleys. "Eastern Virginians," Preston declared to his eastern audience, "are purchasing there lands and settling their families & slaves up on them instead of emigrating as formerly to the west, and transferring your numbers and your wealth beyond your borders and jurisdiction."[42]

Preston then noted what he claimed to be a second major result of railroad expansion on population. Out-migration from Southwest Virginia to the Deep South, Texas, and the Midwest long had worried the region's boosters. Internal improvements and better access to eastern markets, the boosters hoped, would reverse the trend. With railroad expansion now a reality, Preston claimed success. Their "prospect of wealth enlarged and rendered certain" by the railroad, Southwest Virginians were remaining at home, Preston claimed.[43] He declared that

> year after year we beheld the anxious, straggling crowd, pressing forward ... in continuous crowds of carriages and waggons—rich and poor, young & old, white & black, master & slave, hastening ... to their financial *Eldorado* and Elesian of the west; Tile we seemed as we beheld the stream to be left; desolate and alone, amid the depopulation and abandoned scenes of our youth.
>
> The drama has ended. Tis but an occasional emigrant we meet ... experience and *observation have taught our people*.[44]

Table 11. Changes in Southwest Virginia's White
Population, 1850–60

	Net Increase	Percentage Increase
Boone	1,627	53.3
Buchanan[1]	2,762	—
Carroll	1,993	52.7
Fayette	1,936	51.2
Floyd	1,744	29.1
Giles	180	3.1
Grayson	1,511	24.6
Greenbrier	1,951	22.8
Lee	755	8.0
Logan	1,256	35.6
McDowell[1]	1,535	—
Mercer	2,410	60.0
Monroe	474	5.2
Montgomery	1,429	21.0
Pulaski	201	5.6
Raleigh	1,562	90.3
Russell	-1,736	-16.0
Scott	2,208	23.7
Smyth	834	12.1
Tazewell	-182	-2.1
Washington	1,727	14.0
Wise[1]	4,416	—
Wyoming	1,212	76.6
Wythe	368	3.8
Total	32,173	23.5

1. Did not exist in 1850.

Source: *Seventh Census*, 256–57; *Eighth Census: Population*, 516–18.

Was Preston correct? Most Southwest Virginians rejected his rosy appraisal of out-migration, and in fact concluded that the problem actually had worsened, especially among nonlandowners. The *Wytheville Times* bitterly reported in 1857 an "immense rush to the

West," especially of emigrants bound for Texas and California.[45] The Midwest drew off Southwest Virginians as well. From Monroe County, John Echols wrote that "emigration to the North West is so immense that real estate is coming into the market with great rapidity." He noted that Illinois and Wisconsin especially attracted emigrants from Monroe.[46] Olmsted reported a constant stream of queries regarding California and Texas.[47]

Observers who judged out-migration increasing also cited the railroad as the leading factor. As the iron rails expanded westward, land values skyrocketed. In the upper valley counties through which the railroad ran, land values jumped 62.6 percent from 1850 to 1856. The largest increases were in Preston's native Montgomery and Pulaski, but adjoining counties experienced similar developments. Scott County land values, for example, increased 116.7 percent over the same six-year period. As land values jumped, profit seeking encouraged landlords to drive away tenants and either sell the land to newcomers from the east or put it into production themselves. Yeomen hard-pressed to pay the higher taxes that went along with rising land values often had no choice but to sell.[48] Herdsmen especially were hard hit. As even Preston admitted, "The grazing lands are beginning to be surrendered to the plow . . ." with stock shoved aside to "the second rate land."[49] While many mountaineers abandoned Virginia as a result, still others moved into the less commercialized sections of the Alleghany plateau and Blue Ridge subregions. The population of those areas increased quickly enough in the 1850s for the state to create three new counties, Buchanan, McDowell, and Wise, on the fringes of the plateau subregion.[50]

Crucially, Southwest Virginians moved up and down the economic ladder as well as from place to place in the decade. Two distinct trends are detailed in tables 12 through 15. In Floyd County, tenancy grew. From 1850 to 1860, the percentage of tenants rose to 34.2 percent of the county's population, 39.4 percent of self-proclaimed "farmers." These were gains of 6.5 percent and 8.5 percent respectively. Meanwhile, Floyd's laborers had all but disappeared. Comprising 4.6 percent of the population in 1850, laborers in 1860 made up only 0.3 percent of the total.[51]

Quite a different shift took place elsewhere, however. Tenancy declined 12.8 percent in Washington County and 26.7 percent in Raleigh County from 1850 to 1860. Many ex-tenants managed to move into the landowning yeomanry. In Washington County, the percentage of "farmers" who owned their land increased 9.4 percent. Yeoman growth was even greater in Raleigh County, where the percentage of landowning "farmers" increased 22.1 percent. All was not rosy, however, for

Table 12. Percentage of Farmers in Counties
Sampled, 1860

	Floyd	Raleigh	Washington
Yeomen	48.0	40.3	32.1
Tenants	34.2	21.3	27.2
Laborers	0.3	21.8	12.0
Total	82.5	83.4	71.3

Source: Federal Manuscript Census Sample

Table 13. Percentage of Yeomen and Tenants
among Self-described "Farmers" in Counties
Sampled, 1860

	Floyd	Raleigh	Washington
Yeomen	60.6	67.7	53.9
Tenants	39.4	32.3	46.1

Source: Federal Manuscript Census Sample

as the yeomanry grew, so did the laboring class. The percentage of laborers grew 3.6 percent in Washington County to comprise 12 percent of the population in 1860. Marginalization was even greater in
Raleigh, where laborers made up 21.8 percent of the population in
1860, a whopping 17.7 percent increase. Clearly, former tenants unable to buy increasingly expensive land were being forced off their rented farms and into day labor.[52]

Moreover, it was being done without compassion or grace. Olmsted described the sad situation of several Washington County laborers.
He reported breakfasting with a "well-informed, thoughtful gentleman"
and his laborers. The landowner spent most of the morning downgrad-
ing the laborers to their face, calling them lazy and stupid, and charg-
ing that they were unable to work without supervision. Only the poor
quality of white workers, he added, necessitated southerners' dependence on slavery. Olmsted concluded "his white hands all were seat-
ed with us at the breakfast table; coarse, dirty, silent, embarrassed, and
embarrassing men."[53]

Table 14. Change in Percentage of Farmers in
Counties Sampled, 1850–60

	Floyd	Raleigh	Washington
Yeomen	-3.7	1.3	-2.5
Tenants	7.0	-26.7	-12.8
Laborers	-4.3	17.1	3.6
Total	-1.0	-8.3	-11.7

Source: Federal Manuscript Census Sample

Table 15. Change in Percentage of Yeomen and
Tenants among Self-described "Farmers" in
Counties Sampled, 1850–60

	Floyd	Raleigh	Washington
Yeomen	-8.5	22.1	9.4
Tenants	8.5	-22.1	-9.4

Source: Federal Manuscript Census Sample

Displaced agriculturalists dramatized most potently the darker side of railroad expansion, what William L. Barney has called a "modernization crisis." While closer market connections had meant profit and expansion for some Southwest Virginians, a deeper immersion in the tobacco and wheat economies, they had been disastrous for others. Deprived of their now over-priced land, driven into tenancy or day labor, many Southwest mountaineers retreated deeper into the mountains, away from the intrusive and for them, disastrous commercial way of life the railroad made possible. In such places, like Logan County, traditional noncapitalist ways survived, as if by spite, well after the Civil War.[54]

Yet, another option availed itself to Southwest Virginians. If the greater commercialization of agriculture was one result of mountain railroad expansion and the modernization crisis, two others were urbanization and industrialization. By 1860, some mountaineers had left the land entirely and gone to town.

3

"Numerous Interesting Points on the Line": Towns, Tourism, and Industries

In September 1857, the first installment of an anonymous, seven-part novella appeared in *Harper's New Monthly Magazine*. "A Winter in the South" told the story of eastern Virginia Squire Anthony Broadacre, his family, and adventurous friend Bob Larkin. In the winter of 1856–57, the Broadacre-Larkin party embarked on a southern tour, with New Orleans the ultimate destination. Not long into the journey, in Lynchburg, they debated their next move. The squire wanted to remain on the canal to Buchanan and only then catch a stage to a Virginia and Tennessee Railroad depot. Larkin, gazetteer in hand, disagreed. Noting "numerous interesting points on the line, or within striking distance of its stations, which they might visit if so disposed," the younger Larkin favored boarding the newly completed railroad immediately. In the end, the group took the train.[1]

The travelers left for Southwest Virginia the next morning. Christiansburg, Montgomery County's seat, was their first stop. Tempted to stop there and visit nearby Salt Pond Mountain, one of the marvels listed in Larkin's gazetteer, the party nonetheless decided to continue on to Abingdon, where relatives waited. The desire to see "interesting points" got the best of Larkin, however, who left the Broadacres at Pulaski County's Newbern station, determined to see the celebrated New River Cliffs. He promised to rejoin them in a few days.

"'We are now in Abingdon,'" daughter Annette Broadacre wrote a friend, "'a neat, pleasant-looking little town, but very dull, nothing to do and nothing to see, and very little sociability.'"[2] Not surprisingly, they were happy when Larkin returned with tales of the cliffs. He also discussed Newbern, "rather a lonesome-looking village, situated on a hill." On the following morning, Broadacre and Larkin took a side trip to the village of Saltville, center of Southwest Virginia's nationally-known salt industry. Both the beauty of the surroundings and the technological wonders of the salt-making process fascinated them.[3]

Not so Bristol. As the second installment of the story picked up, the group had arrived at "straggling, half-finished village, which has lately sprung up at the terminus of the Virginia and Tennessee Railroad." The entire scene was uncultured and chaotic; "straggling railroad tracks, trains of empty and loaded cars, engines puffing and fuming, vast piles of wood, machine-shops and taverns. There are warehouses full of wheat and corn, great herds of grunting unambitious swine . . . crowds of busy men drinking "bald-face" and chewing tobacco, speculators in land and pork, insolent stage-drivers, gaping country folks, babbling politicians, careless negroes."[4]

Whether largely fiction or fact, "A Winter in the South" still effectively depicts a far different Southwest Virginia than the mountain agricultural region we have thus far encountered. Small towns and industries, by necessity more integrated into the larger capitalist market than the rural hinterlands, were sprinkled throughout the region and had been since the beginnings of settlement. As Van Beck Hall has noted, by 1830, there were already significant differences in western Virginia between counties with towns and those without, particularly in regard to economic diversification and commercialization. Urbanization and industrialization thus had originated long before the railroad, but the transformations of the 1850s added to the growth and importance of urban marketing centers. The Southwest Virginia that tourists such as the Broadacres visited in 1856 was that being made by the railroad.[5]

The wagons full of Southwest Virginia produce that rumbled along the region's poor roads for Baltimore and Philadelphia did not return empty. Commercial farmers used a portion of their profits to purchase store goods, notably tea and coffee, kitchenware, and clothing.[6] Merchants, not farmers, became Southwest Virginia's major shippers, however. Peddlers had entered the region soon after its settlement. With the opening of roads and an ever-increasing demand for outside goods, furnishing merchants, often the same former peddlers, quickly located in Southwest Virginia and opened stores. These merchants acquired goods through barter or cash, transported them to outside markets, sold them, and used the profits to restock their stores.[7]

Pack, Anderson, and Vawter, for example, operated a drygoods store in Fayette County in the late 1840s. The firm accepted in trade a wide assortment of items from customers, including beeswax, chestnuts, hides, tallow, and even home-manufactured gloves and socks. In return, consumers could purchase a plethora of goods: books, boots, calico, flannel, or silk cloth, coffee, combs, cotton, farm implements, knitting pins, nails, shoes, soap, sugar, tableware, tumblers, and tobacco. The merchants also stood ready to loan money at interest or supply credit to their customers. In this manner, the merchant credit system established itself in Southwest Virginia early on. Anne Royall for one took a dim view of such merchants and their credit system. She accused the "foreigners" of "taking in the people of Greenbriar with admirable skill. Having rendered Monroe [County] insolvent, they have come to try the range . . . of Greenbriar, and bid fair to strip her as bare as they have her daughter."[8]

Pack, Anderson and Vawter was a rural concern, but merchant capitalism in Southwest Virginia generally was an urban phenomenon. Although the region contained no cities before the Civil War, it did boast several towns of note. Abingdon, in Washington County, was the largest and most important. In 1850, Abingdon contained about two thousand people, over two hundred buildings, many of them brick, four churches, and a macadamized road. Featherstonhaugh had dismissed Abingdon in 1835 as a "straggling village," but a few years later his fellow Briton Buckingham could "hardly conceive a more eligible spot for [a poor] immigrant family from England . . . to settle in." He noted with praise its hotels, "pretty villa-residences," Whiggish newspaper, and natural history museum.[9]

The Abingdon area also boasted the region's first institution of higher learning, John Gilmer's alma mater, Emory and Henry College. Motivated by the desire to educate its youth in a wholesome nearby environment, the Holston Conference of the Methodist church founded the college in 1836. For a brief time, Emory and Henry was one of the most progressive institutions in the nation, boasting both a student employment program based on the theories of Swiss educational reformer Johann Pestalozzi and a staff of New Englanders from Wesleyan College. Within a few years, however, the new notions had gone by the wayside, and the college quickly metamorphosed into a typical southern institution, with a clientele partially from the deep South and slave servants in abundance.[10]

The valley subregion contained three other important towns, Christiansburg, Newbern, and Wytheville. Second in population to Abingdon, Wytheville contained eight stores, four churches, and two newspapers. Its free-thinkers were notorious among the region's more religious population. Newbern, in Pulaski County, and Montgomery County's Christiansburg were centers of local trade and government.

In the mountainous counties of the plateau subregion, Lewisburg was highly significant as western Virginia's judicial center. Peterstown and Union were also important.[11]

Southwest Virginia's towns, all county seats, functioned chiefly as local centers of government, law, and politics. The importance of county courts in Virginia before the reform constitution of 1851 magnified the significance of these towns. They became home for many members of the region's elite, but especially those involved in the practice of law. Many of the elite Campbells, Floyds, and Prestons called Abingdon home.[12]

Anne Royall had the misfortune to ride into Union on a court day in 1826 to mail a letter and as a result left a vivid portrait of the activities on one of these traditional meeting days. Seeking lodging, she discovered "one tavern only in the place, and every room engaged by the lawyers, and what nots of the country; all but one . . . immediately over the bar room." Thus fixed, she began to listen to the combined babble of "talking, singing, laughing, drinking, and swearing. . . . the whole scene one continual buz." Shoemakers argued about their wares, and two would-be geographers debated the proper pronunciation of "Mississippi." When court adjourned, a new crowd swept in to add to the raucous confusion.[13]

Besides attorneys, other professionals found themselves drawn to the towns. In 1850, for example, Abingdon's population included not only twelve lawyers, but also five clergymen, five doctors, three teachers, two dentists, and two newspaper editors. This small group of elite townsmen, often allied with the planter class through marriage, acquired wealth and power far beyond their numbers. Only 1.3 percent of the sampled population in Raleigh County, 2.1 percent in Floyd, and 3.7 percent in Washington, they nonetheless controlled a disproportionate amount of realty ranging from 29 percent to, in Raleigh County, 67 percent. In all three counties, the mean value of land owned by professionals was higher than that owned by landowning farmers (tables 16 and 17).[14]

Towns also served as commercial entrepôts. Merchants were most visible in this capacity—Abingdon had eleven in 1850—but townspeople not directly involved in trade still profited by establishing taverns and inns, and servicing drovers and travelers. More importantly, Southwest Virginia towns contained a host of artisans ready to supply their neighbors with various goods and services. In 1850, for example, Abingdon contained fifteen carpenters, eleven wagonmakers, ten blacksmiths, five painters, five printers, butchers, brickmasons, cabinetmakers, jewelers, saddlers, stone masons, tailors, and tanners, among

Table 16. Sampled "Professional"
Occupations, 1850

Bank clerk	1
Clerk of court	1
Constable	1
Dentist	1
Doctor	2
Editor	1
Hotel keeper	1
Lawyer	3
Merchant	10
Overseer	1
Professor	1
Poet	1
Teacher	2

Source: Federal Manuscript Census Sample

Table 17. Mean Value in Dollars of Real Estate Owned, by Occupation, in Counties Sampled, 1850

	Floyd	Raleigh	Washington
Landowning farmer	1,406.08	1,010.17	1,942.28
Category 4 Farmer	1,085.88	595.59	1,743.07
Laborer	66.67	0	108.44
Professional	2,807.14	5,030.00	2,051.00
Craftsmen	690.91	505.71	281.31
No occupation	87.23	143.32	778.18

Source: Federal Manuscript Census Sample

others. (For a sense of their numbers regionwide, see table 18.) In the overall sample, 2.3 percent of Raleigh Countians, 6.7 percent of Floyd's residents, and 7.9 percent of Washington Countians engaged in artisan professions.[15]

Towns also supplied social intercourse through schools, church activities, lectures, and fraternal organizations.[16] Samuel Keys of Wytheville noted the importance of the Odd Fellows in counteract-

Table 18. Sampled "Artisan" Occupations, 1850

Barber	1	Miller	6
Bed maker	1	Millwright	2
Blacksmith	12	Potter	1
Bricklayer	1	Shingle maker	1
Brickmason	1	Shoemaker	4
Cabinet maker	3	Stonemason	1
Carpenter	13	Tailor	4
Coach maker	1	Tanner	2
Cooper	1	Wagoner	4
Coppersmith	1	Wagon maker	2
Gunsmith	1	Wheelwright	1
Hatter	1	Woodchopper	1
Ironmaker	2		

Source: Federal Manuscript Census Sample

ing "dull times."[17] And from his estate in rugged Logan County, William Gaston Caperton confessed his desire to rent out the land and move back to Union. Surrounded by no one but his slaves and "plain, ignorant, and un-cultivated" mountaineers, Caperton and especially his wife longed for the "cultivated & polished society" of Union. He complained that the closest church stood in Peterstown, the nearest doctor ten miles away, and the nearest school twenty.[18]

Before 1850, these townspeople as a group sang the virtues of railroad construction. To them, railroads provided a golden opportunity to increase their profits and their economic hegemony over the rural hinterlands. As the *Abingdon Virginian* presented the case, the railroad would mean more money in the farmers' pockets, cash that would not remain there long. The influx of money into the region, the *Virginian* asserted, would signal the death knell of the barter system. Merchants, doctors, attorneys, and schoolmasters could demand cash for their services. These groups would be the ultimate beneficiaries of a regional railroad, and the majority of mountaineers would remain snugly in the professionals' hands.[19]

By 1860, many of these hopes were coming true. The 1850s were boom years for Southwest Virginia towns located on the railroad or connected to it by the local road network. Throughout the region, the percentage of townspeople in nonagricultural occupations grew. While the trend was barely noticeable in some counties—Floyd's nonfarming population grew 1 percent—great changes took place elsewhere. The nonfarming populations of Raleigh and Washington counties grew 8.3 percent and 11.7 percent respectively during the 1850s. In Raleigh, the professional class grew 3.9 percent and the artisan group 3.8 percent. In Washington, the already large professional class grew only 2.2 percent, but the artisan population increased 6.6 percent.[20]

Existing towns benefited. Abingdon and Wytheville particularly expanded as their importance as trade centers increased. In 1858, the *Wytheville Times* noted that since the completion of the railroad, Wytheville had added thirty new homes, ten more in the town's "suburbs," and several new commercial establishments. Everywhere the *Times* looked, it saw the "spirit of enterprise" at work.[21]

Even more dramatic, however, was the genesis and swift development of new towns. Some, such as Cambria, Christiansburg's depot, and Washington County's Glade Spring, at the southern terminus of the Saltworks Branch, grew into small but active villages. Most spectacular was the explosive growth of the twin cities at the railroad's western terminus, Goodson, Virginia, and Bristol, Tennessee, usually lumped together as "Bristol." Located on the vacated site of a Cherokee village, the area in 1850 boasted only a post office and stagecoach stop owned by Presbyterian minister James King. Both King and his Virginia neighbor, General Assembly railroad advocate Samuel E. Goodson, ardently desired the western terminus of the railroad. They repeatedly wined and dined railroad surveyors in order to gain their friendship. Meanwhile, King's nephew, Joseph R. Anderson, decided to get in on the act as well. In 1852, Anderson purchased a hundred-acre tract from his uncle, with fifty-two acres in Virginia and the rest across the line. Not long after, the railroad chose the spot for the terminus. Anderson moved there in 1853, built a house and store, and had the tract laid out into 216 lots, each available for one hundred dollars.[22]

The area grew quickly. By 1856, when the two towns incorporated, they jointly formed a "thriving little village" of seven hundred people and 125 buildings.[23] Two years later, the site became home to the eastern terminus of the completed East Tennessee and Virginia Railroad as well. James M. Johnston, a newcomer from the Piedmont on the make in the boom town, left a description reminiscent of that in "A Winter in the South" but one laced with more bawdy affection: "They have here, a Presbyterian church, a Campellite church and a Methodist church, with plenty of preaching and praying—two large 10 pin saloons and I don't know how many barrooms besides four Hotels—The Exchange keeps no liquor—considering all things Bristol is, however, a pretty decent place."[24]

As far as commerce was concerned, Johnston described "excitement" and "fast times." Capitalist expansion in turn gave rise to a professional class in Bristol. Johnston met several acquaintances from his native Albermarle County including his old schoolmaster, recently returned from five years in Illinois.[25] Another Piedmont native out to make a splash in the boom town was Goodson's first attorney, John S. Mosby, destined to gain fame as the Confederacy's "Gray Ghost."[26]

Overall, the importance of merchant capitalism and the varied attitudes and activities of townspeople suggest that "Jeffersonian" Southwest Virginia knew its heretical moments. More Hamiltonian agents were at work as well. Notably, several machines were at work in the garden.

The Broadacre-Larkin party discovered that Southwest Virginia contained industries as well as towns. To be sure, most of them were small, localized operations. Most localities of any size in the southern mountains boasted distilleries, grist mills, sawmills, and tanneries. These small but vital concerns offered processing services to farmers in the area, grinding the farmer's corn or distilling it into whiskey. Larger, more commercially oriented industries also operated in Southwest Virginia. Hat manufactories were located in Scott and Washington counties. The latter also possessed a woolen manufactory and two cotton manufactories. Two boot and shoe factories produced footwear in Tazewell County. Gap Mills in Monroe County was something of an industrial center, containing a distillery, a fulling mill, a flour mill, an oil mill, a sawmill, a tannery, and a woolen factory. Local farmers profited from these establishments by supplying raw materials and rented slaves to the industrialists.[27]

Three major industries, however, dwarfed these pursuits. Lead mining was one. The lead mines of Wythe County, centered around the village of Austinville, had provided a processed product to American buyers since the 1750s. The American revolutionaries utilized Wythe County lead extensively in weapons manufacture. The mines continued to be important. In 1850, Wythe's two leading lead companies produced four hundred tons of their product, worth thirty-seven thousand dollars. The industry was in trouble, nonetheless. Suicidal competition between the local mine owners ate into profits. Short-lived consolidation agreements among the rivals, diversification into timbering, and company stores (the latter principally involving liquor sales) kept the industrialists afloat through the mid-forties, but the breakdown of their arrangement in 1848 brought a new round of competition. Producers outside the region made matters worse; western mines could produce and sell lead for less than could the Southwest Virginians.[28]

Southwest Virginia's iron industry faced similar problems. With the region, and especially the Holston River valley, rich in iron ore, the Wythe area excelled before the Revolution in iron manufacture and boasted numerous furnaces. Like the lead industry, the ironmongers only encountered serious competition after 1800. New York, New Jersey, and notably Pennsylvania iron makers, using coke rather than charcoal and coal power rather than water power, took the lead in the domestic industry. Scottish iron makers offered stiff competition as well. Southwest Virginia's largely unexploited coal fields offered little aid to the region's iron manufacturers. To add to their woes, new mines along the Mississippi River opened up. Southwest Virginia's rivals faced relatively low transportation costs due to their proximity to water transportation. The iron industry was in better health than the lead, having produced 950 tons of iron in 1850, but the patient still required a shot in the arm.[29]

Southwest Virginia's third important nonagricultural industry was the related production of salt and plaster. Thomas L. Preston and his relatives, Wyndham Robertson, and members of the elite King and Trigg families owned and operated salt works and plaster mines along the Smyth County–Washington County line which produced a combined total of over 465,000 bushels of salt and 200,000 tons of plaster in 1850. These mines formed the basis for the manufacturing village of Saltville described in "A Winter in the South." Unlike the lead and iron industries, the saltworks' outlook appeared healthy. Buyers throughout the mid-Atlantic, midwestern, and Deep South states favored Southwest Virginia salt, and plaster was coming into its own as a fertilizer for tobacco.[30]

All of these valley subregion industrialists coveted a railroad as a means to cut transportation costs and thus compete more successfully with their out-of-state competitors. Mule-drawn wagons hauled the region's iron, lead, plaster, and salt to Lynchburg and the canal over the same roads favored by farmers and drovers. The salt works in addition shipped salt by boat down the Holston River, a hazardous enterprise that resulted in several lost boats every year. A railroad would reverse the decline of Southwest Virginia's industries, and give them new life.[31]

Once completed, the railroad fulfilled these hopes. The V&T negated the necessity of overland transportation of lead and shot to Lynchburg, aiding the lead industry tremendously. Transportation costs fell by more than half. At the same time, the overall industry received a boost when one of the industrialists, Alexander Pierce, sold all but one of his Wythe County holdings in 1854. All the remaining owners except A. S. Fulton combined their operations into the Wythe Union Lead Mine Company, incorporating in 1860. In that year the industry produced 480 tons of lead and an additional 100 tons of lead shot, and enjoyed unrivaled prosperity.[32]

Pierce left lead mining to devote his time and money to mining copper in Carroll County. In 1853 and 1854, the county's "Copper Mining Mania" began.[33] Carroll County's population jumped as would-be copper kings swept into the area, including businessmen from Maryland and Tennessee. Several mines opened for business, a few across the line in Floyd and Grayson counties. In 1855, the copper mines produced 1000 tons of copper, all of which was shipped to market via the railroad once hauled to the nearest depot. Profits were such that in September 1855, the railroad board commissioned Gill to "reconnoitre" the area between the main trunk of the railway and the copper region in order to determine if a branch line like the saltworks branch would prove profitable. Gill reported one month later that he could build such a branch, but he doubted if the mines held enough copper to make the branch worthwhile to the railroad. The directors agreed, and dropped the idea. Gill's decision may have been short-sighted; in 1860, production had increased to 27,680 tons.[34]

The railroad's effects on the regional iron industry closely resembled those of the copper and lead industries. In 1860, the Wythe mines produced 922.5 tons of pig iron, iron castings, and nails. The railroad negated the necessity of overland transportation of pig iron and iron products, lowered expenses, and in time made the acquisition of coal and ore easier.[35]

The construction of the railroad and the Saltworks Branch proved a boon to the regional salt and plaster industry despite a lower output in 1860 than in 1850. In 1853, before the railroad reached the works, members of the Preston family had offered its seven-thousand-acre saltworks to English buyers. Admitting their high transportation costs, the owners assured potential buyers that the railroad eventually would provide cheap and reliable transportation of salt. No takers accepted the offer. In 1856, Thomas Preston clearly was happy about it, as the railroad and branch had markedly changed his and the industry's fortunes. A railroad director, Preston had enriched himself by securing both the Abingdon and Saltville depots on his land. He then deepened his involvement in the increasingly profitable industry by first renting the rival King saltworks, and then purchasing his relatives' holdings. With fully three-quarters of the salt and plaster mines, Preston established a virtual monopoly on the trade. His resultant debt and poor management, however, left him bankrupt within four years. In 1860, the salt monopoly passed to Stewart, Palmer, and Company, who formed the Holston Salt and Plaster Company. They produced 360,000 bushels of salt in that year. Meanwhile Robertson, with his former agent, B. K. Buchanan, continued to operate his mines.[36]

The railroad also contributed to the establishment of new industries. In addition to the usual distilleries, flour mills, saw mills, smithies, and tanneries, as well as copper mining, in 1860 the region boasted manufacturers of agricultural implements, carriages and wagons, clothing, firearms, pottery, finished tobacco, and other products. Like planters, manufacturers from outside the region found the territory inviting. In 1854, Nathan and Sarah Look, originally natives of Massachusetts, moved to Montgomery County from the Valley to manufacture brooms and cheese. The Looks shipped their wares back East on the unfinished railroad. Two years later, the family moved further westward to Smyth County. Smyth County also attracted a twelve-loom textile mill operated by the F. and H. Fries Company of Salem, North Carolina. Telegraph service connected the region's industries to eastern buyers.[37]

By far the most promising new industry was coal mining. In 1853, the Preston family opened coal mines on its holdings in Logan, Russell, and Tazewell counties, expecting a yield of six hundred thousand bushels in the first year of operation. Workers delivered the mined coal to Cincinnati by boat. Eager to exploit the new industry for its own profits, the railroad aggressively encouraged new mining operations. In 1854, it commissioned a study of coal fields in Montgomery County that encouraged the directors to consider a branch to the area. Although Montgomery's yields remained small by postwar standards, totaling eighty thousand bushels in 1860, the railroad's close connections with mining companies, as well as its coal mine boosterism, set a precedent for the future. The railroad's final post–Civil War incarnation, the Norfolk and Western Railroad, established its reputation and fortune primarily as a coal carrier.[38]

As coal and the development of Appalachia are so closely entwined, the relationship between the Virginia and Tennessee Railroad and Southwest Virginia's nascent coal industry alone symbolically suggests the need for a modification of the current explanation of Appalachia's genesis. The conclusion is inescapable that the precedents and first victories of mountain industrialism occurred in the late 1840s and 1850s in Southwest Virginia. An influx of extraregional capital, aggressive railroad policies favored by industrially minded politicians, economic and geographic dislocations of traditionally minded mountaineers, and the beginnings of resource exploitation for outside profit, all pointed to as characteristics of the post-1870 period, were present in Southwest Virginia in the 1850s. The industrialization of Appalachia began in 1853, when the Virginia and Tennessee Railroad broke ground in Lynchburg, not twenty years later when timber interests appeared elsewhere in the southern mountains. Moreover, just as in the postwar period, outsiders were on hand to observe.[39]

Had the Broadacre-Larkin party traveled in the summer instead of the winter, they no doubt would have "gone to the waters." Since the early nineteenth century, and especially after 1832, Southwest Virginia drew the upper crust of southern society to its scenic mountains and fashionable hot springs. While a few resorts operated east of the mountains, the majority did business in Southwest Virginia, clustered into sections of Greenbrier and Monroe counties.[40]

Visitors ostensibly went to the waters for their health. Doctors praised the warm, bitter fluids as veritable cure-alls. In truth, the hot springs functioned more as playgrounds than hospitals. During the summer social season, the southern aristocracy hobnobbed, danced, arranged marriages, drank, gambled, and admired the scenery.[41] Buckingham, who disapproved of the entire scene, described the springs' patrons "lounging idly about, too indolent of body for active exercise, too indolent of mind for animated conversation, and evincing an appearance of the greatest lassitude and weariness in every look and tone."[42]

Southwest Virginia furnished springs for every taste and time of the social season. Fashionable visitors started just east of the region's border with the Shenandoah Valley at Warm Springs, spent a night or two, and crossed the mountains to the "great lion," White Sulphur Springs. Located in Greenbrier County, the popular White generally overflowed with upward of six hundred guests. After a sojourn at White Sulphur Springs, patrons fanned out to other spas. Deep southerners, particularly South Carolinians, favored Salt Sulphur Springs and Gray Sulphur Springs, the former with a section of guest cabins called "Nullification Row."[43] Southerners more willing to rub elbows with Yankees chose Red Sulphur Springs, while those weary of crowds could slip away to the less fashionable Blue Sulphur Springs. During the last week in August, the elite rejoined one another at Sweet Springs, oldest of the spas, before returning to their homes.[44] Few agreed with Featherstonhaugh, who found the food "disgusting," the southern guests "self-sanctified, canting jackasses," and the scene as a whole possessed of "all the filth and nastiness of a badly conducted hospital."[45]

The hot springs produced several ripples in the local economy. Anne Royall professed to believe that the mere presence of so many "people of taste and refinement" could not help but trickle down to the simple mountaineers, bringing "a fund of amusement and instruction home to the doors of [the region's] inhabitants." Yet, as she ruefully confessed, the only visible effect among the residents was an ever-increasing demand for the "foreign luxuries" the elite conspicuously brought with them. Royall blamed this desire for outside goods as the chief catalyst for the Greenbrier Valley's integration into the larger economy.[46]

The resorts touched the local economy more directly. The springs provided ready markets for local meats and vegetables. Featherstonhaugh observed drovers arriving at White Sulphur Springs with twenty to fifty head of cattle per herd, which they sold to the management for three cents per pound, a price as good as that available in Richmond. In addition, local entrepreneurs rented slaves out as domestic servants, provided carriages for guests' transportation, and furnished room and board to travelers awaiting vacancies at the resorts.[47]

Moreover, springs' guests anxious for a diversion fueled a nascent tourism industry elsewhere in the region. No visit to Southwest Virginia was complete, writers counseled, without a stop at Hawk's Nest, magnificently perched a thousand feet above the New River in Fayette County. Organ Cave, fifteen miles south of White Sulphur Springs, also found popularity. The Bob Larkins employed local guides to lead them to these and other attractions.[48]

Southwest Virginia's hot springs faced the same transportation bottleneck as townspeople and industrialists. While reaching the springs from the North or East was relatively easy through a combination of canal boats, railroads, and stagecoaches, getting there from the South, as most patrons had to do, was another matter. Travelers faced two lamentable choices. One was to journey by steamboat to Guyandotte, on the Ohio River, and then trek overland via coach. The alternative was to travel by coach entirely, usually down the valley on the Valley Road until reaching a connecting road. Both trips were arduous.[49] Buckingham swore that he "had practically felt all the sufferings . . . that bad vehicles, bad roads, bad beds, bad fare, and dirty and uncivil attendants could inflict."[50] Count Francesco Arese, a Milanese noble and associate of France's Louis Napoleon, compared the inhabitants of his coach to "anchovies in a keg." He warned readers, "You can hang on, grip on, cling on as much as you are able, you will land every evening shattered, bruised, done up!" The roads to the springs, Arese concluded, were "horrible."[51]

Descriptions such as these were not likely to stimulate business. Thus, despite their profits, the springs operators joined other Southwest Virginians in their ardent desire for a regional railroad. In 1852, DeBow editorialized: "Let the South stand by the Virginia Springs. The rail-roads will soon bring them to our doors. No rude waiters jostle us, no insolent parvenues, no tricks and deceptions, no starvation, nor "Maine laws," no abolition praters, but congenial associations."[52]

The completed railroad eagerly capitalized on such sentiments. Its advertisements promised Richmonders that they could leave the capital at dawn and arrive at White Sulphur Springs by dark through a combination of the railroad and coaches. The railroad then helped feed the new arrivals by making the purchase of store goods easier for management. The railroad and turnpikes made Wytheville a center of grocery buying and slave hiring for the springs.[53]

In addition to aiding the existing springs, the railroad also furthered their expansion. In the 1850s, a dozen new springs opened for business, almost all located near the railroad. Montgomery County took the lead with three. Giles, Grayson, Pulaski, Russell, Scott, Tazewell, and Wythe counties also boasted new springs of their own. Montgomery White Sulphur Springs soon took the lead among the newcomers and became a serious challenger to the older, established resorts. Among its conveniences was a 1.75 mile, mule drawn, narrow gauge railroad running from the hotel to the V&T's Big Tunnel station. The railroad and the expanded tourism industry had linked symbolically.[54]

Urbanization and industrialization, in sum, grew dramatically during the 1850s as results of the railroad and its links to the wider South. Those links led to something else as well, something peculiar to southern modernization—expansion of the "peculiar institution," slavery.

4

"A Source of Great Economy":
The Railroad and Slavery

NOT ALL OF Southwest Virginia's mountaineers were white. African Americans also have called Southwest Virginia home since the beginnings of settlement. The 1790 census, the nation's first, found 1,787 slaves, about 6 percent of the total population, in Southwest Virginia's then four counties. It also identified thirty-nine nonwhite "free persons." The numbers and percentages of slaves in the region grew steadily from 1790 until the Civil War. In 1830, the region's slaveholders held 12,060 bondsmen, 12.3 percent of the population. By 1850, as tables 19 and 20 show, the numbers were 16,442 and 10.6 percent respectively, hardly negligible. The lower percentage was due to the greater increase of white population than any lessening of slavery's importance. Over the same period, in comparison, Virginia's total percentage of slave population fell at an even faster rate, from 38.8 percent to 33.3 percent.[1] Looking backward from 1851, the *Richmond Enquirer* not surprisingly found "the relative increase of the slaves in the whole of Western Virginia . . . remarkable."[2]

Black Southwest Virginians, roughly one-tenth of the region's antebellum population, are usually ignored nonetheless. Contemporaries played down the presence of slavery in the region for political reasons. The eastern opponents of constitutional reform in 1830, for example, found it useful to depict transmontane Virginia as largely all-white and all-but-abolitionist in sympathies. Slavery's opponents, men such as Ossawatomie John Brown and James W. Taylor, then picked up on the image. After the Civil War, influential writers enshrined the stereotype of nearly all-white, antislavery Appalachia.[3]

A few observers, of course, did recognize the "remarkable" presence and importance of slavery in the region. In *Journey in the Back Country*, Olmsted's negative preconceptions to be sure always skewed his interpretations; often he saw only what he wanted to see, which in

Table 19. Southwest Virginia Slave Population, 1850–60

County	1850	1860	Net Change	Percentage Change
Boone	183	158	-25	-13.7
Buchanan[1]	—	30	—	—
Carroll	154	262	108	70.1
Fayette	156	271	115	73.7
Floyd	443	475	32	7.2
Giles	657	778	121	18.4
Grayson	499	547	48	9.6
Greenbrier	1,317	1,525	208	15.6
Lee	787	824	37	4.7
Logan	87	148	61	70.1
McDowell[1]	—	0	—	—
Mercer	177	362	185	104.5
Monroe	1,061	1,114	53	5.0
Montgomery	1,471	2,219	748	50.9
Pulaski	1,471	1,589	118	8.2
Raleigh	23	57	34	147.8
Russell	982	1,099	117	11.9
Scott	473	490	17	3.6
Smyth	1,064	1,037	-27	-2.5
Tazewell	1,060	1,202	142	13.4
Washington	2,131	2,547	416	19.5
Wise[1]	—	66	—	—
Wyoming	61	64	3	4.9
Wythe	2,185	2,162	-23	-1.0
Total	16,442	19,026	2,584	15.7

1. Did not exist in 1850.

Source: *Seventh Census*, 256–57; *Eighth Census: Population*, 516–18.

this case were nonslaveholders' resentment of the master class and occasionally in East Tennessee even abolitionist ideas. Yet even he had to admit that in Southwest Virginia, slaves and slaveholders were much more in evidence as he traveled through the valley subregion, and moreover that the Southwest Virginia whites he met were never openly antislavery.[4]

An additional observer was a native Southwest Virginian, George

Table 20. Slavery in Virginia, 1850–60

Region	1850		1860		Percentage Change[1]
	No.	%	No.	%	
Northwest	8,002	3.8	6,448	2.5	-19.4
Southwest	16,442	10.6	19,026	10.3	15.7
Total Trans-Alleghany	24,444	6.8	25,474	5.2	-1.6
Valley	38,798	18.7	37,204	17.0	-4.1
Piedmont	232,655	50.7	248,849	50.1	7.0
Tidewater	178,861	44.6	179,502	42.0	0.5
Total	474,571	33.3	491,028	30.8	3.5

1. Defined as (1860 total - 1850 total) ÷ 1850 total.

Source: *Seventh Census,* 256–57; *Eighth Census: Population,* 516–18.

W. L. Bickley. Through a mixture of fact and ideology, Bickley placed slavery even closer to the heart of mountain life. Best remembered as the unstable founder of the notorious Knights of the Golden Circle, a shadow organization dedicated to the expansion of slavery throughout the western hemisphere, Bickley was born in Russell County in 1819. He ran away from home as a youth only to return to the region in the late 1840s to practice medicine in Jeffersonville, Tazewell County. Before leaving again for Ohio in 1851, he registered a notable first, writing the pioneer history of his native region in collaboration with a local historical society.[5]

Considering Bickley's later activities and obvious mental instability, his *History of the Settlement and Indian Wars of Tazewell County, Virginia* remains remarkably useful, including as it did voluminous information on the region's geography, climate, economy, educational facilities, and customs. The author's real goals in writing the book, however, were largely political and pro-slavery. Denouncing the eastern Virginia politicians who for most of the century had controlled the state government, Bickley wanted to convince his fellow Southwest Virginians to separate politically from Virginia and form a new state in conjunction with the equally disgruntled mountain residents of Eastern Kentucky, Western North Carolina, and East Tennessee—but not Northwestern Virginia. Bickley pointedly excluded the heart of the future state of West

Virginia, from his new state scheme. Because of slavery, he felt, the two regions were much too different. Whereas the Northwest increasingly was becoming free territory, slavery occupied a central place in southwestern society. Indeed he made a point of condemning contemporaries for the common practice of ignoring Southwest Virginia and equating "West" with the antislavery "Northwest."[6]

That one of the most notorious advocates of slavery in Civil War–era America was a Southwest Virginia mountaineer should have dramatized both the differences between Northwest and Southwest Virginia and the importance of the institution in Appalachia to later observers. Only recently however have scholars reaffirmed the importance of slavery in mountain society. That understanding is crucial. If one is to understand why Southwest Virginia embraced the Confederate cause in 1861, the centrality of slavery must be acknowledged. With slavery already an important fact of mountain life in Southwest Virginia by 1850, the role of the railroad was to provide still greater opportunities for slave-based staple agriculture, and as a result facilitate the institution's growth through the 1850s, a decade when the institution stagnated elsewhere in the state. Here lies a seeming paradox if one fails to recognize the distinctive character of southern modernization or simplistically equates modernization with "progress." In Southwest Virginia, as elsewhere in the South, modernization and the expansion of an institution as "unmodern" as chattel slavery went hand-in-hand.[7]

"There are more slaves here than I have seen before for several weeks," wrote Olmsted outside of Abingdon as he emerged from East Tennessee to complete his journey in the highlands.[8] It was true. While slaveholding in Southwest Virginia was not as extensive as it was in the nonmountain sections of the South, of all sections of the southern mountain region, Southwest Virginia was among the leaders in both the most slaves and the most slaveholders. Approximately 11.2 percent of the householders in the 1850 sample were slaveowners. To be sure, most of these masters owned but a few slaves; the median sample holding was three, although the situation of course varied from county to county. Moreover, there were slaveowners in areas such as Washington County who would have qualified as planters anywhere in the South. Washington Countian Eliza White, for example, owned sixty-five slaves in 1850, and her neighbor John Preston held forty-six. Overall, slavery was most extensive in the valley subregion. As shown in tables 21 and 22, 352 Washington Countians owned slaves,

Table 21. Slaveholders in Counties Sampled, 1850

	Holdings	Number	
Floyd	1–9	103	(92%)
	10–19	8	(7%)
	20+	1	(1%)
		112	
Raleigh	1–9	8	(100%)
	10–19	0	(0%)
	20+	0	(0%)
		8	
Washington	1–9	285	(81%)
	10–19	52	(15%)
	20+	15	(4%)
		352	

Source: Federal Manuscript Census Sample

67 owned ten or more, and 15 owned twenty or more. In contrast, only 112 Floyd Countians belonged to the slaveowning class, and only Joseph Howard owned more than twenty slaves. The contrast was even greater in Raleigh County, where only 8 owned slaves in 1850. With 6 bondsmen, Archibald Walker was Raleigh's leading master.[9] While many of the three counties' leading masters fit Olmsted's description of mountain masters, "chiefly professional men, shop-keepers, and men in office, who are also land owners," most identified themselves as farmers (table 22).[10]

As valley subregion slaveholders owned more slaves, they also controlled much more wealth than their peers elsewhere in the region. Washington County's ten leading masters owned a mean of $28,175 of real property in a county where the overall mean was $761 and the mean of all slaveowners $2,753. In contrast, the mean of Raleigh County's eight slaveowners was $2,699. While far above Raleigh's overall mean holding, $453, the figure still was not substantial; indeed, Raleigh's elite's land holdings were comparable in worth to those of the average Washington County master. Moreover, the gap between rich and poor in the plateau was not as significant. Slaveholding, then,

Table 22. Leading Slaveholders in Counties Sampled, 1850

	Occupation	Number of Slaves
Floyd		
Joseph Howard	Merchant	24
Harvey Deskins	Farmer	14
Peter Guarrant	Farmer	14
Thomas Helms	No occupation	13
Archibald Hylton	Farmer	13
Ira Howard	Merchant	12
James Furgerson	?	11
Joseph Kennerly	Farmer	11
Job Wells	Farmer	11
Asa Howard	Merchant	9
Raleigh		
Archibald Walker	Farmer	6
Henry Gillaspie	Lawyer	5
James Beavers	Farmer	3
Sarah Pack	No occupation	3
Lemuel Jarrel	Farmer	2
Clark Tench	Farmer	2
John Anderson	Merchant?	1
Alfred Beckley	Superior court clerk	1
Washington		
Eliza White	No occupation	65
John Preston	Farmer	46
James King	Minister	38
William Byars	Farmer	37
John Baker	Farmer	33
Wyndham Robertson	Farmer	31
Frances Campbell	Farmer	29
Whitley Fulton	Farmer	28
James P. Strother	Farmer	23
William Harvey	Merchant	22
Allen McCoy	?	22

Source: Federal Manuscript Census Sample

while it approximated the situation of the black belt elite in the valley, grew more egalitarian as it penetrated the mountains.[11]

This expansion continued both numerically and geographically through the 1850s. Most basic was the simple growth of the region's slave population from 1850 to 1860. In 1860, Southwest Virginia as a whole contained 20,532 black residents, of whom only 1,506 were free (tables 19 and 20). This meant an increase of 2,584 slaves and 232 free blacks in the decade. Considered as percentages, this translates into a 15.7 percent rate of increase in the number of slaves. This figure does not appear especially remarkable at first. Over the same ten years, for example, Texas's slave population increased 213.9 percent, Arkansas' 135.9 percent, and Florida's 57.1 percent. When compared with older states such as Georgia and Tennessee, however, as well as the rest of Virginia, Southwest Virginia's growing slave population takes on new significance. Statewide, slavery grew from 1850 to 1860 at only a 3.5 percent rate. In the Tidewater, growth had stagnated, and in the Valley and especially the Northwest, slavery had declined. The rate of growth in the Piedmont, while more substantial, was less than half that of Southwest Virginia. In short, although the real numbers were comparatively smaller in Southwest Virginia, the institution nonetheless evinced a vitality noticeably absent in the rest of the commonwealth. If slavery indeed had peaked in Virginia and entered a period of decline, as William W. Freehling recently implied, it nonetheless showed surprising vigor in the Southwest.[12]

Slavery did not grow at a uniform rate across the region (tables 23 and 24). In the Blue Ridge subregion, Carroll County's copper rush led to a sizable increase in the county's slave laborers from 154 to 262, a 70.1 percent rate of growth. In Floyd and Grayson counties, however, increases in the white population far outstripped slave population growth. In 1850, for example, 113 Floyd County slaveowners owned 444 slaves. Ten years later, the numbers of both groups had increased roughly by only thirty. The mean and median sample slaveholdings in Floyd were exactly the same as those in 1850, 3.4 and 2 respectively. With twenty-two slaves, Joseph Howard remained the county's leading master and the only owner of more than twenty slaves. Meanwhile, the white population had increased by almost 30 percent. In Floyd, as with the growth of white tenantry, very little had changed.[13]

While slavery remained in stasis in the Blue Ridge subregion as a whole, however, one indicator suggests that future growth was in the offing. The rates of natural increase among slaves, computed from the percentage of slaves under age ten compared to the total slave population and displayed in table 25, were 35.6 percent and 33.4 percent

Table 23. Slaveholders in Counties Sampled, 1860

	Holdings	Number	
Floyd	1-9	135	(94%)
	10-19	8	(5%)
	20+	1	(1%)
		144	
Raleigh	1-9	21	(100%)
	10-19	0	(0%)
	20+	0	(0%)
		21	
Washington	1-9	330	(85%)
	10-19	42	(11%)
	20+	18	(5%)
		390	

Source: Federal Manuscript Census Sample

in Floyd and Grayson respectively, higher than the statewide average of 30.5 percent. As Inscoe has noted, a higher than average rate of natural increase reflected confidence among slaveholders that slavery was a safe and profitable investment for the future. In other words, the white tide sweeping into Floyd and Grayson counties did not deter those counties' slaveholders from deepening their involvement in the peculiar institution.[14]

Nor did a lack of substantial growth mean widespread opposition to the institution. Robley D. Evans, for example, a future officer in the Union Navy, was the son of one Floyd County master, a physician who owned a dozen slaves. Most of the Evans' neighbors were nonslaveholders who "as a rule were poor and did their own farm work." Yet all of them carefully maintained the sanctity of the institution in the county, at least according to Evans. "There were two things one must not do," he remembered, "—steal horses or interfere with his neighbors slaves."[15]

A different situation existed in the valley subregion counties, which together already held half of the entire region's slaves. Two distinct

Table 24. Leading Slaveholders in Counties Sampled, 1860

	Occupation	Number of Slaves
Floyd		
Joseph Howard	Farmer	22
Pleasant Howard	No occupation	19
Thomas Franklin	?	15
Archibald Hylton	Farmer	15
Ira Hylton	Merchant	14
Job Wells	Farmer	13
John Helms	Farmer	11
Noah Moore	Farmer	10
Harvey Deskins	Farmer	9
Lewis Livesey	Farmer	9
Raleigh		
John Manser	Doctor/Farmer	9
Jenifer Smoot	Collector	7
William Ferguson	Farmer	5
Isom Dobins	Farmer	4
Thomas Hundley	Farmer	4
"Morris and Johnson"	?	4
Daniel Shumake	County clerk	4
Elizabeth Walker	Spinster	4
William Bruffy	Doctor	3
Edward Prince	Merchant	3
Washington		
Wyndham Robertson	Gentleman	72
John Preston	Farmer	46
William Y.C. White	Farmer	45
George Litchfield	?	42
James P. Strother	Farmer	39
Adam Hickman	Gentleman	36
Whitley Fulton	Farmer	35
William A. Preston	Farmer	31
Newton White	Farmer	31
James White	Doctor	28

Source: Federal Manuscript Census Sample

Table 25. Slaves under Age Ten in Southwest Virginia, 1860

| County | Number of Slaves | | Percentage of Total |
	Under Age Ten	Total	
Boone	60	158	38.0
Buchanan	13	30	43.3
Carroll	83	262	31.7
Fayette	86	271	31.7
Floyd	169	475	35.6
Giles	247	778	31.7
Grayson	183	547	33.4
Greenbrier	449	1,525	29.4
Lee	300	824	36.4
Logan	53	148	35.8
McDowell	0	0	—
Mercer	132	362	36.5
Monroe	357	1,114	32.0
Montgomery	734	2,219	33.1
Pulaski	538	1,589	33.9
Raleigh	15	57	26.3
Russell	389	1,099	35.4
Scott	123	490	25.1
Smyth	326	1,037	31.4
Tazewell	398	1,202	33.1
Washington	788	2,547	30.9
Wise	24	66	36.4
Wyoming	19	64	30.0
Wythe	693	2,162	32.1
Total	5,699	19,026	30.0
Total for Virginia	149,725	490,865	30.5

Source: *Eighth Census: Population,* 508–15.

trends may be discerned. Two counties experienced major slave growth. Montgomery County gained 748 slaves, a 50.9 percent increase that far outpaced the county's 21 percent gain in white population. At the opposite end of the valley subregion, Washington County, Southwest Virginia's leading slave county in 1860, added 418 slaves, a 19.5 percent increase. In Washington County, 390 slaveowners owned 2,547 slaves in 1860. While the mean sampled holding was 6.5 and the median 4, 60 residents of the county owned more than ten slaves, and 18 owned over 20. With 72 slaves, Wyndham Robertson now reigned as the county's leading planter. In the other three counties of the valley subregion, however, slave populations experienced little dramatic change. Pulaski County gained 118 slaves, Smyth lost 27 slaves, and Wythe lost 23 slaves. Again, however, the rates of natural increase in these three counties were higher than Virginia's overall rate.[16]

The counties of the Allegheny Plateau experienced the widest fluctuations. One can simplify analysis somewhat by considering the subregion in 1860 as further subdivided into eastern and western halves, as Paul Salstrom has done. In the more rugged western section of the plateau subregion, Russell and Tazewell counties' slave populations underwent significant growth. Russell gained 117 slaves in the decade and Tazewell added 142. Notably, these two counties were those best connected to the railroad through a road network that linked them to Abingdon. As one moved away from the railroad, however, the importance of slavery declined noticeably. The entire remainder of the western plateau gained only 152 slaves in the decade. McDowell County was all-white in 1860, and Buchanan, Wise, and Wyoming nearly so.[17]

Had the western plateau then become an impenetrable mountain wall against slavery expansion? The region's slaveholders felt much differently than their neighbors. Among these slaveholders, one found the highest rates of natural increase among the slave population in all of Southwest Virginia. Only McDowell County, with no slaves, and Scott County, with a rate of 25.1 percent, had averages smaller than the statewide average. Elsewhere, the rates varied from Logan County's 35.8 percent to Buchanan County's whopping 43.3 percent. Boone County's rate of natural increase was 38.0 percent. In these counties, in other words, slavery generated little enthusiasm among most of the rapidly growing white population, many of whom in fact had fled the developing commercial, slave-intensive nexus, but aroused strong faith in the system among the subregion's few slaveholders. More than most of the state's masters, the slaveowners of Boone, Buchanan, Logan, and Wise counties confidently emphasized the breeding or purchase of slave children, human investments whose dates of maturity, literally as well as figuratively, were several years in the future. Clearly they believed that slavery, not free white labor, would be the wave of the future in the western plateau.[18]

A different situation developed in the eastern half of the Allegheny

Plateau subregion. Because of a somewhat gentler landscape, more reliable road and river transportation, and a longer history of settlement and commercial enterprise, some counties in this area already were involved substantially with slave-based agriculture and commerce. In 1850, Greenbrier County held 1317 slaves, making it the non–upper valley county with the largest slave population. Only Montgomery, Washington, and Wythe counties possessed more slaves in 1850. With 1061 slaves, Monroe County followed close behind. To their west, however, Fayette, Mercer, and Raleigh counties lagged behind, together holding only 356 slaves.[19]

By 1860, Greenbrier had added an additional 208 slaves, and Monroe 53. The rates of slave population growth in these counties were moderate, 15.8 percent and 5 percent respectively. The real story occurred just to the west, where tobacco cultivation captured the economy. Just as in the Tidewater, tobacco meant slave labor. By 1860, Fayette County contained 115 additional slaves, a 73.7 percent rate of growth. Mercer, with 185 new slaves, exhibited a growth rate of 104.5 percent.[20]

Most interesting of all was Raleigh County. In 1850, only 8 slaveowners and 23 slaves lived there. Ten years later, the number of masters had almost tripled, and the slave population had increased to 57, a 147.8 percent rate of growth. When calculated with real numbers as small as these, percentages can distort as much as they reveal. Still, when considered along with Fayette's and Mercer's, Raleigh's experience strongly suggests that slavery had started to take a strong hold in the three plateau counties along the New River. To be sure, Raleigh County's 21 slaveowners had a long way to go to match a Wyndham Robertson. With 9 slaves, doctor-farmer John Manser was Raleigh's leading slaveowner in 1860. A further indicator that slavery was only in its infancy in Raleigh County was the relatively advanced age of its slaves. In Floyd, by way of comparison, the mean slave age was eighteen. In contrast, the mean slave in Raleigh was age twenty-eight. Moreover, with one exception, Raleigh's rate of natural increase was the lowest in the region.[21]

All in all, the Seventh and Eighth Censuses reveal that slavery in Southwest Virginia was spreading out of the counties where the institution already had established itself and was establishing a foothold in more mountainous parts of the region. It grew at a dramatic rate along the New River, in the line of counties just north of the upper valley subregion, in Montgomery County, and in Carroll County's mining camps. Ahead of the onrushing tide of Piedmont-style, slave-based capitalism, whites unable or unwilling to take part in the new

order removed to the more rugged areas of the Blue Ridge and Allegheny Plateau subregions, swelling those counties' white populations. Even
there, however, slavery and all that accompanied the institution could
not be escaped forever. The elite of the plateau subregion were increasing their investments in slavery with eyes toward a future expansion
of their own. Had civil war not destroyed slavery in the 1860s, it certainly would have continued its march into the Southwest Virginia
mountains.

If one is to fully comprehend slavery in Southwest Virginia, one
must do more than count. What was mountain slavery like for the region's expanding slaves? How did the railroad modify the work and
lives of slaves? In the absence of slave accounts, one is forced to depend upon the biased records of white Southwest Virginians, accounts
of outside observers, and secondary scholarship. Opinions expressed
in these sources vary. W. J. Cash maintained that white mountaineers'
treatment of blacks was worse than in the wider South. Some antebellum travelers, such as the English Quaker abolitionist Joseph John
Gurney, found little difference whatsoever in the South's peculiar institution as practiced in its mountain form. Noting slaves' "miserable
clothing" in cold weather, Gurney concluded that the institution was
just as bad in the springs area as elsewhere. Most observers, however,
concluded that mountain slavery was somewhat milder than in the
lowlands. Despite his hatred of the institution, Olmsted called mountain slavery "the mild and segregated form," and wrote that mountain slaves' "habits more resemble those of ordinary free laborers, they
exercise more responsibility, and both in soul and intellect they are
more elevated."[22]

What was the true situation? Just as elsewhere in the South, evidence suggests that the slave experience differed from owner to owner. Some masters seem to have accorded their slaves decent treatment
and perhaps even developed bonds of affection. One Lewisburg master asked his brother to purchase "ten Sows big with Pig" in Charleston for his slaves.[23] John Echols trusted two slaves named Dick and
George enough to allow them to deliver horses to George Henry Caperton without any white supervision.[24] Most striking of all was the dispute over the treatment of slaves between U.S. Army officer Alexander
W. Reynolds and his sister, Sallie Patton. Stationed in Texas in the late
1850s, Reynolds demanded that his sister forward to him his three
slaves. Citing his alleged inability to care for them, and especially the
slave Jim, Patton refused. Reynolds was furious. "I have never known

you to take such heartfelt interest in any thing," he wrote, "as you appear to take in your dear darling negroes. Your brother is but a secondary consideration in comparison to them."[25]

Most slaveowners were willing to go only so far, however. Ex-governor David Campbell was known as a kind master who "allowed his servants unusual privileges," including allowing them to sell wood and hogs. When a slave named Page was caught stealing chickens and hogs from neighbors, however, Campbell determined that the "reckless scoundrel" be "taken out of the country, as a matter of safety to the community." Referring to Page's mother, who had helped hide the accused, Campbell added that "I would send old Hannah off but she is too old to treat very harshly." He also approved the whipping of two other slaves who helped hide Page from the authorities.[26]

Page was not alone. Three of John Barnes's Tazewell County slaves were jailed for attacking their young overseer as he whipped one of them. Escaping, the three fought another white man and set dogs on others. Their fate too was to be sold to buyers in the deep South.[27]

The fate of Page and the Barnes slaves demonstrates that the threat of sale "down the river" could be as egregious a punishment as the lash. Such sales would have been easy, as Southwest Virginia was an important route in the slave trade. Eastern Virginia and Maryland slaves generally passed through the valley subregion on the Valley Road on their way to the deep South. George Featherstonhaugh, traveling in Southwest Virginia in the 1830s, encountered the "singular spectacle" of slave drivers shepherding three hundred slaves across the New River from Montgomery to Pulaski County. The slaves forded the river manacled and chained together in double files, while all the while forced to sing to banjo accompaniment. John Armfield, the slave trader, eventually sold the slaves in Natchez, Mississippi, and in Louisiana.[28]

One should note, however, that most sales must have taken place between Southwest Virginians. As John C. Inscoe noted in his study of Western North Carolina, that region's higher than average rate of natural increase, coupled with a rate of increase in the slave population faster than the state's as a whole, strongly suggests that most regional masters were selling intraregionally. The sale of slaves in these cases usually emanated from the death of the master.[29]

Many Southwest Virginia slaveowners, of course, expressed discomfort with selling slaves and the resultant tragic effect on the black family. There is little evidence, however, that this ultimately kept Southwest Virginia's masters from breaking up families when it was in the owners' best interests. The heirs of William Preston, for example, coolly divided his eighty slaves among themselves and then swapped and sold to neighbors. Likewise, Monroe County attorney and legislator Allen Caperton took the slaves from one estate across the state to Richmond to sell just as the dead owner's will stipulated.[30] Referring to another estate, also to be disposed of in the state capital, one relative asked Caperton, "Will you sell them to traders or try to sell them privately, that is to persons who are not trading in Negroes?" He then proceeded to suggest good sale prices.[31]

Indeed, price reigned uppermost. When the Panic of 1857 depressed slave prices, the *Abingdon Democrat* reported as encouraging good news that a young woman and her two children had sold in Russell County for $1905, "pretty well for hard times."[32] Overall, Olmsted reported that "Slaves . . . were 'unprofitable property' in the mountains, except as they increase and improve in salable value. Two men . . . spoke of the sale of negroes in the same sentence with that of cattle and swine."[33]

Slaves, of course, could prove profitable to owners in other ways than direct sale. Masters sometimes used their human property as collateral to obtain loans. Planter James P. Strother of Smyth County assured a potential lender in a credit reference that the subject in question had "a tolerably good plantation in Washington [County] & at least one negro man who is young and valuable, perhaps he may have other negroes."[34]

More common was the practice of loaning or hiring out slaves to others; family members, fellow owners, industrialists, and nonmasters unable to amass enough capital to enter the master class. "I believe your Pa hired a negro boy at hillsville," one Wythe Countian wrote in 1851, "gives 50 dollars a year and clothes him."[35] Wythe County slaveowner Richard W. Sanders hired slaves himself for planting, and at the same time hired out two of his slaves to neighbors, in one case to a mine operator. Hiring transactions generally occurred at a public place such as a courthouse on the first day of the year. Owners usually agreed to furnish clothing and pay doctor bills, although at times this was the hirer's responsibility. In order to maximize profits, some masters, like Caperton, took their slaves across the state to Richmond to hire them out. Inscoe has noted, however, that most mountain slaveowners wanted to keep their property nearby, where they could maintain some control.[36]

Whether working for the owner or hired out, slaves filled a wide variety of roles in Southwest Virginia. Like most slaves elsewhere in the South, they toiled as agricultural laborers. On mountain farms, however, this meant a wider array of tasks than on a Deep South cotton plantation. Slaves had to be versatile; they generally tended several crops, instead of one staple, herded livestock, constructed buildings and fences, made bricks and shingles, and engaged in various other handicrafts or household industries. Large farmers such as the Tazewell County Floyds used slaves as couriers, often trusted with cash and items of value. Slaves also worked in mines and in industrial operations, and served as domestic servants in both private homes and hotels. The hot springs particularly hired many slaves as cooks and domestics; many ill slaves were provided free of charge in exchange for an anticipated cure. As one Southwest Virginian told Olmsted, most whites believed that a white person willing to work as a domestic servant probably was not worth hiring.[37] "In fact," Olmsted added, "no girl hereabouts, whose character was good, would ever hire out to do menial service."[38]

The railroad provided more avenues for slave labor. Its construction provided a new market for slaveowners wishing to rent out their human property. Indeed, the completed railroad functioned as a silent monument to the abilities and tenacity of the black laborers who performed most of the line's construction and maintenance. Hired slaves cut wood, graded, broke up stone for ballast, laid track, and cleared snow from obstructed tracks. The skilled toiled as blacksmiths, carpenters, and mechanics. Many also served on train crews as freight hands and brakemen. The railroad generally paid owners two hundred dollars per year for hired slaves, an estimated labor savings of 50 percent. By 1856, 435 of the railroad's 643 workers were hired slaves. Envisioned by whites, it was black Southwest Virginians who made the dream of a mountain railroad a reality.[39]

Indeed, the railroad hired so many slaves that other hirers had trouble obtaining workers. Olmsted described a conversation with an overseer near Abingdon. The overseer, stick in hand, supervised seven wheat cradlers, five black and two white. He explained that the "niggers had all been hired by the railroad, at $200 a year." Olmsted also accused the railroad of driving its slave laborers hard. Another one of his hosts, an east Tennessee farmer apparently living near the Virginia line, described a railroad contractor "who had some sixty hands which he had hired in Old Virginny. . . . everybody who saw them at work, said he drove them till they could hardly stand, and did not give them half what they ought to have to eat."[40]

Chief Engineer Garnett found hired slaves "a source of great economy" to the railroad, but noted one glaring disadvantage. In 1853, he wrote, "it makes it difficult to collect a force of white laborers on the same work, where a considerable number of slaves are employed."[41] Many of the railroad's hired whites, often Irish immigrants, opposed working side by side with blacks. In cases where the railroad had to choose due to cost or conflict, the white laborers generally lost out. In March 1857, for example, the railroad determined to drop one of its five gangs of freight train hands, as only four had proved necessary. Four crews were black, and one was made up of whites. President and Acting General Superintendent J. Robin McDaniel fired the whites.[42]

Slave laborers cost the railroad less, then, but they were not without financial liabilities. The railroad, like all hirers, agreed to certain stipulations required by owners. It agreed, for example, to furnish the slaves of a master named Brown four pairs of shoes per slave each year. The railroad, often unwillingly, also bore the responsibility in case of injury or death, frequent occurrences on the line. In January 1857, for example, slaves hired to clear snow off tracks contracted frostbite. Their angry owners required compensation, but the railroad refused to pay. The V&T successfully argued that the slaves themselves were responsible by rushing to a warming fire too quickly.[43]

The Virginia and Tennessee Railroad impacted on the state's slave economy in a second manner as well. As had other railroads in the state, it became a carrier of choice in the slave trade. To encourage business among slave traders, the railroad entered into an agreement with several other southern railways, whereby it would carry small slave children free of charge. The railroads used this policy as an incentive to capture the slave trade.[44]

Finally, beyond economics, there were political implications. We have seen that Henry A. Wise and his fellow nonregional railroad supporters envisioned ideological as well as numerical gains for slavery when they threw their support to Southwest Virginia's railroad. Slavery expansion was a means to a united Virginia and through that, a united South. With the V&T's crucial link completed, its boosters broadened their vistas. William M. Burwell, for example, advocated "direct trade" via steamship through the port of Norfolk to Europe. "The supremacy of New-York is . . . to be fought with the capital and competition of England, France, and Germany," he wrote. The railroad, by linking Norfolk to the southern interior, had made such a vision possible, Burwell affirmed.[45]

A second, related scheme advocated by Burwell and his friends was a canal across the Tehuantepec isthmus of Mexico, linking southern ports with the goods and gold of California, weakening New York merchants, and expanding the potential area of slavery expansion, Bickley's "golden circle." Burwell again credited the Virginia and Tennessee Railroad in making the Tehuantepec canal a real possibility. The railroad itself embraced the two schemes, as it found them good publicity. The names chosen for the line's engines illustrate this. Most bore the names of regional locales—"Bristol," "Holston," "Montgomery," "Norfolk"—railroad officials, or swift animals. However, the railroad also gave locomotives names such as "El Paso," "Mazeppa," "San Francisco," "St. Nazaire," and "Tehuantepec." Thus, the locomotives racing past Southwest Virginians constantly reminded them of both their southern links and future glories.[46]

These glories, not incidentally, were to be won as Virginians. While Bickley and perhaps most other white Southwest Virginians flirted with the idea of state secession in 1850, they had a decade later made their peace with the eastern part of the state. Political changes emanating from economic commercialization and slavery expansion had firmly linked Southwest Virginia to Richmond by the secession winter of 1860–61. If the V&T was the medium for such a transformation, then, it also was Southwest Virginia's iron road to secession and civil war. These political implications will be examined next.

5

"No Other Chance for Us": Secession

Fʀᴏᴍ Gʀᴇᴇɴʙʀɪᴇʀ and Monroe counties came calls for secession if demands went unmet.[1] Still other Southwest Virginians delineated the choice of honorable opposition or submission.[2] On the floor of the convention itself, western leaders proclaimed that "if . . . the gentleman is for war, let the God of Battles decide it, hilt to hilt." Panic, threats, and violence were in the air.[3]

What is so striking about this scene is that it did not occur during Virginia's Secession Convention of 1861, as one might expect, but rather a decade earlier, during the effort to hammer out a new state constitution. Called in response to Governor John B. Floyd's Message of 1849, the Constitutional Convention of 1850–51 nearly tore Virginia in two before achieving success. Easterners, having adroitly gerrymandered a majority of convention seats, continued their advocacy of the so-called mixed basis, which apportioned representation according to a mixture of population and taxes paid. Faced with the necessity of a new constitution, they hoped to seize control of the reform machinery and shape it to their section's interests. Meanwhile, as in 1830, westerners demanded change.[4] "[A] convention will be called," Washington County General Assembly Delegate Isaac B. Dunn wrote, "The S.W. will drive down their peggs upon the white basis."[5]

Called to order in October 1850, the proceedings reached their crescendo early in 1851. From February until early May, increasingly angry delegates took the floor daily to defend oratorically the mixed or white basis. Mixed-basis supporters depicted their opponents as traitors and Jacobins sworn to destroy property rights, weaken slavery to the point of extinction, and surrender Virginia to northern rule. The white-basis camp answered that their opposition were antirepublican traitors to the ideals of 1776. Southwest Virginia delegates, all for the white basis, assured easterners that they were not abolitionists, but also warned that mountaineers might turn to abolition in the future to spite a tyrannical East. In April, with no settlement in sight and sectional bitterness increasing, the reform caucus, nearly all mountaineers, agreed to walk out, go home, and prepare for state secession if they were denied the white basis. Back home in Southwest Virginia, public meetings and newspapers endorsed the rumored walkout. Only at the last minute did a compromise salvage the convention and perhaps the state as well.[6]

Over 90 percent of Southwest Virginians perceived the constitution that followed favorably, as demonstrated with their heavy vote in favor of ratification, shown in table 26. It gave them most of what they wanted: white manhood suffrage, county court reform, the abolishment of the hated Executive Council. It made most executive and judicial offices elective, including positions on the Board of Public Works. The basis compromise mandated a House of Delegates apportioned on the white basis, a Senate arbitrarily controlled by the east but without enough votes to override the West when the two houses met jointly, and a promise to reapportion after 1865. Eastern fears were allayed somewhat by a tax break aimed specifically at slaveholders.[7]

What followed was a remarkable, decade-long rapprochement between cismontane and Southwest Virginia, fostering political ties that approximated the iron rails of the Virginia and Tennessee Railroad. Like the Alabamians J. Mills Thornton has described, Virginians on both sides in 1850 and 1851 had perceived their opponents as corrupt would-be tyrants who threatened the revolutionary legacy of liberty. Thus, Southwest Virginians perceived the reform forces' victory in the convention as a real triumph of the common man over the aristocrats. In truth, the triumph was somewhat hollow. Virginia's slaveholding minority continued to control the state government through a judicious use of Democratic patronage and a closed party nominating process. The only real transfer of power was to members of the western elite, men like John B. Floyd and Allen Caperton. Nonetheless, as so often is the case, the perception mattered more than the reality. Southwest Virginians believed that they finally had a representative, responsive state government friendly to their interests. As they reconciled with Richmond politically, the commercial ties developing between the southwest and the capital reinforced the rapprochement, just in time for secession and war.[8]

As we have seen, railroad construction in Southwest Virginia resulted at least in part from escalating national tensions over slavery. Extraregional proponents of both constitutional reform and capitalist ex-

Table 26. Vote on Constitution of 1851 in Southwest
Virginia, October 23–25, 1851

County	For	Against
Boone	159	62
Carroll	608	5
Fayette	436	19
Floyd	295	36
Giles	428	106
Grayson	589	13
Greenbrier	641	91
Lee	698	90
Logan	261	84
Mercer	339	85
Monroe	516	130
Montgomery	566	12
Pulaski	251	6
Raleigh	125	51
Russell	488	177
Scott	726	79
Smyth	790	2
Tazewell	679	36
Washington	1,083	12
Wyoming	116	29
Wythe	543	43
Total	10,337	1,168
Total for Virginia	70,253	10,523

Source: Gaines, "Virginia Constitutional Convention,"
Appendix 4.

pansion through internal improvements made no secret that they ultimately envisioned a united South dedicated to the preservation of
slavery. Southwest Virginians, while more concerned with the material benefits of railroads and reform, equally feared the northern abolitionist threat symbolized in the Wilmot Proviso and the debate over
California. During the national and state crises of 1850 and 1851, latent fears of abolitionists began to metamorphose into cathartic "crises of fear." Just after Virginia's new constitution seemingly had re-

solved the state's sectional crisis, three black men killed three white men in Grayson County, allegedly at the instigation of two abolitionists named Bacon and Cook. "The awakened wrath of the citizens of Grayson has been terrible as the storm," the *Wytheville Republican* reported, "and before it like reeds before the hurricane everything suspected of being tainted with Abolition, has bowed or been swept away."[9]

Periodic political traumas revolving around the slavery issue raised the stress level of the region to still newer heights throughout the decade. Since the advent of Andrew Jackson, Southwest Virginia had been the most Democratic part of the commonwealth. Only Greenbrier and to an extent Fayette, Monroe, and Montgomery counties had voted Whig consistently. With southwest Democrats favoring internal improvements as much as their Whig counterparts, excluding the canal, which was popular only in the Whiggish Kanawha Valley, party loyalty generally was determined instead through the personal influence and rivalries of local politicians such as the Democratic Floyds or Whigs Allen Caperton and William Ballard Preston, and by national issues, emphasized over state issues to avoid internal party divisions. In regard to the latter, Whigs tended more toward unionism. Democratic leaders in contrast often belonged to the more militant, states-rights wing of their party, which made national affairs even more central to regional politics. After his highly visible support of internal improvements and constitutional reform, southwestern Democrats also looked to the Tidewater's Henry A. Wise for leadership. Ironically, Southwest Virginia became the center of Wise's support.[10]

Southwest Virginia's two congressmen, Democrats Henry A. Edmundson and Fayette McMullen, took a strong southern stand during the Compromise of 1850 debates. Both supported the Texas–New Mexico "Little Omnibus" bill, the act establishing Utah Territory, and the new Fugitive Slave Law. They opposed the admission of California as a free state and the abolition of the slave trade in the District of Columbia.[11]

Later, the Kansas-Nebraska Act of 1854 and the storm of northern outrage that followed provided new rallying cries for regional defenders of slavery. Wise, in his gubernatorial campaign the following year, added fuel to the fire. Wise's opponent, Know-Nothing Thomas S. Flournoy, still subscribed to the passe doctrine of slavery as a necessary evil. With characteristic hyperbole, Wise transformed Flournoy into a godless abolitionist and equated the Know-Nothings with abolitionists and aristocrats. The rhetoric proved especially effective in Southwest Virginia, where the campaign grew heated and violent. Par-

Table 27. Gubernatorial Vote in Southwest Virginia, 1855

County	Flournoy (Know-Nothing)	Wise (Democrat)
Boone	138	280
Carroll	311	657
Fayette	301	271
Floyd	447	566
Giles	405	418
Grayson	266	553
Greenbrier	870	533
Lee	377	1,113
Logan	76	366
Mercer	350	417
Monroe	891	577
Montgomery	592	660
Pulaski	272	305
Raleigh	259	80
Russell	580	989
Scott	509	797
Smyth	571	654
Tazewell	189	1,102
Washington	928	1,284
Wyoming	116	82
Wythe	724	829
Total	9,192	12,533
Total for Virginia	73,244	83,424

Source: *Richmond Enquirer,* June 8, 1855; May 27, 1859.

tisan mobs scuffled at the slightest provocation. In Abingdon, one man was stabbed during a political brawl. In the end, Wise won a narrow victory, securing 53 percent of the statewide vote. As table 27 demonstrates, Wise's margin in Southwest Virginia was greater, 12,533 to 9,192. Only five counties, Fayette, Greenbrier, Monroe, Raleigh, and Wyoming, all in the eastern half of the Allegheny Plateau subregion, returned Know-Nothing majorities. In contrast, Wise's largest majorities occurred in the rugged western half of the plateau.[12]

The year 1856 provided Southwest Virginia little respite. Congressman Edmundson was implicated in Preston Brooks' caning of Charles Sumner. Later that year, John C. Frémont's candidacy persuaded even formerly hard-line unionists like David Campbell that a Republican victory, empowering the abolitionists, would justify southern secession. Campbell fretted over rumors of Republican activity in Russell County, but consoled himself with the reflection that the Republican threat had further cemented the tenuous bond between slaveowners and nonowners.[13] Bleeding Kansas produced the same effect. In the summer and fall of 1857, according to the *Wytheville Times,* Kansas came "to occupy public attention almost exclusively."[14]

To replace Wise as governor in 1859, the Democrats nominated Lexington newspaper editor John Letcher, one of the reform leaders in the 1850–51 convention. It soon became apparent that the nominee possessed serious liabilities. Wise despised Letcher for the latter's refusal to support him in the 1855 race.[15] Dismissing Letcher as one of the "pimps of the Hunter clique," in reference to R. M. T. Hunter's wing of the state party, Wise refused to support Letcher in turn.[16]

His public excuse was slavery. In 1847, Letcher briefly endorsed a friend's antislavery pamphlet, which linked slavery to eastern domination of Virginia. Letcher repudiated the so-called Ruffner Pamphlet quickly, but the stain would not disappear. In 1859, it gave both Wise and the *Richmond Enquirer* reason to portray Letcher as untrustworthy on slavery. The remnant of the Whig and Know-Nothing parties, now styled simply the Opposition, also focused on the Ruffner Pamphlet. The Opposition nominated prominent pro-slavery advocate William L. Goggin to oppose Letcher and hoped to ride the slavery issue to victory.[17]

The tactic worked to a point, but not well enough. Letcher edged Goggin with approximately five thousand votes to spare, but as table 28 shows, Letcher's totals were over six thousand votes less statewide than Wise's totals four years before. Moreover, although Letcher ran better than Wise in the Northwest and in parts of the Valley, he fared poorly in Southwest Virginia. There, Goggin topped Letcher 11,474 to 10,152, a net Democratic loss of over two thousand votes from 1855. In Southwest Virginia, the perception of Letcher as a closet free-soiler, Wise's antagonism, and John B. Floyd's obvious distaste for Letcher all doomed the Democracy to regional defeat. For thousands of Southwest Virginians, loyalty to slavery had overcome loyalty to party.[18]

Southwest Virginia in 1859 was not a nest of fire-eaters, of course. Conservative voices still could be heard. The *Wytheville Times* declared

Table 28. Gubernatorial Vote in Southwest Virginia, 1859

County	Goggin (Opposition)	Letcher (Democrat)
Boone	150	292
Buchanan	73	164
Carroll	461	344
Fayette	346	385
Floyd	522	339
Giles	463	352
Grayson	384	497
Greenbrier	889	779
Lee	688	624
Logan	94	480
McDowell	115	33
Mercer	557	429
Monroe	845	672
Montgomery	615	388
Pulaski	314	239
Raleigh	381	148
Russell	751	404
Scott	600	559
Smyth	598	454
Tazewell	541	621
Washington	966	870
Wise	208	266
Wyoming	170	78
Wythe	743	775
Total	11,474	10,152
Total for Virginia	71,543	77,112

Source: *Richmond Enquirer,* June 14, 1859; Nov. 6, 1860.

itself "equally opposed to the ultraist of the North and the fire-eaters of the South. The labors of both are equally pernicious, and would result in the most disastrous consequences."[19] David Campbell agreed, musing that the best thing that could happen to the United States would be the forcible ejection of Massachusetts and South Carolina from the union. Nonetheless, while most Southwest Virginians remained loyal to the union, their unionism increasingly came with qualifications attached. Like other southerners, they demanded federal guarantees of slavery's survival as the price of their loyalty to the union.[20]

Then came John Brown, who, it is worth noting, incorrectly saw the southern mountain region as a homogeneous, antislavery enclave a half-century before William Goodell Frost popularized the concept of "Appalachia." In the mid-1840s, Brown conceived a scheme of guerrilla bands attacking slaveowners from bases high in the Allegheny Mountains. Brown hoped to carry slaves through the hills to freedom in the aftermath of these raids. In 1857, he confided to Frederick Douglass that "These mountains are the basis of my plan. God has given the strength of the hills to freedom; they were placed here for the emancipation of the negro."[21]

Brown continued to modify his plan after Douglass's initial rebuff. By 1858, he had decided to attack the federal arsenal at Harper's Ferry, Virginia, in the northwestern part of the state. Once inside the arsenal, Brown planned to arm himself and his followers and then move deep into the mountains. Convinced that slaves required only a spark to rise up against their masters, Brown expected them to flock to his banner. Sympathetic mountain whites would join him as well. He then would drive south, through Southwest Virginia, to perhaps Florida or Texas. Eventually, the southern mountains would become a black state. On October 16, 1859, Brown struck. Instead of recruits, militiamen and U.S. Marines converged on Harper's Ferry to capture Brown.[22]

Panic swept the South in the wake of Harper's Ferry. Here was the abolitionist onslaught southerners had feared for years. The northern tendency to laud the executed Brown as a martyred saint only compounded the panic. Southwest Virginia reacted in the same manner as the rest of the slave South. Wild rumors of slave rebellions and Republican involvement in the raid appeared as fact in local newspapers. Locally, suspected abolitionists received threats, particularly if they were outsiders. Mechanic Matthew Fitzgerald of Wytheville wrote his local newspaper to deny charges of abolitionist activity, labeling the rumors deliberate attempts to destroy his business.[23] In Bristol, a terrified James M. Johnston arranged a public meeting at a ten-pin alley to denounce a citizens' committee charge of pro-Brown activity as "false—false as hell." Johnston finally convinced his informal jury of his innocence when he linked the evidence against him to "a jew nigger trader."[24]

Attention and concern focused on the status of the local militia.

Before Harper's Ferry, interest in militia duty was slight, much to the vexation of militia proponents. Governor Wise's rousing of the companies in preparation for a northern invasion in the aftermath of Harper's Ferry changed the situation overnight.[25] Fifteen-year-old militiaman John Caperton wrote his mother: "Great excitement is prevailing every where in this neighborhood and every company is in redineys at a moment warning. You know that two thousand troops have come down from the North to rescue Brown and Gov. Wise has gone to Harpers Ferry with a thousand soldiers and several companis have received orders to come on to morrow close around us. We have just recieved our uniform I think it is beautiful we look like a set of soldiers as we are."[26]

Another militiaman, James N. Bosang of the Pulaski Guards, remembered that "we hoped to be ordered into service to be present at [Brown's] hanging, but greatly to our disappointment were not."[27]

The militaristic response to John Brown's raid is a familiar story. The anxieties produced by Harper's Ferry found outlets in lesser-known responses as well. Some Southwest Virginians found refuge in religion. Writing from Carroll County in December 1859, "Spectator" grumbled that his neighbors had yet to respond to Harper's Ferry in the appropriate, "warlike" manner. He appealed to Carroll Countians to form a volunteer company in the manner of other Southwest Virginians. Instead, in January 1860, the largest religious revival in the county's history broke out. By March, the revivals were spilling over into neighboring counties.[28]

Militarism and religious fervor often went hand in hand. In February 1860, the Reverend W. D. Roedel of the Wytheville Female College used the occasion of a flag presentation to a local militia company to condemn Brown's abolitionist supporters as "monstrous" servants of the anti-Christ. Their goal was to destroy Christian America and replace it with a "Utopian anarchy" of free-thinking paganism. Their plot had to be resisted, with force if necessary. Roedel, in the name of God, advocated a stronger militia system, boycotts of northern goods, and the suppression of godless publications such as the *New York Tribune*.[29]

The 1860 presidential race followed. In Virginia, including Southwest Virginia, the contest essentially boiled down to a two-man race between John Bell, representing old-line Whigs, and Southern Democrat John C. Breckinridge. Supporters of both candidates depicted their man as both the only true representative of the South and slavery and the only realistic challenger to Abraham Lincoln and the Republicans. The other southerner emerged in campaign rhetoric as a submissionist not to be trusted in regard to slavery. Among the politicians who spoke in Southwest Virginia was William Lowndes Yancey, the "prince of fire-eaters," who stumped the region for Breckinridge. Emory and Henry College students poured into Abingdon to hear the fire-eater, and returned to campus enthralled with his oratory and arguments.[30]

By autumn, however, most Southwest Virginians had resigned themselves to the fact that Lincoln would win the election. What should they do in response? Some initially counseled moderation, still unsure of exactly where Lincoln stood. Leonidas Baugh wrote in the *Abingdon Democrat* that while he despised the idea of Republican victory, Virginia should ride out the storm in the union.[31] Dissenters, however, rejected moderation. Many were women. Alise Caperton wrote that "some persons think that *Virginia* will go to the north but *never never* if I was Virginia. I would fight a *thousand years* before I would go to the north."[32]

Virginians went to the polls on November 6, 1860 and Bell won the state with something over three hundred votes, 74,701 to 74,379 (table 29). Douglas polled about sixteen thousand votes, and Lincoln 1,929. Southwest Virginia, however, gave a 1,510 vote majority to Breckinridge. The Kentuckian finished strongest in the western half of the Allegheny Plateau subregion, where slaves were few. Bell, in contrast, found his largest majorities in the eastern plateau and the eastern valley counties of Montgomery and Pulaski, where slavery was numerically stronger. Clearly, a vote for Breckinridge was not simply a vote for slavery and secession. Rather, the canvass reflected continuing loyalties to the voters' traditional parties. Of all the counties won by Bell, only Giles had gone Democratic in the gubernatorial races of 1855 and 1859. The others traditionally were Whig.[33]

Southwest Virginians expressed anxious confusion in the aftermath of Lincoln's victory. Monroe County minister S. R. Houston thought the "affairs of the South yet more threatening; the people crazy with excitement. . . . Newspapers full of accounts about the excitement in the cotton states. A dissolution of the Union seems inevitable! Then what?"[34] The *Wytheville Times,* a Bell organ, retracted six months of dire predictions concerning a Republican victory and nervously assured Southwest Virginia that Lincoln was a conservative who would not threaten southern slavery. Even if he tried, the *Times* added, Congress would stop him.[35]

Stephen A. Douglas struck the same note. On November 28, the weary Douglas traveled through Southwest Virginia on the Virginia and Tennessee Railroad, en route to Washington. He spent the night in Wytheville. On the following morning, as he waited for his train, the

Table 29. Presidential Vote in Southwest Virginia, 1860

County	Bell	Breckinridge	Douglas	Lincoln
Boone	121	204	24	0
Buchanan	14	134	19	0
Carroll	315	729	11	0
Fayette	381	241	65	0
Floyd	384	400	36	0
Giles	366	244	63	0
Grayson	315	547	16	0
Greenbrier	993	505	133	0
Lee	462	894	10	0
Logan	100	271	6	0
McDowell	35	37	0	0
Mercer	443	432	13	0
Monroe	693	520	83	0
Montgomery	712	425	74	0
Pulaski	332	250	5	0
Raleigh	230	69	14	0
Russell	473	526	0	0
Scott	491	594	91	0
Smyth	446	496	49	0
Tazewell	306	934	0	0
Washington	916	1,178	56	0
Wise	102	363	8	0
Wyoming	60	29	9	0
Wythe	617	795	22	0
Total	9,307	10,817	807	0
Total for Virginia	74,701	74,379	16,292	1,929

Source: *Richmond Enquirer,* Nov. 16, 20, Dec. 4, 25, 1860; *Tribune Almanac for 1861,* 50–51.

Illinois senator spoke for twenty minutes in opposition to secession. With a Democratic-controlled Congress and Supreme Court opposed to Republican policies, Douglas asserted, Lincoln was "powerless for evil."[36]

As 1860 came to a close, however, Southwest Virginians more and more ignored moderate advice like Douglas's. The regional mood soured, and turned angry. Public meetings in Pulaski, Smyth, and Wythe counties denounced northern aggression, including the election of a purely sectional president, demanded the repeal of unfavorable northern legislation, and endorsed a Virginia convention to consider secession.[37]

On January 7, 1861, the General Assembly convened in special session. Ostensibly, Governor Letcher called the legislature together to discuss the sale of the James River and Kanawha Canal to a French company. First on the session's unofficial agenda, however, was the response to Lincoln's election. Letcher tried to squash the growing sentiment for a secession convention, which he considered unwarranted. Instead, he argued that Virginia should continue to work for a national convention that would draft union-saving amendments to the U.S. Constitution.[38]

In his message to the legislature, Letcher spoke along lines that would become the standard argument of Virginia's conditional unionists. He condemned the North for precipitating the crisis, but assigned nearly equal blame to the Deep South's fire-eaters. South Carolina and Mississippi, he argued, wanted to coerce Virginia into their planned southern confederacy. The commonwealth had to resist them as strongly as it did Lincoln. If the union did collapse, he went on, Virginia should not unite with a Deep South confederacy, but instead form a new union with the border slave states, the Old Northwest, the middle Atlantic states, and the western territories. Essentially, Letcher wanted to form a new union without New England or the Deep South.[39]

The General Assembly, controlled by Breckinridge Democrats, rejected Letcher's advice. A secession convention became the first order of business. On the evening of the legislature's first day, a joint resolution favoring a convention went down to defeat 71 to 31, with opponents arguing that the matter required some discussion. Most of Southwest Virginia's delegation however favored the resolution. The House of Delegates then established a committee, which included two Southwest Virginians, to discuss the convention issue. The committee required only two days to report a convention bill, which passed 109 to 30. Only two Southwest Virginians, William J. Dickenson of Russell, Wise, and Buchanan counties, and Henry W. Holdway of Scott and Wise counties, voted against the bill. The opposition came primarily from Northwest Virginia delegates.[40] On January 21, after the secession of five southern states, the legislature adopted a joint resolution stating that if all efforts to save the union proved "abortive . . . every consideration of honor and interest demand that Virginia shall unite her destiny with the slaveholding states of the south." Thus, the General Assembly completely repudiated Letcher.[41]

The convention bill gave neither unionists nor secessionists much time to organize. On February 4, Virginians would vote twice in regard to secession. They would first choose delegates to the convention, and then decide if the convention's final decision needed to be approved by the voters. Historians have pointed to the latter issue, termed "reference," as a crucial gauge of unionism in Virginia in early 1861.[42]

On one side of the secession question stood the immediatist secessionists. Perceiving Lincoln as the pawn of a militant abolitionist conspiracy aimed at eradicating slavery and thus the southern way of life, immediatists expected the worst with his victory. His purely sectional triumph seemed to confirm that the entire North, not just the abolitionist fringe, desired the subjection of the South. Continued control of the executive branch would enable the Republicans to enact hateful policies and undermine slaveholders through the federal patronage. Instead of checking militant abolitionism, as it had at Harper's Ferry, Washington under the Republicans would place itself in the vanguard of the struggle against slavery. Immediatists concluded that the South had only two responses—cowardly submission or honorable secession.[43]

Indeed, considerations of honor lay at the heart of the immediatist response. They felt the North's antislavery activities and support of Lincoln to be deliberate insults and humiliations. They believed that northerners saw southerners as inferior, second-class citizens, and that inferior status was about to be written into law. Southerners yearned to silence the insults, erase their shame, and vindicate themselves. Honor demanded that the South accept no more abuse.[44]

Images of honor and shame permeated immediatist rhetoric. "I see how it all is—we are emasculated," Henry A. Wise wrote after the convention act passed. "The Convention will do nothing. There is no alternative but for those true to the South . . . to organize & arm themselves, & I fear that cant be done without state authority. Were a people ever so insulted as we are now by N.Y. Ohio & all?"[45]

Southwest Virginia's immediatists agreed. John B. Floyd, with trembling hands, told a Smyth County meeting that the federal government was now openly antisouthern, and he saw "no other chance for us but combined action of the South in rearing up a confederacy."[46] In Wytheville, William H. Cook defended secession as "the only proper course." Virginia had to "take such a course as will resound to her fame, & identify her with her southern sisters. . . . the slave states ought to act all together." Cook suspected that his Wythe County neighbors disagreed, but he expected Tazewell County to "redeem South western Virginia."[47]

In Smyth County, immediatist attorney James W. Sheffey argued that the "northerns have ignored southern principals and treated them with as much disrespect as it is possible for them to do, and their treatment to southern principals they nullify the Constitution. . . . Virginia must go with the south." One of Sheffey's auditors was young John S. Apperson, a newcomer to the region from the Piedmont and an ardent secessionist. "The North has injured and insulted the South and refused to make amends," he wrote in his diary. "The South has determined to bear it no longer." Reference, he believed, was "superflous altogether, in fact wrong. . . . we have not the time for a convention."[48]

The *Abingdon Democrat* expressed the hope that the convention delegates would not dishonor the state or its "men of old." To submit to the black Republicans, the newspaper stressed, would be cowardly, disgraceful, and humiliating. Virginians had grown up listening to the tales of the commonwealth's revolutionary heroes. What would the present generation of Virginians tell their children?[49]

In opposition to the immediatists was a loose coalition of conditional and unconditional unionists. Like their rivals, unionists acted out of anger, fear, class and economic interests, and considerations of honor. Only their perceptions and responses differed. Harper's Ferry mortified unionists as deeply as it had secessionists. The unionists argued, however, that the union remained the best bulwark protecting the South from Brown-style fanatics, even under a Republican administration. If Virginia seceded, however, the state would throw open its frontiers to the militant abolitionists, and no federal authorities would be there to stop the raiders. The fugitive slave problem would increase as well. Finally, if hostilities broke out between the North and South, slavery would not survive. Virginia would become a de facto free state, dependent on undesirable white laborers.[50] "How would you like the idea of Pat and Bridget instead of Rose and Sambo?" Sarah A. Preston asked her sister, Harriet Caperton.[51]

Unionists departed from immediatist secessionists further by blaming the Deep South nearly as much as the North for the crisis. They also feared the economic consequences of secession, which would cut off the state's farmers, drovers, and planters from their lucrative northern markets and tie the state's pro-tariff manufacturers to a government controlled by cotton-planting free-traders. Moreover, Virginia's slave exports would collapse if the southern confederacy reopened the

African slave trade, as many feared. As a result, former Whigs in the middle class drew especially toward unionism.[52]

Honor played a crucial role in Virginia unionism as well. Immediatists depicted unionists as unmanly cowards, submissionists, and abolitionists. Unionists vehemently denied the allegations, and felt it necessary to defend their honor. To prove their honorable intentions, most cismontane and Southwest Virginia unionists attached a long list of professed conditions to their unionism, which led to their crude but illustrative moniker "wait-a-bits." If Lincoln indeed attempted to coerce the seceded states or put the abolitionist program into effect, secession would be a justified last resort. In the meantime, they waited in hopes that compromise attempts such as the Virginia-sponsored Washington Peace Conference, the Crittenden Compromise Resolutions, or private initiatives could create an honorable solution to the national crisis. To be "honorable," any compromise agreement had to include measures to safeguard slavery permanently from northern or federal interference and promises of no federal coercion of the Deep South. Historians have debated ever since whether this attitude reflected genuine unionism. In retrospect, a more accurate name might have been "conservative secessionist." Virginians of this mindset were willing, even desperate, to give Lincoln his chance, but only one. This "wait-a-bit" attitude dominated Southwest Virginia unionist ranks.[53]

Renewed rumors of compromise aided unionists at the polls on February 4. The statewide returns revealed a significant setback for immediatism. As the *Abingdon Democrat* put it, immediatism had "been badly whipped . . . almost annihilated."[54] Of one hundred forty-two delegates elected, only forty-six can be identified as immediatists. Moreover, reference won with a vote of 103,236 to 46,386. Unionism fared especially well in the Northwest and Valley. Southwest Virginia, like the Tidewater and Piedmont, was more divided. Reference and "wait-a-bits" won their largest margins in Whig/Constitutional Union counties like Mercer, Monroe, Montgomery, Washington, and Wyoming. Some counties that had gone strongly for Breckinridge, such as Boone and Lee, also went for the union. Democratic counties such as Buchanan, Carroll, McDowell, Smyth, and Tazewell, however, opposed reference.[55]

On the whole, Southwest Virginians and especially old-line Whigs had expressed their desire to remain in the union at least temporarily, in order to give the Republicans an opportunity to bow to the South's demands and save the nation. Half of Southwest Virginia's twenty-two convention delegates were moderate "wait-a-bits." The conditionalists far outpaced the region's unconditional unionists, who elected only four delegates. Seven elected immediatists pressed the moderates more closely. Judged from a different vantage point, in other words, eighteen of Southwest Virginia's twenty-two delegates would support secession under the right conditions.[56]

The results nonetheless disgusted Southwest Virginia immediatists. John B. Floyd wrote William M. Burwell that "the southern cause has sustained a fearful defeat in Va at the last election." Floyd, more than his fellows, saw everything he had worked for as governor collapsing before his eyes. "When Halifax & Pittsylvania [Piedmont counties] declare to Tazewell & Logan that the *question* of slavery is not worth quarreling about," he wrote, "these last named counties will be prepared to go a little farther & believe that the *negro himself* is not worth quarreling for!" Unionism, Floyd feared, was about to reverse Southwest Virginia's integration into the South's staple, slave-based economy.[57]

Tension led to violence. In Smyth County, a mob of immediatists terrorized a self-proclaimed abolitionist and unionists gathered to retaliate.[58] In Abingdon, immediatists hoisted a secessionist flag to welcome the town's February court. Unionist William B. Clark, declaring that "that d——d rag . . . [was] not the flag of our fathers," tore it down. Cooler heads intervened to prevent a riot.[59]

On February 13, amid rising tension, the Virginia secession convention gathered in Richmond. Among the delegates was former President John Tyler, two former cabinet officers, and twelve ex-congressmen. Approximately a quarter of the delegates were immediatists, another quarter unconditional unionists, largely from the northwest, and the remaining half moderate "wait-a-bits." Three-fourths of the delegates owned slaves, but lawyers, not planters, dominated the roll. Southwest Virginia's contingent reflected the convention's larger divisions. Of the region's twenty-two delegates, at least fourteen were attorneys. Only four identified themselves as agriculturalists.[60]

Southwest Virginians hoped the convention would decide the issue one way or the other in a few days. Instead, it dragged on until May. Henry T. Shanks, the modern historian of Virginia's secession, divided the deliberations into three phases of roughly equal duration. The first period, lasting until March 9, was a period of delay. A majority of delegates waited to judge the results of national compromise measures and to hear Lincoln's inaugural speech on March 4. In the interim, delegates established their positions on the right of secession and the question of coercion.[61]

Southwest Virginians from the first played a somewhat larger role in the secession convention than they had during the constitutional convention of 1850–51. One of the first Southwest Virginians to speak was Smyth County immediatist James W. Sheffey. On February 27, Sheffey declared "the Union is no more! The Union is dissolved! Seven states have seceded, and established a provisional Government. That fact practically dissolves the Union." He argued that Virginia, situated between the free states and the new confederacy, could not hope to remain neutral for long. The commonwealth must choose the South and secession. Perhaps only then, he told unionists, would northern conservatives, "if there be such there," silence the abolitionists, mitigate the South's grievances, and restore the union.[62]

Sheffey blamed Lincoln. Because of his silence, no one knew if Lincoln planned to coerce the seceded states. The president-elect had been as "Silent as an Oriental despot and mysterious as the veiled prophet of Khorassan. . . . No voice from Springfield . . . to tell us what his future purposes are." There were rumors, however, and the rumors pointed to coercion. Virginia had to be prepared, as coercion had to result in Virginia's secession.[63]

Additionally, Sheffey dealt with the question of Southwest Virginia's loyalty to the state. Already, northwesterners had renewed their threats of dissolution of the state, just as they had in 1851. This time, Sheffey promised, the Southwest would not join them, as the region's delegates had ten years before. Fortified by the mountains, the descendants of the heroes of King's Mountain would defend southern rights to the last, even if eastern Virginia faltered.[64]

On March 1, Monroe County immediatist John Echols introduced resolutions demanding that Congress recognize the Confederacy's independence and begin negotiations on the questions of the African slave trade and navigation of the Mississippi River. Echols hoped for peaceful dissolution of the nation.[65] Three days later, Lincoln dashed Echols' hopes. Promising to "hold, occupy, and possess" federal property in the South, Lincoln's inaugural struck southerners as a declaration of war. Southwest Virginians grew angrier. Immediatists hastily organized meetings across the region to plan resistance to coercion. Pro-secession resolutions from these meetings appeared on convention delegates' desks. As a result, Benjamin Wysor of Pulaski County introduced a secession ordinance in the convention on March 8. The convention referred Wysor's ordinance to the Committee on Federal Relations.[66]

The day after Wysor's ordinance, that committee made its long-awaited report, and the convention shifted into a second phase marked by unionist control. The report, while defending the right of a state to secede, opposed immediate secession. Instead, the moderate majority again endorsed a national convention to settle the crisis through constitutional amendments along the lines of the Crittenden Compromise. The report also endorsed a border state convention. Both the report and new hopes of compromise in the convention, hopes buoyed by Secretary of State William H. Seward's secret promises of no coercion, strengthened convention unionists.[67]

On March 26, Southwest Virginian William Ballard Preston, an acknowledged leader of the "wait-a-bits," delivered a lengthy speech in opposition to hasty secession. Preston acknowledged the right of secession, but depicted it as a last resort. The convention's legal mandate from the people, he asserted, was only to compose proposed constitutional amendments that would undercut abolitionist agitation, "restoring the friendly feelings of the two sections." Preston attempted to convince the convention that a firm response to the North from Virginia, neither warlike nor submissive, would convince the North to acquiesce to the South's many demands. If the effort failed, Virginia then could leave the union.[68] Pressed by the immediatist Wise, Preston repeated and defended his argument. According to the *Richmond Daily Dispatch,* Preston declared that the only difference between Wise and himself "was that [Wise] had no hope, while he had hope from both sections and would never give up until time and blood shall set a seal upon the efforts in behalf of the Union."[69]

The day after Preston's speech, the convention began resolution-by-resolution voting on the Committee on Federal Relations' report. The key vote occurred on April 4, when immediatist leader Lewis E. Harvie of Amelia County attempted to introduce a secession ordinance as a substitute for the report's sixth resolution, which expressed hope for sectional reconciliation. Unionists and moderates combined to defeat Harvie 88 to 45, with twenty-one delegates not voting. Harvie gave up hope that Virginia would ever secede.[70]

Seven Southwest Virginians supported Harvie's secession ordinance: William P. Cecil of Tazewell, McDowell, and Buchanan counties; Manilius Chapman of Giles County; Samuel L. Graham of Tazewell County; Fielden L. Hale of Carroll County; Sheffey; and Wysor. Thirteen Southwest Virginians, including Preston, opposed it. Thus, as late as eight days before Fort Sumter, Southwest Virginia's divided delegation, like the convention as a whole, opposed immediate secession. Unionism appeared to be fully in the ascendancy.[71]

In retrospect, it is clear that unionism in fact was on its last legs. First of all, the convention no longer truly reflected public opinion. Excluding the residents of the northwestern counties, Virginians had moved more toward endorsing secession since the February election of delegates. Newspapers whipped up anti-Lincoln sentiment, especially in Southwest Virginia. The convention, meanwhile, had turned inward and grown more cautious and conservative.[72]

Second, state sectionalism had reappeared to factionalize delegates. Northwestern unionists, led by John S. Carlile, Alexander H. H. Stuart, and Waitman T. Willey, took the opportunity of the convention to reopen the Pandora's Box closed by the Constitutional Convention of 1850–51. Specifically, the northwesterners initiated a campaign for constitutional reform, including the complete white basis of representation and repeal of the tax break given slaveowners in 1851. Northwestern secessionists joined their fellow Northwest Virginians in the hope that constitutional reform would make secession more palatable to their constituents. Essentially, the Northwest's unionists demanded constitutional reform in exchange for promises of their loyalty to Virginia.[73]

Ten years before, Southwest Virginians had joined their northwestern brethren to make similar threats. Now a decade into the new constitution and connected to Richmond's markets by railroad, the issue clearly made Southwest Virginia's delegates uncomfortable. On the one hand, they generally did desire the reforms in question. On April 5, every Southwest Virginian save Robert E. Kent of Wythe County voted against an eastern attempt to close debate on reform. Yet on the other hand, most believed that the question should be settled later, after a secession ordinance had been adopted or finally rejected.[74]

In explaining his dissenting April 5 vote, Kent best explained what had changed. Slavery, he maintained, had "undergone a very great change in my part of the State. It is an institution to which my people are very much attached . . . and are anxious to foster it."[75]

Finally, and more important for the unionists, Lincoln refused to give moderates the guarantees of no coercion that were critical to their platform. In early April, the convention began to receive reports that Seward to the contrary, Lincoln was taking an increasingly hard-line on Forts Pickens and Sumter. The reports frightened unionists to the extent that Preston proposed sending a committee of three to Washington to meet with his old friend Lincoln and determine just what the president's plans were. On April 8, the convention agreed, and dispatched Preston, unconditionalist Alexander Stuart, and immediatist George Wythe Randolph to meet with Lincoln. By that date, however, Lincoln indeed had decided to reinforce Fort Sumter. By the time the commission reached Washington, Fort Sumter was under fire. Lincoln informed the Virginians in writing that if the reports were true, he intended to meet force with force.[76]

Excited pro-secession demonstrations erupted across the state. In

Montgomery County, the Christiansburg *New Star,* whose title referred to a hoped-for new star in the Confederate Stars and Bars, declared that war had come and Virginia must choose sides immediately.[77] The convention first learned of Fort Sumter on April 13, just after the introduction of four petitions from Southwest Virginia, three of which favored secession. At the end of the day, Pulaski's Wysor submitted a resolution that Virginians "make common cause with their brethren of the Confederate States . . . most unjustly assailed in a war of self-defence."[78] When the convention reconvened on April 15, all had heard that Lincoln had called for seventy-five thousand troops to put down the southern rebellion. Here was the coercion moderates dreaded. Hoping that the proclamation was a hoax of Richmond's secessionist newspapers, unionists managed to obtain an adjournment. On the following day, national newspapers confirmed the story.[79]

As a result of Lincoln's call for troops, secessionist fury swept Southwest Virginia. Christiansburg resident James C. Taylor wrote Governor Letcher that "Our community has been thrown into the most intense excitement by the news, that Lincoln has made a recquisition from Va. . . . Please do not ask us to join a northern army to fight our southern friends, neighbors, fathers, & brothers."[80] Meanwhile, in Smyth County, John Apperson described "Excitement . . . at its pitch in regard to national affairs. Every house in Marion nearly has a secession flag floating over it. Men are excited to the highest pitch of their animal power, and well they may."[81]

On April 17, Montgomery County doctor and Mexican War veteran Harvy Black warned a crowd that "long columns armed now are marching with bayonets fixed upon our country's bleeding bosom. . . . the last bond that held us together as a people has been rapped [ripped?] asunder." Because of the abolitionists, Lincoln and his "cabalistic, hell-answering cabinet" planned to violently coerce the South into submission with Virginia's help. The commonwealth had to refuse. "Here to-day we cast the die and pass the Rubicon! And when we run up the stars and stripes of the S. Confederacy, we declare ourselves no longer subject to the rule of Abraham Lincoln, or his republican murderers."[82]

In Richmond the convention crossed its own Rubicon. On the table lay William Ballard Preston's secession ordinance, reluctantly introduced the day before. Shaken by Lincoln's proclamation and convinced that a Wise-organized "Spontaneous Peoples' Convention" planned to stage a coup, depose Letcher, and replace the convention, the delegates approved the ordinance 88 to 55. Only four Southwest Virginians, Colbert Fugate of Scott County, English-born James Law-

son of Logan, Boone, and Wyoming counties, Samuel Price of Greenbrier County, and John D. Sharp of Lee County, voted against the ordinance, and they later signed it. The region's eleven "wait-a-bits" in
contrast had waited enough. They rejected their conditional unionism in the face of Lincoln's "coercion" and public outcry. Overall, nearly half of the antisecession votes in the convention came from northwestern delegates. Three days later, most of these northwestern
Virginians quietly slipped out of Richmond and returned home to create a new, unionist state.[83]

Fully freed from previous restraints and anxieties, white Southwest
Virginians fervently rallied to their new colors. Companies created to
stop John Brown quickly mustered and offered their services to Richmond. Support for secession cut across Southwest Virginia's subregional
boundaries. From the Blue Ridge subregion, Floyd County militia captain S. A. Buckingham wrote Letcher that "patriotism" had united Virginia. "I participate," he wrote, " in that glorious feeling of enthusiasm that now warms the Southern blood and fires the Southern
hearth."[84]

In the valley subregion, the companies formed in the wake of Harper's Ferry mustered. At Emory and Henry College, every student save
two sons of East Tennessee unionist William L. Brownlow joined southern regiments. In Abingdon, William B. Clark, the man who had torn
down a Confederate flag two months before, also enlisted. All expressed
their eagerness for action.[85] "For god sake order the twenty sixth Brigade," R. T. Preston telegraphed Letcher from Christiansburg.[86]

Units moved out quickly. On April 16, the Pulaski Guards gathered
in Newbern. "The boys were coming nearly all night." James N. Bosang
remembered. "Oh, what a day the next was! The tears, the farewells,
the parting with loved ones, the heartaches of those who were to be
left." In Dublin, the Guards boarded a train for Richmond: "We moved
off amid the flutter of handkerchiefs, fans, canes and every demon-
stration they could make. . . . We were going to war."[87]

Such support for secession was also evident in the Allegheny Plateau subregion. "The war spirit is abroad in our midst," Marion
Mathews wrote from Lewisburg.[88] "There is but one sentiment here,"
wrote another Lewisburg resident. "Every man, young & old is ready
to start at a moments warning to defend the old Commonwealth."[89]

From Fayette County, Thomas Mathews assured Letcher that he
could count on the loyalty of the Allegheny Plateau Virginians of
Southwest Virginia. Fayette County's mountaineers had "been as your-
self of divided antecedents and proclivities, as long as a union-bond
existed between Virginia and the union of our fathers." With that bond

snapped, Mathews's neighbors, "no longer citizens of the union, hold themselves as fellow citizens of *Virginia*."[90]

Through May and into June, Southwest Virginia's "war spirit" continued unabated. New volunteer companies and home guard units organized. Gender proved to be no barrier, as a group of Montgomery County women attempted to establish a home guard unit of their own.[91] Another woman, Washington Countian Polly Branson, remembered that "I was opposed to secession, but after the state seceded, I was for the side my boys were on."[92]

Support for secession in Southwest Virginia was not total, however. Dissent did exist, especially among pacifist religious groups such as the German Baptist Church, or "Dunkards." In the plateau subregion, a minority of residents clung unconditionaly to the union. In Greenbrier County, men refused to serve in a newly created home guard unit. Men from Buchanan, Russell, and Wise counties slipped into Kentucky to avoid military service, many later to join unionist Kentucky regiments.[93] From Wise County, A. F. Henderson wrote Letcher of "some disaffected persons in this county who avowe that they will 'fight for Linkon and die in his cause.'"[94]

Other unconditional unionists surprisingly expected to fight for Lincoln under Virginia's flag. P. F. Caldwell wrote Letcher from Lewisburg offering to raise a regiment of cavalry to form part of Virginia's quota as announced by Lincoln in his April 15 proclamation. He informed Letcher that he had already placed advertisements in the local newspapers headlined *"Defend the Government,—Stand by the Constitution— Support the Union,* against those who are trying to *usurp* the *first*—destroy the *second* & dissolve the *last*." Across the back of Caldwell's letter, someone in the government scribbled "Union man who wants to raise a company of cavalry to fight against Va."[95]

Unconditional unionism was not only a plateau phenomenon. In Washington County, unionists at first worked openly. Like Lewisburg's Caldwell, Abingdon's John A. Campbell began to raise a unionist Virginia regiment. Campbell gathered nearly two hundred men before Virginia authorities forced the unit to disband. According to John B. Floyd, his hometown was full of such unionists who hoped to slow Virginia's mobilization.[96]

Unconditional unionists presented an immediate threat to mountain secessionists, especially those left behind when the soldiers marched away. They wanted unionism suppressed with force. Martha J. Gilmer wrote her soldier brothers in disgust at the numbers of unionists and slackers in Russell County. She expressed the hope that the government would force the unionists into Confederate service, or worse. "You had a nought union people around you to fight with out the yankes," she wrote, "if you go back to larelhill to run the yankes off I want you all to kill all the wimmen kill them that brought beanes and milk and ever traiter you see."[97]

In Montgomery County, meanwhile, William Ballard Preston's extended family worried about their neighbors, the Price family. According to slave informants, the Prices were unionists and abolitionists. "Dr. Otey says that he has negro evidence that they are inciting the slaves to rebellion," Mary Eliza Caperton wrote. According to Otey's source, one Price had told a slave that the war was about Lincoln's wish to free the slaves. The man then tried to give the slave a pistol. The influence apparently had some effect, as at least one Preston slave declared Lincoln to be a "second Christ." Further, none of the Prices had attempted to enlist in local military units, a fact Caperton saw as corroborating the rumors. She also reported that local secessionists were determined to make sure that the Prices voted in favor of secession on May 23, the "reference" ballot. If they voted for the union, "there will be blood spilled in Montgomery. Dr. Otey had on a large navy pistol & a large knife buckled around his waist."[98]

Repression such as that threatened by Otey's "large navy pistol" silenced unionists on May 23. Postmasters opened mail. At least one Price was jailed. Other unionists later reported being threatened with the loss of their property, and even death, if they voted against secession. Secessionists threatened Wythe County Unionist Andrew Brally with drowning and Russell Countian Aaron Hendricks with shooting. At several polls, armed troops stood watch. Not surprisingly, the vote resulted in a landslide for secession.[99]

Disunionist fervor could not remain at a fever pitch for much longer, however. As the companies left the region, to "much lamentation" according to John Echols,[100] fears of defeat, slave uprisings and famine surfaced. Initial military defeats such as the loss of Northwest Virginia took an added toll. Gloom and melancholy descended. Mary Eliza Caperton and Sarah Ann Preston expected General George B. McClellan's Ohio force in the northwest to reach Montgomery County momentarily. At the same time, however, a grim determination to resist the Yankees developed. Preston vowed to tear up the railroad's tracks to slow the northern advance.[101]

Among the soldiers, Floyd Countian S. L. Walton of the Forty-second Virginia Infantry best caught the mood. Walton promised to remain true to the southern cause. From camp in Lynchburg, he swore that "be fore i would dizert i would sufer to be shot i volunteered to fight for My Country an My Wife an My Father an My Mother an My

Brother and frens." When the Civil War began, most white Southwest Virginians, despite class, gender, or subregional orientation, agreed with Preston and Walton.[102]

Secessionist sentiment in Southwest Virginia, in short, emanated from a combination of honor-based politics, a state constitution that erased to an extent east-west sectionalism, binding the regions tenuously, and modernization. In further commercializing Southwest Virginia, and linking it to Richmond's markets, the railroad had made the region more like the rest of Virginia and the South. Secession was a natural, expected response in a region where devotion to slavery and the cash crop had been renewed and deepened. The railroad was not through with Southwest Virginia either. Union armies were on the march, and their target was the Virginia and Tennessee Railroad. Having brought greater commercialism, expanded slavery, and ultimately secession to the region, the railroad now would bring war and defeat.

6

"Our Land in Every Part Groaning": The Civil War Begins, 1861–62

BEFORE DAWN on July 21, 1861, Union General Irvin McDowell's raw army splashed across northern Virginia's sluggish Bull Run Creek and struck P. G. T. Beauregard's smaller Confederate force. The first major battle of the American Civil War had commenced with the Federals driving. By early afternoon, Beauregard's lines of weary volunteers verged on collapse. Then, at 2 P.M., General Thomas J. Jackson brought his fresh Confederate brigade into position on Henry House Hill. "Look!" South Carolinian Barnard Bee cried to his beaten men, "There is Jackson standing like a stone wall! Rally behind the Virginians!" Rally they did. Jackson's brigade stopped the Union advance and then drove the exhausted Yankees backward. When Beauregard ordered a counterattack, the Federal retreat disintegrated into a disorganized rout. Victory went to the "Secesh," and southerners heaped praise and credit on Jackson and his men, henceforth immortalized as the "Stonewall Brigade."[1]

The Fourth Virginia Infantry formed the center of Jackson's stone wall. With the Twenty-Seventh Virginia Infantry, the Fourth Virginia bore the brunt of the fighting and sustained the most casualties on Henry House Hill. Notably, it was a Southwest Virginia regiment; eight of its ten companies hailed from Grayson, Montgomery, Pulaski, Smyth, and Wythe counties. Moreover, Floyd and Greenbrier county men fought in other "Stonewall" regiments. In one sense, then, Southwest Virginia saved the Confederacy at Manassas.[2]

An estimated fifteen thousand Southwest Virginians went on to see action in at least ninety-nine infantry companies, four artillery batteries, and seven companies of cavalry. The Southwest's mountaineers fought in nearly all the celebrated battles of the war's eastern theater, as well as Chickamauga and the Atlanta Campaign, and, at least according to John W. Daniel of the Twenty-Seventh Virginia, originated and popularized the high, piercing battle cry Union soldiers feared as the "rebel yell." Away from the better-known battlefields with names like Manassas, Antietam, Gettysburg, Cedar Creek, and Petersburg, however, other Southwest Virginians participated in a lesser known theater. Mountain fire-fights, ruthless guerrilla raids, random violence, confused loyalties, and desolation characterized the Civil War within Southwest Virginia. Part of the larger war in the "Appalachian" southern mountains, it was a brutal affair that brought few of its participants glory or fame. It was, and is, a largely forgotten war.[3]

Military and political events and resultant civilian reactions divided Southwest Virginia's Civil War into three phases. The first lasted from Virginia's secession in April, 1861 through the winter of 1861–62. During this initial period, Southwest Virginia received its baptism of fire. Military defeats and the resulting loss of territory, hunger and privation, an embryonic guerrilla war, and Confederate impressment policies all combined to stun the region's population, especially in the plateau subregion. War in reality proved to be quite different from the idealized, quick, and easy crusade portrayed from pulpits and stumps in the heady days of April. The second phase encompassed the period from the renewal of Federal operations in the region in March and April 1862, to May 1864. During this two-year interval, defeatism spread from the plateau counties across the region. Military conscription, the appearance of paramilitary bands of deserters, charges of government favoritism toward the wealthy, and profiteering scandals led Southwest Virginians to question the motives and competency of their state and national governments. Increasingly, the war began to seem "a rich man's war and a poor man's fight" to the region's impoverished majority. Support for the two governments in Richmond decreased to the point where many mountaineers began to protest and even passively resist Richmond's policies in what Paul D. Escott has called "a quiet rebellion of the common people." The final phase, encompassing essentially the last year of the war, saw both the final collapse of slavery and the Confederacy created to protect the institution. The ideological accord created by internal improvement policies and constitutional reform in the 1850s broke down almost completely under the strain of war and the conviction that the unsympathetic state and Confederate governments had deserted the region. Political antagonism returned to the fore. The complementary economic ties survived, however, setting the stage for the postwar economic exploitation that characterized the development of "Appalachia."[4]

In the 1850s, the Virginia and Tennessee Railroad brought Southwest Virginia both capitalist commercial expansion and a renewed commitment to slavery. In 1861, the railroad brought Southwest Virginia to the attention of the Union Army.

When Virginia seceded in April 1861, the V&T assumed new strategic importance, as many of its supporters had predicted since the mid-1840s. As the new Confederacy's single most important east-west connector, the railroad shuttled troops and supplies to both eastern and western fronts. In time, the V&T became the chief supply line for Confederate forces in Virginia. As a result, the war proved to be highly profitable for the railroad. Despite tripled labor costs resulting from the military drain on manpower, profits doubled in the first year of the war. The company managed to pay off its million dollar debt to the state in 1863 and cut its total funded debt by nearly one-and-a-half million dollars. Federal destruction only reversed the railroad's fortunes in the last few months of war.[5]

Southwest Virginia's railroad link to the rest of Virginia and other southern states meant similar economic booms for other capitalists. The region became a leading supplier of Confederate war material. Farmers in unoccupied areas produced corn, wheat, and vegetables for soldiers and civilians outside the region. Southwest Virginia grains provided the chief source of bread for Confederate armies in the war's eastern theater. Demand outpaced supply to such an extent that in late 1864, the War Department dispatched soldiers to the region to raise additional supplies of corn and potatoes. Overall, Southwest Virginia functioned as a major Confederate breadbasket.[6]

Livestock were in just as much demand. Confederate units in Virginia and Tennessee provided constant markets for beef cattle. Robert E. Lee's Army of Northern Virginia, Richmonders, and other eastern Virginians depended on Southwest Virginia for beef, and the hog market boomed as well.[7] In December 1862, James M. Johnston wrote from Bristol that "hogs are now all the rage here—they say everybody is agent for the government to buy pork and there are thousands of hogs on the road to this place, and they are killing from three to four hundred . . . daily."[8]

Thus, the war brought unheard of profits and status to those fortunate Southwest Virginia farmers in a position to avoid military service or occupation. Their success led inevitably, however, to resentment on the part of mountaineers affected adversely by the war. Moreover, the capitalism primed by the railroad in the 1850s placed many in a paradoxical relationship with Confederate authorities. Military officials, while desperately in need of regional produce, complained constant-ly that Southwest Virginia farmers hoarded supplies in anticipation of higher prices, charged exorbitantly, and avoided militia or regular ser-vice. These charges eventually provided the justification for impress-ment and conscription.[9]

Southwest Virginia's industrialists shared in the wartime economic bonanza. Regional mineral companies became leading suppliers of raw materials vital to the war effort. Southwest Virginia's lead mines, the Confederacy's only source of lead for ammunition, produced over three million pounds of lead during the conflict. The region's iron industry provided tons of pig iron to Richmond's celebrated Tredegar Iron Works, the South's most significant ordnance manufacturer. Again, however, the success of these firms triggered resentment. The War De-partment considered the industries of such importance that it grant-ed numerous exemptions from military service to workers and man-agers. The tendency on the part of the industrialists to seek higher prices on the black market also created indignation.[10]

The region's salt industry operated under similar conditions. The saltworks, most privately managed by Stuart, Buchanan & Company for most of the war, functioned as the Confederacy's leading supplier of salt. Demand from state and Confederate officials kept the furnac-es running at full blast and underlay the construction of four new fur-naces during the war. In time, the wells produced so much salt that the railroad was unable to keep up with shipments. Yet, salt shortages and inflationary prices characterized salt production almost immedi-ately, leading many mountaineers and state legislators to believe—cor-rectly—that the management was using the war to make a financial killing on the black market. During the second phase of the regional war, salt became a burning and divisive issue.[11]

The Union high command quickly grasped the importance of the railroad Lincoln called "the gut of the Confederacy." Control of the V&T and possession of the region would close the Rebels' main sup-ply line, secure Southwest Virginia's resources for the Union, provide a back door to Richmond, and create an opportunity to accomplish the president's cherished goal of liberating largely unionist East Ten-nessee. In setting such lofty goals, however, as T. Harry Williams point-ed out, the Federal brass from the first seriously underestimated the physical obstacles to success the mountains presented.[12] General Ja-cob D. Cox wrote years later that fellow officers in the theater such as George B. McClellan and William S. Rosecrans underestimated the to-pography when they planned their thrust toward the railroad and

Knoxville. "Looking only at a map," Cox wrote, "it seemed an easy thing to do."[13]

It did seem easy at first. On May 26, 1861, only three days after Virginia voters approved secession, McClellan's Ohio army crossed the Ohio River into Northwest Virginia. Linking up with regiments of northwestern unionists, McClellan ran off a small Confederate force at Phillipi on June 3, and raced south. By mid-July, McClellan's army, now divided into wings led by Cox and Rosecrans, occupied almost all of Northwest Virginia, and Cox pressed on the Southwest. McClellan's success, illustrated in map 3, produced two critical results. His occupation of the Northwest permitted unionists from that area to meet safely in Wheeling, the first step toward the creation of their new unionist state. At the same time, McClellan's victories, small in retrospect but seemingly major at the time, made him a national hero in his and others' minds. On July 23, he turned over command to Rosecrans and left for Washington and command of the Army of the Potomac.[14]

Rosecrans proposed to continue the army's swift advance to Wytheville, destroy the railroad between Wytheville and Abingdon, and sweep on into East Tennessee. Standing in his way were three quasi-independent Confederate commands under William W. Loring, a regular army veteran, and two political generals, none other than Henry A. Wise and John B. Floyd. The two politicians clashed immediately and unrealistically for the glory of winning back the Northwest.[15] "G—— d—— him," Floyd swore, "why does he [Wise] come to *my country*? Why does he not stay in the east. . . . I don't want the d—— rascal here, I will not stand it."[16]

Not surprisingly, the Confederate effort to reconquer Northwest Virginia failed. Personal rivalries hampered the Rebels at every turn. In August, Virginia's Robert E. Lee arrived at Loring's headquarters to coordinate the disjointed southern effort in the mountains. Lee initially hoped that Loring would go on the offensive, but the latter refused, exasperating Lee. Floyd proved more eager to fight, but he lacked the skills necessary to accomplish much. On September 10, Rosecrans attacked Floyd's entrenchments on the north bank of the Gauley River at Carnifex Ferry. Floyd's Rebels repulsed five vicious assaults before nightfall, but then beat a hasty retreat, low on ammunition. Floyd immediately blamed Wise, who, judging Floyd's position with the river at his back suicidal, repeatedly refused to send reinforcements.[17]

Floyd and Wise then fell back twenty miles into Fayette County, unable to even agree on a position to dig in and wait for Rosecrans's certain advance. Lee hurried south from his own failed Cheat Mountain campaign to cajole Floyd and Wise into cooperating in a coun-

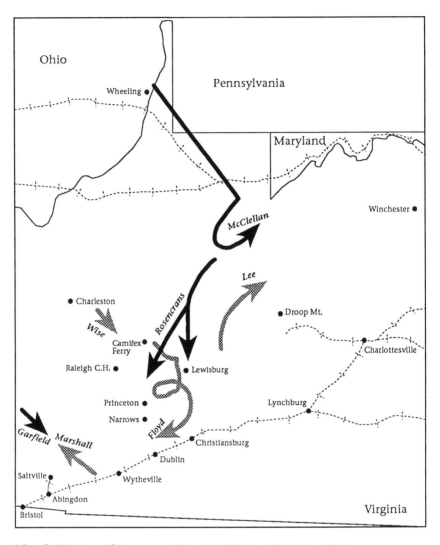

Map 3. Major military operations in Western Virginia, 1861.

teroffensive. After Richmond recalled Wise, Lee planned a new campaign, but bad weather, a measles epidemic in the ranks, and demoralization eventually convinced him to throw up works and let Rosecrans do the attacking. In October, after scouts discovered that Rosecrans had disappeared, Richmond recalled the momentarily disgraced Lee and left Floyd in charge. Rosecrans, however, had only pulled back temporarily to regroup and rest his tired, sick army. Late in the month, Floyd renewed his retreat with Rosecrans at his heels.

By December 5, Floyd was in Dublin, having abandoned the entire eastern plateau. Rosecrans only advanced as far as Raleigh County, however, before going into winter quarters. Leaving Cox and a small contingent of troops in control of key positions, Rosecrans returned to Wheeling.[18] The contest for the railroad, the "jugular vein of rebeldom" as Rutherford B. Hayes of the Twenty-third Ohio Infantry called it, paused until spring.[19]

The contest in the Kanawha Valley was not the only scene of action in Southwest Virginia during the first months of the war. Kentuckian Humphrey Marshall commanded the "Army of Eastern Kentucky," composed of Kentuckians and Southwest Virginians, along the borders of the two states. Convinced that a Confederate incursion into eastern Kentucky would rally the populace to the Stars and Bars, Marshall led his hungry, poorly armed force into Kentucky in November 1861. His Virginians, notably those of the Twenty-eighth Virginia Infantry, balked, hesitant to leave their families and homes behind in winter. Marshall left the critical mountain passes connecting the two states in the hands of Lee, Scott, and Wise county militiamen who had refused to join regular units or leave home.[20]

To block Marshall, Union General Don Carlos Buell selected Ohioan James A. Garfield, who got his brigade on the scene quickly and maneuvered Marshall back toward Virginia. On January 10, 1862, Garfield routed Marshall at Middle Creek, Kentucky, and sent the Rebels reeling back into the Old Dominion.[21] Suddenly a national hero, Garfield planned to resume his advance in the spring and destroy the Virginia and Tennessee Railroad, "the grand lever on which the rebellion hangs."[22]

Confederate military reverses in the northern and western most counties of Southwest Virginia's plateau subregion shocked and angered the region's residents, deflating the exuberant pro-secession sentiment that characterized the previous summer. In the valley subregion to be sure, conditions still remained relatively good. Shortages of food—especially salt for civilian consumption—inflation, and the black market caused the most complaints. These Southwest Virginians were spared the hardships experienced by those mountaineers living closer to the warring armies, where the situation quickly grew critical. In Lee, Russell, Scott, and Wise counties, Marshall's army quickly exhausted local food supplies. Civilians hoarded the little that remained, leading inevitably to high inflation and military impressment of food and forage. The situation was so bad that when Richmond ordered Marshall to fall back no further than the Kentucky-Virginia line after Middle Creek, the general refused, responding that the country-

side twenty miles around was absolutely devoid of supplies. He retreated much deeper into the plateau, only to discover the situation nearly as bad as that which he had left. His soldiers quite simply had picked
the area clean.[23]

Hunger, inflation, impressment, and defeat all combined to shock
the Big Sandy Valley. Resistance to militia service symbolized the area's dilemma. While still sympathetic to the southern cause, many men
refused to abandon their families until spring, especially in order to
march into Kentucky. By March 1862, Marshall had grown so exas-
perated with this resistance that with the permission of Jefferson Davis,
Governor Letcher, and Lee, he imposed draconian measures. Marshall
ordered all male residents of the area and outlying counties, aged eighteen to forty-five, to muster with arms. He requisitioned all available
food, forage, wagons, and horses. Those who refused to comply could
face military court-martial. Compliance however lagged. In May, the
government resorted to martial law.[24] "The people of that part of Virginia are heartily sick of the rebellion, and have not generally responded to [Marshall's] call," Garfield reported.[25]

Dissatisfaction with Marshall provided the area's unconditional
unionist minority with an opportunity to emerge from the shadows.
Up to nine hundred men fled to largely unionist eastern Kentucky.
Others remained at home. Marshall reported that Buchanan and Wise
county unionists had organized companies to fight for Lincoln. As for
elsewhere, he warned "that there are many in Washington [County],
and . . . in the lower part of Lee they march through with drums and
fifes and with colors flying."[26]

A similar situation developed at the northern front in Fayette,
Greenbrier, Monroe, and Raleigh counties, where conditions also worsened quickly. Both armies carried off food, forage, and other supplies
from local mountaineers, but the Confederates impressed and stole
with short-sighted zeal. "I got with the Regiment on Monday and
found them all drunk as usual," Tazewell County native Charles A.
Fudge of the Forty-fifth Virginia Infantry reported. He went on to describe widespread pillaging and robberies of local secessionist families'
homes by drunken Rebel soldiers. Angry confrontations between soldiers and the citizens the army supposedly was there to protect resulted.[27] Likewise, after Carnifex Ferry, Leonidas Baugh complained that
the "havoc and desolation produced by an army is alarming. Every
apple is swept out of the orchard near us, and miles of fencing is burnt
to the ground—the rails being taken for firewood. People's houses are
taken with or without leave for the sick and even gardens are ransacked
and every vegetable taken out. This is done by our own soldiers. The

Yankees fairlly gut the houses & lay waste the farms of secessionists. . . . Our soldiers depredate on *all*."[28] So much for winning the hearts and minds of the populace to the Confederacy.

By winter, a typhoid epidemic had further submerged the four counties in misery. Slavery also began to collapse. Many slaves took advantage of the nearness of Federal lines to escape. Owners vainly warned the slaves that Yankees were crueler than southerners, and would cut off their arms to make them useless to the South, or else sell them in Cuba to pay for the war. Runaway slaves poured into Union camps regardless. The Federals refused to return or resell the "contrabands," but did send some on north to work as personal servants for white families in Ohio. Hayes, for example, provided an escaped slave to a relative.[29] He concluded that "Slavery is getting death-blows. As an 'institution,' it perishes in this war."[30]

Many whites fled as quickly as slaves, albeit for vastly different reasons. The secessionist majority abandoned entire towns to their few unconditional unionist neighbors at the approach of Federal columns and fled south into rebel-held areas. Raleigh Court House was a ghost town after Yankee occupation; Boone and Logan Court Houses went up in flames. Some mountaineers left the South entirely and left for the peaceful vistas of the Midwest or the Far West.[31] For those who remained, the winter of 1861–62 was like no other they had experienced. Hayes shrewdly noted those on whom the war had taken the greatest toll. He wrote his mother, "The poor women excite our sympathy constantly. A great share of the calamities of war fall on the women. I see women unused to hard labor gathering corn to keep starvation from the door."[32]

Hungry families meant demoralization in and desertion from the ranks. When McClellan smashed through Northwest Virginia with ease, hundreds of southwestern soldiers took off for home to defend their families. In the baggage left behind at Carnifex Ferry, Hayes found "letters, diaries, etc., etc., in Floyd's trunks and desks [which] show that their situation is desperate. Thousands are in the army who are heartilly sick of the whole business."[33]

Hundreds of the "heartilly sick" in Fayette and Raleigh counties crossed over to the Federals. The Forty-eighth Virginia Infantry, for example, saw twenty of its men don Union blue. While some turncoats claimed to have been prewar unionists forced into uniform, Hayes as well as fellow officer E. P. Scammon concluded that most of them were in fact fair-weather secessionists demoralized by defeat and deprivation. Hayes suspected that most area Confederate soldiers who deserted would have remained in gray if properly fed and led. "People come twenty-five miles to take the oath," he confided to his diary. "How much is due to a returning sense of loyalty and how much is due to the want of coffee and salt, is more than I know. They are sick of the war, ready for peace and a return to the old Union."[34]

Henry A. Wise suggested the same. Writing Lee, Wise confessed that he questioned the loyalty of the entire Kanawha Valley, that Boone County was "nearly as bad" and that "part of Greenbrier is awful." The mountaineers of those counties were "submitting, subdued, and debased." He argued however that the people of Fayette and Raleigh were not truly unionists, but rather afraid of the conquering Federals. "The people demand that the Yankees shall not be fired upon, lest it exasperate them," Wise reported.[35]

Others remained in the ranks but with little devotion to the Confederate cause. Greenbrier County unionist John Sanner reported that "I spoke to some of the militia that I dare trust, and they told me it was their intention not to fight, unless it would be 'to shoot some of their d—n—d officers,' who had dragged them from home."[36]

That resurgent unionism did not characterize all of the plateau's residents, however, was demonstrated painfully with the violence of an escalating guerrilla war that threatened the survival of entire communities. Unionist and secessionist neighbors of the plateau harassed, robbed, and killed each other seemingly at will.[37] Guerrilla activities, according to Garfield, turned the Big Sandy region into "a home of fiends, and converted this war into a black hole in which to murder any man that any soldier from envy, lust or revenge, hated."[38]

Garfield's comment, of course, said as much about the union soldier's attitude toward the mountaineers around him as it did explain the outbreak of guerrilla violence. The poverty created by the war, the sudden brutality of the partisan conflict, and the decidedly un-northern culture of the southern mountains quickly convinced Federals that mountain Virginians were little better than savages. Garfield dismissed the soldiers in Marshall's army as "men of no brains . . . whose lives are not worth to the country what the bullet would cost to kill them."[39] One of his men, Frank H. Mason, described "utter degradation" and "primeval barbarism" and compared mountaineers unfavorably to "the happy barbarians of the Pacific isles."[40] Another, Illinoisan James D. Cox, curtly dismissed mountaineers as "trash."[41]

Union soldiers in the Greenbrier and Kanawha valleys held similar beliefs. Hayes wrote home about the region's magnificent scenery almost as much as he did of the war, but possessed no parallel infatuation with the mountains' population. In his eyes, most mountaineers were "a good-for-nothing people. . . . Unenterprising, lazy, narrow, listless, and ignorant." Southwest Virginia's slaves, Hayes insisted, possessed more intelligence and character than their white owners. Like his compatriots in Kentucky, he took pains to suggest that mountaineers were barely the racial equals of northerners.[42]

Negative perceptions of mountaineers as savage, ignorant, and barely caucasian, their lives worth less than a union-issued Minie ball, combined with the escalating guerrilla war to produce disastrous results. Federal soldiers reserved a special loathing for the so-called "bushwhackers," civilian partisans who harassed enemy soldiers, kidnapped and robbed unionists, cut supply and communication lines, and ambushed small bodies of troops. In northern eyes, bushwhackers were the lowest form of human life, cowardly outlaws who refused to play fairly. Rosecrans, who believed in the rules, generally believed in using civil courts to try ostensible noncombatants. When these courts released captured partisans, as they often did, Federals began to wonder why *they* had to play by the rules. Frustrated and angry Union soldiers, particularly mountain unionists but Ohioans as well, yearned to strike back.[43] One Federal called for a force "to meet them in their own mode of warfare, [to] . . . clean that region."[44] Another concurred, noting that his unionist mountaineers "are anxious to try the job on."[45]

The Lincoln administration encountered great difficulty in coming to grips with the developing problem. Some, like Rosecrans and Lincoln himself, favored a "soft" policy of civilian trials and attitudes designed to ease the transition of the areas in question back into the union. The military, however, favored a "hard" policy of military trials followed invariably by execution, the complete depopulation of trouble spots, and a no-prisoners policy in the field. They encouraged hostage taking as well. In a *de facto* manner, the hard-liners won.[46]

Southwest Virginia produced a prototypical hard liner in 1861. Nearly three years before Sherman and Philip H. Sheridan allegedly invented "total war" in Georgia and Virginia's Shenandoah Valley, George Crook pointed the way in the Greenbrier Valley. Crook was a veteran Indian fighter who had served in the Pacific Northwest's Rogue River War. In September 1861, he became Colonel of the Thirty-sixth Ohio Infantry. Faced with the bushwhackers, and beset with the same prejudices as his men, Crook put his previous training into practice. What worked against one race of savages, he concluded, would work against another. He later recalled, "Being fresh from the Indian country where I had more or less experience with that kind of warfare, I set to work organizing for the task." Crook sent spies out to identify suspected bushwhackers. Once identified, he dispatched soldiers to arrest the suspects. The hitch was that he also had imposed a no-prisoners policy: "when an officer returned from a scout he would report that they had caught so-and-so, but in bringing him in he slipped off a log and broke his neck, or that he was killed by an accidental discharge of one of the men's guns, and many like reports. But they never brought back any more prisoners."[47]

Inevitably, Crook's war against the bushwhackers expanded into a more general war of terror against the entire population. The bushwhackers wore no uniforms, thus any civilian became a suspect. Crook admitted that in fighting the guerrillas, his soldiers burned out the entire northwestern county of Webster, launched indiscriminate ambushes of civilians in Greenbrier County, and purposely "spread terror" throughout the region.[48]

The first year of the Civil War in Southwest Virginia brought both geographic and class cleavages. For most mountaineers of the valley and Blue Ridge subregions, the war had meant flush economic activity at best and irritating shortages and inflation at worst. Commitment to secession and the Confederacy remained strong, although military reverses worried some residents. Quite a different situation had developed in those parts of the plateau subregion traversed by the armies, however. In those counties, battle, foraging soldiers and inflation left many civilians near famine. Many of the hungry were soldiers' families. As a result, many fighting men expressed reluctance to leave their loved ones behind, and some deserted. Mass depopulations occurred as mountaineers fled hunger and Federal occupation. For those who remained, a bitter internecine conflict brought more violence. Who was to blame? Citing military failures, uncontrolled troops, and sheer incompetence, some Southwest Virginians blamed the Virginia and Confederate governments. While many reembraced the old Union, still more stood by the Confederacy but also expressed war-weariness, resignation, and defeatism. The lower, nonslaveowning classes bore the brunt of the suffering, although there was enough to go around. "Could we have believed a few years ago," Sarah Preston wrote at the end of 1861, "that we would have lived through the past eight months? Our land in every part groaning because of this awful war! Surely not! . . . God is scourging the land! He is angry with us." Looking ahead, Preston could see little hope, but only "a *fearful struggle*" looming. As the spring of 1862 dawned, many Southwest Virginians like Preston looked to the battlefields and to their government to see if the plateau's woes would become the norm for the entire region.[49]

7

"What Will Become of the Poor and Widows?": Deprivation and Defeat, 1862–65

On August 30, 1862, as the Second Battle of Manassas drew to a close, a victorious Stonewall Jackson and his staff rode across the battlefield. Noticing a wounded Confederate struggling up a railroad embankment "where the fight had been so hot," in Henry Kyd Douglas's words, Jackson approached the soldier and asked him if he was wounded. "Yes, General," he replied, "but have we whipped 'em? . . . I belong to the Fourth Virginia, your old brigade, General. I have been wounded four times but never before as bad as this. I hope I will soon be able to follow you again." Tenderly, Jackson ordered his staff to quickly secure medical aid for the suffering soldier.[1]

As a member of the Fourth Virginia, the soldier almost certainly was one of the Stonewall Brigade's Southwest Virginians. His devotion to duty, and to his commander, clearly touched both Douglas and Jackson. Here was a potent symbol of the Confederacy's will to win. Back in Southwest Virginia, however, the folks back home were playing out quite a different scene.

Military events beginning in the spring of 1862 did nothing to better Southwest Virginia's worsening predicament (map 4). The region's war entered a new, second phase with a new round of Confederate defeats. Along the Kentucky-Virginia frontier, James A. Garfield's Union force resumed limited operations in March. Continued bushwhacker raids from Virginia into Kentucky convinced Garfield to neutralize the guerrilla's main staging area at Pound Gap, just on the border.[2] Humphrey Marshall had left the gap's defenders "very thinly clad, many barefooted, a very few with blankets, no overcoats, a parcel of flint-lock, old

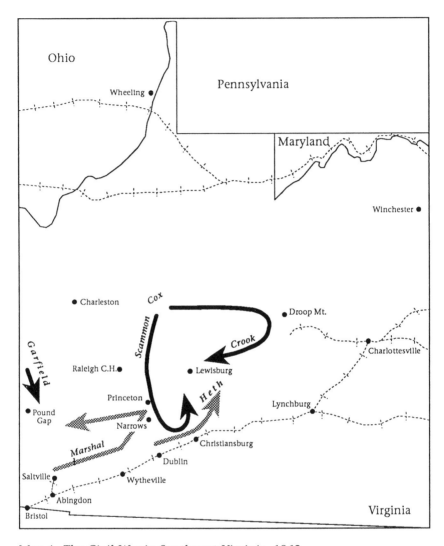

Map 4. The Civil War in Southwest Virginia, 1862.

fashioned muskets and squirrel rifles, altogether a sorry sight." Typhoid, pneumonia, measles, and mumps ravaged the five hundred militiamen.[3] Not surprisingly, when Garfield's sixteen-hundred-man expedition attacked in a snowstorm on March 16, the Rebels threw down their arms and ran. Marshall vainly tried to put the best face on the defeat, recruited new soldiers, and even invaded Kentucky a second time in September to support Generals Braxton Bragg and Edmund Kirby Smith in their

Kentucky invasion. Throughout the incursion into the Bluegrass State, however, Marshall's Virginians again deserted and went home.[4]

Marshall moved into the northern plateau once as well, to fight Jacob Cox. Along the northern front, the Federals, now under command of General John C. Frémont, resumed their drive on the Virginia and Tennessee Railroad and East Tennessee. In April 1862, Frémont ordered Cox's twelve-thousand-man army to push southward along the New River into Giles County, link up with George Crook's second column, and take the railroad. Facing Cox's were the fourteen hundred Confederates and four artillery pieces of Brigadier General Henry Heth's tiny "Army of New River." Realizing his predicament, Heth, an unpopular eastern Virginian, called out the militia, ordered civilians to prepare to burn their crops, and prepared to abandon the rest of the eastern plateau subregion. When Heth begged Lee for supplies and reinforcements, the War Department instead weakened Heth's force by ordering components to Marshall and Kirby Smith. Lee then informed Heth that if Frémont defeated Jackson in the Shenandoah Valley, Heth would have to surrender all of Southwest Virginia and race eastward to save the valley and Lee's left flank. Heth had little faith in Jackson, and almost immediately shipped his supplies to Lynchburg and started east.[5]

Heth's troop movements amazed the Federals, who at that moment were on the march. E. P. Scammon, riding at the head of the advance, reported with glee that Heth was inexplicably pulling out. "There is nothing to stop us this side of the railroad except mud and water," Scammon wrote, begging Cox to order a swift, all-out descent on the Virginia and Tennessee Railroad.[6] Hayes too expressed confidence that he could take Wytheville.[7] "This whole region is completely conquered," Hayes wrote. "Rapid movement is all that is needed to take possession of the railroad and several good counties without opposition."[8]

While Hayes and Scammon finally convinced Cox that the complete conquest of Southwest Virginia was within their grasp, they could not sway Frémont. On May 8, after Stonewall Jackson defeated part of Frémont's Valley force at McDowell, Frémont ordered Scammon and Cox to stop. Hayes at that point had advanced as far as Giles County. Frémont's hesitancy cost the Union Southwest Virginia. Heth had raced back to the region, and on May 10, hit Hayes, who then fell back to join Scammon at the Narrows of the New River in Giles. The two brigades skirmished for several days. Marshall moved up through Tazewell County to reinforce the desperate Heth, captured Princeton, got cold feet, and promptly gave it back to the Yankees. Heth and Marshall had succeeded in frightening Cox, however, to the point where he ordered a general retreat.[9]

Heth quickly turned to eliminate Crook's Federal column, which had spent most of the campaign in Greenbrier County chasing down bushwhackers. On May 23, Heth unsuccessfully attacked Crook in Lewisburg. William W. Loring, assuming command of all troops in Southwest Virginia, raced to Pulaski County and prepared for Cox's expected advance on the railroad.[10]

The attack never came, thanks to Stonewall Jackson. At the end of May, Jackson neared the end of his now-famous Valley Campaign. He had run rings around the Federal opposition and added to his already near-mystical reputation. After the Battle of Winchester, Jackson escaped Frémont and McDowell and disappeared. In reality, he had headed east to support Richmond against McClellan's army on the peninsula. Both Cox and Crook, however, convinced themselves that they were the Stonewall Brigade's next target. Accordingly, they dug in to wait for Jackson. Federal caution, Heth's small army, and Jackson's reputation had combined to save the railroad.[11]

The result was two years of stalemate. From the Union side, Hayes wrote in June 1862, "Flat Top Mountain, twenty miles south of Raleigh, is the boundary line between America and Dixie—between western Virginia, either loyal or subdued, and western Virginia, rebellious and unconquered."[12] The armies went into winter quarters virtually in the same position they occupied the year before. Raids on the railroad replaced occupation as the major component of federal strategy in 1863.[13] The most significant of these raids was John T. Toland's unsuccessful attack on Wytheville in July 1863. Arriving just as the main Confederate force in Southwest Virginia headed north to screen Lee's retreat from Gettysburg, Toland nearly took the town and the railroad by surprise. A hastily-organized defense, however, saved the V&T. As they fled, the Federals burned what they could of Wytheville, angry at both Toland's death and the armed participation of the townspeople. Wytheville emerged in Federal lore as a nest of bushwhackers. "We were fired upon from houses," Scammon reported, "public and private, by the citizens, even by the women." The Federals swore vengeance.[14]

"Wytheville has been one of the most violent Rebel towns from the first," Hayes wrote after the raid. "They always talked of 'no quarter,' 'the black flag,' etc."[15] Observers identified other towns, including Blacksburg, Dublin, Lewisburg, Marion, and, ironically, Union, in the same light. Increasingly, however, and especially in the countryside, divided communities became more the rule during the regional war's second phase. Policies enacted during the period coupled with events to undermine Southwest Virginia's devotion to the southern cause.[16]

Death and defeat on the battlefield continued to undermine confidence and hope. Montgomery Countians petitioned the General Assembly for new military leadership, writing that "the southwest has recently been thrown into a panic by reason of the approach of the enemy—and by reason of the conduct of those charged with our defence."[17] After Jackson's death at Chancellorsville in May 1863, Christiansburg's Ginger Wade wrote that, "gloom has been cast over everybody. . . . Perhaps we put our trust in the man too much . . . but I almost feel like giving up."[18] In late 1863, Mollie Black of Blacksburg wrote of defeats and wondered "When will it end? I think something must be done before spring to bring peace." She added that "even the well off are starting to complain, and if *they* are, what will become of the poor & widows?"[19]

As Mollie Black implied, defeat, privation, and developing class tensions across the region went hand in hand. Mountaineers found increasing difficulty obtaining basic necessities such as grain, coffee, and salt. What was available came at black market prices so high that only the wealthy could afford them. In December 1862, for example, a barrel of flour cost twenty dollars. Crop failures in 1862 deepened distress. Increasing resentment was the fact that the shortages in part resulted from the government buying all available reserves, often for reasons the region's residents opposed. The Confederate government bought up large quantities of grain, for example, to turn into whiskey in government distilleries. Mountaineers also resented the fact that government contracts made a small portion of the population wealthy while the majority went hungry. Finally, the state government compounded the problem with its late, half-hearted efforts at poor relief, which were more conservative, ineffective, and riddled with patronage than programs in other states.[20]

Indicative of the situation was the outcry regarding salt production. "I scarcely know what to say about the Salt works to you," one Wythe Countian wrote, "they have been carrying on the most high handed swindle . . . people ware guilty of."[21] Legislators constantly received complaints that the Saltville enterprises were engaging in extortion and black marketeering, charges that were corroborated after the war by saltworks' stockholder Charles C. Campbell, the railroad's Saltville agent and a unionist. "I bought it low and sold it for all it would bring," he later wrote, a practice that helped Campbell amass a personal fortune worth thirty-seven thousand dollars. In August 1862, as a result of complaints about the activities of men like Campbell, Governor Letcher called a special legislative session to deal with the salt imbroglio. Letcher condemned the saltworks' operators and called for state impressment of the concerns. The General Assembly responded by granting Letcher broad emergency powers to regulate the salt industry.[22]

Letcher, however, proved reluctant to use the powers given him. Visiting Saltville in September 1862, Letcher discovered that Stuart, Buchanan & Company, the major enterprise, had several outstanding contracts with the Confederate government and several southern states. Most Virginians expected Letcher to ignore the contracts and seize the salt for use in Virginia. Letcher refused, however, citing the need for southern unity. Unhappy with the governor's perceived timidity, the legislature stripped him of his salt powers and assigned them to the Board of Public Works. In June 1863 and again in March 1864, the Board impressed some saltworks. Nonetheless, salt remained hard to get and expensive.[23]

Other state and Confederate policies similarly increased privation and resentment. In April 1863, the Confederate Congress levied a "tax-in-kind" of one-tenth of a farmer's annual produce. Enforcement was uneven and inept; southerners living near army camps or railroads bore the brunt of the "tithe." When mountaineers proved especially unwilling to comply, the congress authorized the use of force to collect it. Illegal impressment of supplies above the one-tenth also became frequent. Washington County unionist Aaron Hendricks claimed to have lost forty thousand bushels of corn and 150 horses to impressment. Confederate agents in Southwest Virginia repeatedly seized farmers' entire crops to feed nearby armies, arguing that if the Confederates did not take the supplies, the Yankees would. The General Assembly debated the problem frequently but did little in substance.[24] "I tremble for the fate of the Confederacy," a Grayson Countian wrote, "so much grumbling now exists [regarding] the tax in kind."[25]

Agents impressed slaves as well as food and forage, in order to construct fortifications or mine salt, both dangerous tasks. In March 1863, the state began to issue quotas for each county to fill. Southwest Virginia's slaveholding class, through the county courts, howled. With all the white laborers off in the army, the slaveholders maintained, the region's slaves were all that stood between Southwest Virginia and famine. Not only local people would starve, the courts warned, Lee's army would go hungry as well. Nearly every county court refused to comply with the repeated demands for their slaves.[26]

The slaveowners' desperate struggle to keep their slave investments safe from danger disgusted the region's nonowners, who accused the elite of selfishness. Impressment of a poor man's crop was fine, the slaveholders seemed to be saying, but impressing the wealthy was another matter. Indicative of the widening class resentments resulting from resistance to slave impressment was the letter of Russell Countian G. P. Cowan, who reported that many local yeomen finally had given up on the Confederacy and crossed into Union lines as a result of the controversy.[27]

As they struggled to keep their slaves out of government hands, slaveowners also faced a growing runaway problem. Asserting that they had been "set free by Mr. Lincoln's Proclamation," slaves escaped at every approach of Federal troops. Tazewell County's slaves fled to Kentucky with such frequency that by March 1864, one observer concluded that slavery in the plateau had become a purely voluntary condition.[28] The lack of "loyalty" to masters surprised slaveowners and contributed to negative feelings toward both blacks and slavery. "I was surprised at Jim's leaving you," soldier S. B. Hern wrote Sallie Preston. "Such darkies are uncertain and especially in these times."[29] Disabled veteran G. C. Forsinger of Abingdon blamed slaves from outside the region for subverting the loyalty of his bondsmen. "I had some difficulty in keeping those negroes off the place after night," he wrote, "and had more in keeping my own on it."[30]

Overall, slavery in Southwest Virginia became a negative and divisive element in 1863 and 1864. The southern way of life Southwest Virginians hoped to protect from abolitionists was collapsing under the strain of war. As unionists had warned in the winter of 1860–61, secession and war had undermined the defense of slavery, provided its enemies with greater opportunities to undermine the system, and had driven a wedge between slaveowners and nonowners. For mountaineers who had come to place independence from Washington first, slavery increasingly seemed a liability to the Confederacy. For those who still saw slavery as the war's primary *raison d'être,* the incentive to continue the struggle waned.

Conscription widened the cleavage between classes most of all. In April 1862, at the urging of military officials and newspaper editors, the Confederate Congress passed an act conscripting all men aged eighteen to thirty-five into military service, unless otherwise exempted. The following September, Congress raised the age limit to forty-five. Favoritism toward members of the upper class in granting exemptions caused widespread discontent. Most odious was the exemption granted owners or overseers of twenty or more slaves, which seemed an insult to the small farmer. As a result, compliance lagged. Mountaineers avoided enrollment, sought exemptions from local authorities, and deserted if called up. The military responded with repression and press gang tactics. Those who refused to serve were branded, whipped, even shot. Monroe County delegate Wilson Lively complained in the General Assembly that conscripts from his district had been jailed after their physical examinations and transported under guard to training camp. What Lively did not say was that such behavior probably was necessary to keep the conscripts from escaping.[31]

Letcher, who opposed conscription as unconstitutional, tried to provide Southwest Virginians with a way out. In May 1862, at Letcher's urging, the General Assembly authorized a ten-thousand-man state army free from Confederate control. The Virginia State Line was charged with defending Southwest Virginia, a task many believed regular forces had muffed. To lead the State Line, the legislature chose John B. Floyd, whom Jefferson Davis had cashiered for his embarrassing flight from Fort Donelson. Southwest Virginians still had faith in Floyd, and pronounced him infinitely superior to inept outsiders such as Heth and Marshall. Theoretically, only men not subject to conscription could join the State Line, but in practice, recruiters took anyone, including Kentuckians and deserters from regular units. Regular officers expressed outrage. Recruitment went poorly, however, and the legislature abolished the Line in February, 1863. Four-fifths of the men who had enrolled in the State Line deserted rather than come under Confederate control. Floyd himself died months later.[32]

Meanwhile, the guerrilla war continued and expanded, bringing Southwest Virginians another source of misery. In 1862, the state and Confederate governments officially endorsed guerrilla recruitment and encouraged the formation of partisan units. The sanctions, in retrospect, did more damage than good. First, the bushwhacker units, as Rebel commanders found, were both unruly and unwilling to obey orders from above, creating many headaches and opposition to the guerrillas within the army. Second, they retarded the growth of regular units. Many potential recruits as well as seasoned veterans desired to live the romantic life of the partisan. "Devil Anse" Hatfield of Logan County, to mention one notable example, deserted from the Forty-fifth Virginia Infantry in 1863 to return home and form the partisan Logan Wildcats. Finally, the guerrilla units encouraged the official development of rival unionist "Home Guards" or "scouts" who matched the Rebels blow for blow. By late 1863, bushwhackers and Home Guards roamed the mountains at will, taking hostages, pillaging, and killing. Some were as young as fourteen.[33] "Unless it is stopped," worried Nancy Hunt, a native New Yorker and unionist storekeeper in the utopian Mountain Cove community, "I awfully fear another Lawrence massacre. . . . I have not written of all the havoc that has been made here. It is awful to live the way we do."[34]

Desertion continued to be a problem. Milton Charlton of the Fifty-fourth Virginia Infantry reported that men over the age of thirty-five "are keeping a continual fuss about being kept in service and some of them have left and gone home." When their commander stationed guards to stop desertion, the guards allowed deserters to flee nonetheless. Thus, the guards themselves ended up under arrest. Charlton concluded that "he may put out as many guard as he pleases it will not stop the men from going away."[35]

Adding to the havoc were armed bands of extraregional deserters that appeared in the mountains in 1862. Because of the locations of the main armies, Southwest Virginia became a favorite route home for deserters en route to either the Deep South or the Northeast. The mountains provided a fairly direct path home as well as innumerable places to hide from regular troops or provost officials. Soon, the grapevines of both armies identified Southwest Virginia as a "Deserter Country." Giles, Montgomery, and especially rugged Floyd County soon attracted hundreds of hard-bitten, well-armed deserters from both North and South. Floyd County acquired the nickname "Sisson's Kingdom" for the unionist family that encouraged up to five hundred deserters to join them in defiance of Confederate authority. Other families, notably those belonging to the Dunkard Church, hid deserters in Floyd. In the counties west of Floyd, Federal deserters usually formed the majority. While generally confining their activities to hiding and feeding deserters, local unionists occasionally took more direct action.[36] Montgomery Countian Levi Beckelheimer "assisted in relieving some Union prisoners about May 1863 in Floyd County Virginia. . . . I with some others fired our guns at the Rebels, which caused their release."[37]

Before long, these paramilitary bands of from two to forty deserters and sympathizers commenced a reign of terror separate from but analogous to the guerrilla war. Deserters robbed and killed local residents. County officials pleaded with higher authorities to do something about the outlaw deserters, even if it meant the imposition of martial law. The usual response was to send in troops. In Scott County, Confederate cavalrymen fought companies of deserters in open combat. Lee approved, and advocated a similar response in the center of deserter activity, Floyd County.[38]

Defeatism, hunger, impressment, guerrillas, deserters, and conscription all combined to strike Southwest Virginia a heavy blow. Much of the region's commitment to secession grew out of the economic growth and prosperity slavery offered, and northern threats to that expansion.

By late 1863, hope and prosperity had disappeared for all but a few, replaced by hard times and pessimism. War had proved more terrible than Southwest Virginians imagined. Moreover, their state and national governments, instead of providing the assistance and leadership desired, had contributed to the region's collapse through incompetence, harsh legislation, and apparent favoritism to the elite. Southwest Virginia's congressmen were outspoken in their opposition to the President and his policies but produced few tangible results. To some Southwest Virginians, Jefferson Davis had come to seem as egregious an enemy as Abraham Lincoln.[39]

As a result, Southwest Virginians resisted policies like impressment and conscription that personally affected them adversely. They also began to grasp for straws. Indicative of the region's confused collective psyche was the appearance of ghostly visions and omens. Nancy Hunt, for example, reported from Greenbrier County several accounts of: "something moving in the air that looked like a house door, followed by hundreds of boxes about 2 feet and 4 or 5 feet long, these were followed by millions of men marching on the ground, 4 deep, in double quick time. They were four hours passing. . . . They were unarmed and going towards the north. Some secesh think it means foreign aid. Some Union people think it is the spirits of the slain in battle come to haunt the Rebels."[40]

In 1864, some mountaineers in the haunted region would turn to open rebellion against the Confederacy.

In November 1863, Union forces under William Averell won a decisive victory at Droop Mountain in Pocahontas County, just north of Greenbrier. Droop Mountain, "West Virginia's Gettysburg," effectively ended the threat of major Confederate operations in the eastern plateau counties, secured the continued existence of West Virginia, which had joined the Union the previous July, and set the stage for the Union Army to break at last the stalemate in Southwest Virginia. In May 1864, Federal troops acting on General Ulysses S. Grant's orders began a major raid designed to destroy the Virginia and Tennessee Railroad once and for all (map 5). As modified by Franz Sigel, the plan called for Crook's seven-thousand-man force to destroy the New River Bridge and tear up at least twenty miles of track. Meanwhile, Averell's two-thousand-man mounted force would wreck the saltworks or more track, depending upon resistance. Both groups would then march northeastward along the railroad to rejoin Sigel around Lynchburg. Grant refused to express much optimism due to the necessarily

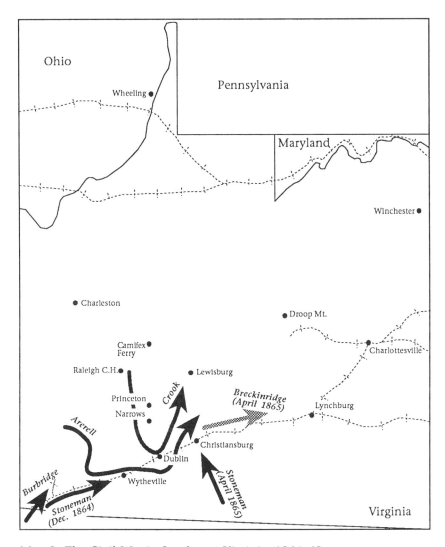

Map 5. The Civil War in Southwest Virginia, 1864–65.

small number of men involved, but hoped the raid at least would serve as a potent diversion.[41]

Facing Averell and Crook was a force of approximately sixty-five hundred effectives under former presidential hopeful John C. Breckinridge, who had just replaced General Samuel Jones. On May 4 after Grant crossed the Rapidan River and moved toward the Wilderness, Lee ordered Breckinridge to move toward Staunton with two-thirds of his effective force. Lee realized that he had left Southwest Virginia wide open to invasion, but regarded the preservation of his army as the primary concern.[42]

Crook meanwhile moved out on May 2, followed two days later by Averell. After skirmishes on May 4 and May 6, Crook routed an entrenched but outnumbered force at Cloyd's Mountain in Pulaski County on May 9 and pushed on toward Dublin and the railroad. On the following day, he reached and burned the railroad's New River Bridge and advanced on Blacksburg as a crowd of escaped local slaves sang in joy.[43]

Averell meanwhile had abandoned his plan to destroy the saltworks when he learned a force twice his size had gathered to stop him. Instead, he decided to avenge his comrade Toland and burn Wytheville. On May 10, Averell attacked the town, but its defenders, augmented by the Saltville force, drove the Federals off after four hours. Averell marched off toward Dublin and, on May 12, entered Christiansburg.[44] "The railroad was destroyed as much as practicable," he reported, "with depots, shops, &c. to a point four miles east of Christiansburg."[45]

Averell spoke too soon. The damage the raiders caused was repaired within a few weeks, largely because Averell and Crook pulled out too quickly. When they learned of fighting in the Wilderness, they automatically assumed that Lee would best Grant and concluded to get out of Southwest Virginia before they could be cut off. In his laden baggage train, Crook carried away thirty horses, fifty head of livestock, one hundred-twenty bushels of corn, ten tons of hay, and seven hundred pounds of tobacco. He destroyed six hundred weapons, sixty thousand rounds of ammunition, wagons, blankets and uniforms. Close to two hundred slaves fled their masters to join the Yankee parade. Besieged by bushwackers, Averell and Crook took hostages to intersperse among their men. Crook additionally ordered every captured bushwacker shot on the spot.[46]

The retreating raiders found Confederate sympathies surprisingly strong after three years of war. Ohioan J. W. Cracraft remembered "The women and what few men were in [Lewisburg] looked very grim as if they would like to have given us their opinion of us Yankees, but . . . they satisfied themselves by looking cross and ugly."[47] As a result, the raiders sought to punish as well as escape. In Greenbrier County, "noted for [its] cruel hatred of Union soldiers throughout the war," Averell's men burned bridges.[48] "You may guess what would be left when ten or twelve thousand hungry men and horses would pass through the country," Federal J. V. Young added, "I have seen the hungry soldier take the last bite from families on the road and leave the women crying—Saying their children must starve while all the men are in the Rebel service. . . . the country is gleaned."[49]

In the aftermath of the Crook-Averell raid, the Federals made two more attempts to destroy the railroad and the salt works. Late in September, a twenty-five-hundred-man force under General Stephen G. Burbridge advanced from Kentucky, via East Tennessee, toward Saltville. On October 2, the Federals drove the town's defenders into their entrenchments before retreating, low on ammunition. Black soldiers of the Fifth U.S. Colored Cavalry bore the brunt of the fighting. Enraged Tennessee Rebels murdered perhaps 150 black prisoners after the battle, a massacre beyond the scale of the better-known affair at Fort Pillow. Five days later, Tennessee bushwhacker Champ Ferguson killed two more wounded black troopers at the Confederate military hospital established at Emory and Henry College. The guerrillas returned the next evening and killed a white officer. Only the intervention of the hospital staff saved the remaining prisoners. Confederate officials, fearing retribution, jailed Ferguson without charges in Saltville, holding him until four days before Appomattox.[50]

Breckinridge retaliated for the Saltville raid by invading East Tennessee in November with a small force of twenty-four hundred, advancing nearly to Knoxville before retiring. The obvious weaknesses of the Rebel force convinced Federal cavalry General George Stoneman that he could advance easily into Southwest Virginia, destroy the salt works, and wreck the railroad once and for all without serious opposition. On December 10, his hastily gathered force moved out. Stoneman advanced up the railroad to Wytheville in six days before retreating to Tennessee. Abingdon, Bristol, Saltville, and Wytheville went up in flames. A local unionist in blue allegedly torched Abingdon.[51] Stoneman claimed to have destroyed all railroad bridges and depots west of the New River, wrecked thirteen locomotives, and "all the foundries, mills, factories, storehouses, wagon and ambulance trains, turnpike bridges, &c, that we could find . . . and many other things too numerous to mention . . . and last, but not least, four pestiferous printing presses." Nine hundred prisoners, slaves, and refugees followed Stoneman back to Tennessee. The raid left the railroad in Southwest Virginia closed for the duration of the war.[52]

Against the backdrop of Federal raids and destruction, the region stumbled through its last year of war. As the Confederacy disintegrated, Southwest Virginians found all their existing difficulties magnified. Federal raiding, pillaging, and occupation stripped much of the region of food. supplies, and personal belongings. Inflation worsened. In Tazewell County in June 1864, bacon sold for five dollars per pound, corn went for fifty dollars per bushel, coffee for twenty dollars per pound, and shoes at a hundred dollars a pair. By the end of the year, one Tazewell soldier's wife was reporting a diet of wild game, apples, corn bread and milk. Hungry residents fled their homes to avoid famine.[53]

Slavery completely collapsed. While many owners continued to challenge escapes as well as government impressment, others resigned themselves to the loss, feeling themselves well rid of their "ungrateful" servants.[54] Susanna Waddell of Monroe County, for example, recorded in her diary on June 30, 1864, that "Nearly all the negroes left with the Yankees. They hitched up the oxen, loaded the wagon with their own & their master's things & went off. . . . I dare say before long those whose servants remained with them, will not be sorry to see them depart."[55] Another die-hard secessionist wrote simply, "I hope the yankees will take all the negroes away."[56]

Resistance to military service intensified. Noting that in Floyd County "they keepe taking the people as fast as they become 18," S. A. Walton proceeded to report the trials of his son Eldred, who, when his harness-making contract ran out, went to work at a tanyard for the exemption. Desertion worsened as well. Many of the men who retreated from Cloyd's Mountain simply kept going until they arrived home. By February 1865, more than half the Confederate troops in Southwest Virginia had deserted. Lee's Southwest Virginians came home in droves as well, anxious to defend their homes. As a result, the authorities adopted even harsher methods to fight desertion. Reserve forces, composed of old men and boys, moved into Montgomery and Floyd counties to arrest deserters and fight the deserter bands. Provost authorities executed captured deserters immediately.[57] Joseph H. Wilson wrote from Floyd in March 1865, that "they shot a deserter from Petersburg they same night he got home and they say that the is a great many deserters a wround here and they say that they are a going to shoot them all. . . . There is a good many home . . . from Petersburg."[58]

Frustration with lawmakers in Richmond grew dramatically in the war's last year, and sometimes evolved into outright disloyalty. The secret Heroes of America organization first spread into the region from North Carolina in 1863 with the goal of overthrowing the Confederate government. HOA members, sometimes called "Red Strings," provided aid to federal soldiers, assisted escaped northern prisoners, and promoted desertion among Rebel units. In April 1864, Floyd County's A. J. Hoback informed the state government that the organization was attempting to take over the county's government through the election of members and control of the police. F. A. Winston was elected as a "a regular Radical" for the office of Sheriff, and Robert W. Whitlow became constable despite the presence of soldiers at the polls and fighting between Confederate troops and armed unionists. Four months later, the Montgomery County Committee of Public Safety warned that the same thing was happening in their county.[59]

In September, an alarmed Secretary of War James A. Seddon assigned two undercover private detectives the task of determining the extent of HOA activity in Southwest Virginia. Posing as northern agents, John B. Williams and Thomas McGill operated for two months in Carroll, Floyd, Giles, Montgomery, and Pulaski counties. They reported that the HOA was rampant in Floyd, Giles, Montgomery, Pulaski, Scott, Washington, and Wythe. Two Confederate regiments, the Twenty-second and Fifty-fourth Virginia Infantry Regiments, also were said to be infested. The detectives also implicated over one hundred prominent citizens including the former Douglas Democrat and "wait-a-bit" secession convention member Daniel H. Hoge, Montgomery County sheriff-elect John Francis, other police and judicial officials, and businessmen. General John Echols, in a cover letter, further charged that the Heroes planned to elect members to the General Assembly, and he blamed HOA members for his recent military reverses in the region, particularly desertion. Seddon wrote Jefferson Davis alleging that like northwestern unionists, the Heroes aimed at a separate state of Southwest Virginia. A shadow government, he charged, already existed.[60]

The HOA thus seemed to pose a serious threat to the Confederate war effort. What should be done to suppress the order in Southwest Virginia? Seddon asked attorney Nicholas F. Bocock to meet with his man on the scene, Major Henry Leory, examine the collected evidence, and offer advice. After reviewing the reports of the detectives as well as additional evidence collected by Leory, Bocock agreed that the HOA was a real threat. He argued nonetheless that specific individuals named in the investigation should not be arrested. First of all, the HOA's network undoubtedly would warn many targets before arrest. More importantly, the evidence was too flimsy and hearsay to be admitted into a civil court. There was, Bocock advised, no strong evidence "that any particular person did or assisted in doing any of the acts proved, it would be almost impossible to fix guilt on any individual so as to secure his conviction . . . there is no evidence and none likely to be obtained to prove who has acted." Bocock concluded that the government's only viable option was to suspend the writ of habeas corpus in the region "until the treason is effectively suppressed."[61] Davis tried to follow through on this advice, but Congress refused to comply.[62]

The historian Henry T. Shanks, relying on the War Department's evidence, concluded that the majority of Southwest Virginians had become hostile to the Confederacy by mid-1864. In accepting the investigation's conclusions uncritically, however, Shanks opened himself up to error. If Echols, Leory, and Seddon had been incorrect, so then would Shanks. This indeed appears to have been the case. No one piece of evidence conclusively negates the War Department's findings, but the combination of several points does present a strong case that the investigation overestimated HOA activity and disloyalty to the Confederacy in the region.

First, one should remember that an overestimation of the strength of disloyal citizens groups hardly would be surprising. Indeed, inflated estimates of the number, size, and importance of such groups were the norm during the war years. Northern counterintelligence routinely interpreted war-weariness as disloyalty and saw all opponents of the Lincoln Administration as traitors. If the North was so prone to hysteria and exaggeration, one should not be surprised to discover a parallel "red string scare" in the South.[63]

Did Echols and Leory similarly overestimate HOA strength in Southwest Virginia? Certainly they had made their minds up even before the investigation began. On September 1, 1864, before Seddon had even approved the undercover investigation, Echols wrote that Leory "has been able to determine with certainty [the] . . . character and existence and extent [of the] secret treasonable association." Nineteen days later, Leory wrote Seddon that "we have a large list of traitors. The adjoining counties are full of these people. I am told there are 800 members of the order in Montgomery County alone." Thus, the detectives' reports only served to mirror and confirm rumors Echols and Leory already believed.[64]

Second, one must question the efficiency of the detectives. During the investigation, while traveling through Pulaski County, the detectives openly broke cover at least once to meet with Leory. Were they observed? Certainly some HOA members suspected that the two men were spies. John Francis refused to keep an appointment with the detectives in Christiansburg for this reason. "We supposed," Williams reported, "he was afraid we were not all right, and we thought the rest of the party seemed to be getting restless and uneasy from some cause or other."[65]

Three days later, while meeting with other admitted HOA members, Francis appeared outside. "Capt. John Francis came while we were there," Williams wrote, "and there was a great deal of private conversation among the party. . . . we were afterward told . . . that they were consulting about killing us if they could find out whether we were spies sent there to find out what they were doing."[66]

Postwar evidence further suggests that the HOA was not as strong in Southwest Virginia as the Confederacy believed. The order did not disappear in the South after Appomattox, but continued on to form the nuclei of mountain Republican parties across the region. The one exception was Southwest Virginia, the only part of "Appalachia" where a viable Republican party did not develop immediately after the war. The absence of widespread Republican activity suggests that the HOA was not particularly widespread in the Southwest. Even when unionists did attempt to organize, they avoided the Republican rubric. In Grayson County, for example, former HOA members attempted to organize a pro–Andrew Johnson Union party in 1867.[67]

Finally, one can point to Southwest Virginia's involvement with the Southern Claims Commission. The United States government created the agency in 1871 to reward aggrieved southern unionists who had provided goods or services to the northern war effort. Convinced that unionism in Southwest Virginia was unimportant, the commission only bothered to appoint a special commissioner to take claims in the region in January 1875, and then only after complaints. By 1880, a total of 220 Southwest Virginians had filed claims. The local special commissioner, Charles C. Campbell, judged most fraudulent, and the commissioners in Washington concurred. Only thirty-nine regional claimants received the commission's seal of approval.[68]

The record of claims filed admittedly is an imperfect gauge of southern unionism. Not all unionists suffered damages. The expense of traveling to make a claim, costly attorney's fees, red tape, and the likelihood of failure all contributed to discourage the filing of viable claims. So stringent was the test of loyalty that even freedmen sometimes failed to pass. Reconstruction was another factor, as many unionists either abandoned their support for the government or were afraid to express it. The twelve admitted HOA members in the War Department report, for example, never filed a claim, although four others named by them did. Nonetheless, the relatively small number of claims filed by Southwest Virginians does suggest that unionist activity was not as widespread as Richmond feared. The regions 220 claims made up only 5.6 percent of all claims filed in Virginia and West Virginia. If anything, this figure suggests that unionism may have been *less* important than elsewhere in the old state.[69]

The claims themselves confirm that impression. Among all the extant files, only one mentions the Heroes of America. Robert W. Whitlow, Floyd County's constable, listed HOA membership in an effort to prove his contributions to the Union. In testimony provided to support Whitlow, F. A. Winston—the Floyd County unionist whose election touched off the War Department investigation—confirmed that Whitlow was a Red String. Despite that information, the commission still rejected his claim. Aside from Whitlow's file, one searches in vain for the HOA. Claimants said nothing about the order, and few implied any organized resistance at all. Rather, the claimants almost always listed activities undertaken as individuals, families, or Dunkard congregations. Hiding Federal escapees topped the list of unionist actions.[70]

What appeared to the detectives to be unionism and disloyalty to the Confederacy were in fact largely war-weariness coupled with strong dissatisfaction with the state and Confederate governments. There is no conclusive evidence that Southwest Virginians were any less loyal to the Confederacy than other southerners, but certainly they were tired of war and disappointed with their leaders. The lawmakers had alienated and seemingly abandoned Southwest Virginians through their "rich man's war, poor man's fight" policies and inability to win the war. Southwest Virginians had entered the war optimistically, only to see their home region relegated to secondary importance, stripped of its resources and manpower, and left to the mercies of Union troops. The decade of contentment with the state government forged by the Constitution of 1851 came to an abrupt halt. Southwest Virginians had placed their trust in it, and in 1864 and 1865 concluded that it had failed them. Like S. A. Walton of Floyd, many were convinced that a return to the Union could be no worse than remaining in the Confederacy, and "if they come the Sooner the better I think."[71]

While the political era of good feelings had vanished, however, and East-Southwest antagonism returned to the fore, the economic bond forged by the railroad survived, albeit in need of great physical repair. That survival, coupled with the return of East-Southwest alienation, is crucial for understanding the region's postwar "Appalachian" history.

Epilogue

AFTER APPOMATTOX, Pulaski Countian James N. Bosang of the Stonewall Brigade left the Union prisoner of war camp at Point Lookout, Maryland, and headed home. A Virginia and Tennessee Railroad engine and tender brought him to Dublin in late July. Arriving in Newbern, his mother wept to see him, the only one of her soldier sons to come home, for "Johnny was dead, and Henry was in Mexico."[1]

Life in Pulaski County during the war clearly had been difficult. "I found my mother, with the five younger children, had been having a hard time and did not have enough to subsist on for one week." Undaunted, Bosang borrowed enough money to go to work as a shoemaker. It was a profitable decision; his neighbors needed shoes.[2]

Bosang was hardly alone, as members of the regional elite expressed similar feelings. "Monroe is greatly changed within a few years," John Echols wrote in 1866, "by deaths & otherwise, & the place has not the same attraction for us which it formerly had." Confronted by defeat and a frightening new world, Echols abandoned the region for the Valley town of Staunton and a bank presidency.[3] Others followed. Continuing a process that began with wartime refugees, many Southwest Virginians bade farewell to their desolate farms and headed for California, Colorado, Indiana, Kansas, Missouri, and Texas. Others left the country entirely. Henry Bosang went to Mexico before settling in California, and former Confederate officers Alexander and Henry Reynolds went even farther, enlisting in the military service of the Khedive of Egypt.[4]

How serious was this postwar out-migration? The regional population statistics suggest that it was substantial enough to retard population growth. In the 1850s, Southwest Virginia's population increased by 22.6 percent. From 1860 to 1870, however, percentage growth in population slowed to a mere 8.9 percent, reaching only 206,336 in the area that had been Southwest Virginia in 1860. While wartime deaths surely account for some of the slowdown, it seems most likely that out-migration was the leading factor.[5]

The population did increase, of course, however slowly. What about the majority who remained? For them, the postwar period largely meant bitterness, dislocations, and perplexing change. Local wounds often failed to heal. Giles Countians, for example, ostracized Lute Porterfield, the unionist who allegedly led Crook's raiders through the region in 1864. Naming his sons after Crook, Edward Everett, James A. Garfield, Allan Pinkerton, and Philip Sheridan did not help community relations either. For the rest of his life, Porterfield went abroad armed, ready for the retribution he expected daily. When he grew wealthy buying up the land of his bankrupt secessionist neighbors, they concluded that he literally had sold his soul to the devil. The line between the Union and Hell apparently remained a thin one in Giles.[6]

The most obvious change in the region was the survival of West Virginia. The new state's unionist founding fathers included nine Southwest Virginia counties in their creation: Boone, Fayette, Greenbrier, Logan, Mercer, Monroe, Raleigh, and Wyoming. As noted earlier, the nine counties left the old commonwealth unwillingly and at gunpoint. The vote for the new state in the five of the nine occupied by federal troops in October 1862, was one hundred to nothing. In 1864, no one in the nine counties voted in the federal presidential election. Loyal Confederates continued to represent the counties in the Virginia General Assembly, and the county courts maintained their authority in the name of the old state. For these Southwest Virginians, West Virginia was a postwar phenomenon.[7]

Perhaps the founding fathers of West Virginia would have served their interests better by leaving the southwesterners in Virginia. Five years after the war, ex-Confederates from the area joined Copperhead Democrats to the north, shoved West Virginia's Radical Republicans aside, and took control of the state. In 1875, former secessionist Allan Caperton went to the U.S. Senate. When he died the following year, another former Rebel, Samuel Price, replaced him. In the same year, Greenbrier County's Henry M. Mathews, a Confederate major in the war, became governor. Under the control of conservatives based in what had been part of Southwest Virginia, West Virginia joined the Solid South.[8]

Economic and social changes occurring at the same time were perhaps more important. After a brief lull, the area's modernization literally picked up steam again. Change increased exponentially as the coal boom hinted at before the war exploded in full force. In the 1870s, the Chesapeake and Ohio Railroad, heir to the old Virginia Central, finally penetrated Fayette and Raleigh counties' coal fields. In the next decade, the Norfolk and Western Railroad, operating from the Virginia and Tennessee Railroad's former trunk, opened up rich fields to the south and west. In addition to mining, large-scale timbering commenced. Timber and mine companies acquired huge tracts of land from the area's residents. By 1925, southern West Virginia reigned as the nation's leading coal producer. The final transformation from agriculture to industry, however, destroyed much of what remained of the region's antebellum culture and society. Self-sufficient farmers became wage laborers, their lives at the mercies of northern corporations and pliant local officials. Widespread poverty and violence resulted.[9] As Ronald D. Eller eloquently wrote, "modernization had come like a storm over the ridges, tossing and uprooting the very structure of mountain life. When the storm had passed, what was left was only a shell of what had been before."[10]

The same transformation essentially occurred in those counties remaining in Virginia, especially in those of the "far southwest" where coal also was plentiful. Elsewhere, timbering played a larger role. As in West Virginia, northern capitalists bought up most available land.[11] Politics in the Old Dominion, meanwhile, reverted to patterns surprisingly reminiscent of the period before 1850. The leading issue once again was money spent for internal improvements, and especially the huge debt that had resulted from antebellum spending on projects like the V&T. In 1870, when Virginia's "Redeemers" took over from the Reconstruction government, the state's prewar debt plus interest topped 45 million dollars. What should be done? "Funders" supported paying off the debt in full, even if it meant that public schools and other state programs fell by the wayside. The Funders publicly justified their position by calling on the state's honor, but privately cared more for restoring the state's credit rating. Bankers, brokers, industrialists, and the urban upper middle class stood at the forefront of the movement. They aimed to create a "new South" based on the northern model. The Funders' continuing campaign for fence-law legislation indicated their antirural bias. [12]

The "Readjusters" opposed the Funders, arguing that the state had a right to negotiate with its creditors to scale down the debt to a manageable level. The North and Britain, after all, were partially responsible for the size of the debt because of wartime destruction and John Bull's failure to support the Confederacy. The Readjusters wanted to maintain Reconstruction-era programs such as free public schools. Four groups tenuously composed the Readjusters. Freedmen unhappy with the weak state Republican party formed one element. At the opposite pole were former states-righters like Henry A. Wise, who opposed mimicking Yankee business methods or truckling to northern bankers as dishonorable. A third element consisted of urban eastern Virginians who wanted schools and state aid. Many were Greenbackers. Their leader, and ultimately the chief Readjuster, was William Mahone, railroad tycoon and former Confederate. Mahone had bankrolled the Funders but switched sides after the Panic of 1873, blaming Funder policies for the loss of his beloved Atlantic, Mississippi, and Ohio Railroad, which included the Virginia and Tennessee Railroad. Finally, there was Southwest Virginia, the stronghold of the movement. Just as before the war, Southwest Virginians wanted public aid for schools, roads, and other improvements. All Readjusters focused on high taxes and corruption in office. Thus, in the 1870s, Southwest Virginia renewed its political struggle with Richmond after a twenty-year hiatus.[13]

The Readjusters briefly gained the upper hand. In 1879, they captured the General Assembly, scaled down the debt, lowered taxes, and increased public aid to schools. In December 1879, Mahone went to the U.S. Senate. The Readjusters' links to the national Republican party and the membership of blacks supplied the Funders, who claimed the "Democratic" mantle, a potent campaign tool, however. In 1883, in a mud-slinging, race-baiting campaign, the Democrats took power. When Southwest Virginia flirted with Populism in the 1890s, the ruling Democrats determined to emasculate Southwest Virginia politically. The 1902 constitution, drafted in great part by future Wilsonian "progressive" Carter Glass, disenfranchised both the state's blacks and half of the white electorate, including large numbers of Southwest Virginians. In essence, the constitution repealed universal manhood suffrage. The conservative Democratic machine, thus protected from black and mountain voters, remained in power into the 1970s, largely under the thumb of U.S. Senator Harry F. Byrd, Senior. The Byrd machine, however, never tamed Southwest Virginia. In the Southwest, a vigorous two-party system survived despite constitutional obstacles. Indeed, the region acquired such a reputation for political belligerence that still today, it is the only part of the United States popularly known by its congressional district number, the "Fighting Ninth."[14]

Crucially, none of this occurred in a vacuum; none of it was new, or startling, or unexpected. Indeed, the point is that these briefly sketched developments—the post–Civil War industrialization of Appalachia and all that came with it—were rooted in the remarkable economic and political transformation that took place in Southwest Virginia in the 1850s as a result of railroad-driven antebellum modernization. One might use the analogy of a snowball. As the snowball rolled down the ridge, it increased in size and speed, but at its core was the original snow. That "core," the Virginia and Tennessee Railroad and its "iron bands and commercial ties," survived the war, and as the railroad metamorphosed into Norfolk and Western, grew into an iron web that firmly bound the region to the rest of the nation.

Indeed, little occurred that did not have antebellum antecedents. When Southwest Virginians went into mines or factories, they only were continuing the shift from "safety first" farming to capitalist roles their fathers chose. When industrialists located in the region, they followed the well-marked trail of the iron, salt, and lead magnates. Bristol, Cambria, and Glade Spring had their later counterparts in the coal towns that eventually dotted the landscape. Coal stoked the Gilded Age vision of a new South that created "Appalachia," but the vision was only a sharper lithograph of that printed in the *Richmond Whig* or *DeBow's Review*. The local colorists and missionaries who descended upon the mountains were only the latest in a long line of George Featherstonhaughs and Bob Larkins, eager to see the curious sights. When political elites courted outsiders and assisted in the exploitation of their land and people, they were following well-established patterns. And the proud defiance that seemed to die on Cemetery Ridge and Cloyd's Mountain flickered anew in the streets of Matewan and on Blair Mountain.

Today, Southwest Virginians and southern West Virginians still deal daily with the consequences of antebellum modernization. Iron bands and commercial ties link us to the past, and to each other.

Methodology

Many of the statistics presented in the text were derived from samples taken from the Federal Manuscript Census for 1850 and 1860. Before utilizing the information available in the manuscript censuses, I first selected appropriate counties for sampling. The eventual choice of Floyd, Raleigh, and Washington counties, none "typical" in any sense, reflected four considerations. First, they reflected as a whole the wide range of county populations in Southwest Virginia. In 1850, Washington County was the region's largest, Raleigh County the smallest, and Floyd County just at the median. Second, in choosing these counties, each of the three geographic subregions could be represented; Blue Ridge, plateau, and valley respectively. Third, the boundary lines of these counties did not change between 1850 and 1860, which I hoped would increase reliability. Finally, each was interesting in a qualitative sense. Floyd with its unionists and deserters, Raleigh's tobacco boom, and Washington County's politicians and visitors all demanded special attention.

Having chosen the counties, I proceeded to draw systematic samples, as opposed to random samples, from Schedule I, the population schedule, with the household functioning as the basic sampling unit. The sampling fraction varied from county to county and from year to year, as I intended to construct individual county samples of roughly four hundred households, yearly samples of twelve hundred, and a total sample of twenty-four households. Historians have come to accept samples of over one thousand as highly reliable. The exact sample sizes were:

Year	County	Sample Size	Household
1850	Floyd	329	Every 3d
1850	Raleigh	296	All
1850	Washington	534	Every 4th
		1159	

1860	Floyd	338	Every 4th
1860	Raleigh	280	Every 2d
1860	Washington	513	Every 5th
		1131	
Total		2290	

For each household, I recorded the age, gender, occupation, birthplace, and real property holdings of the householder, as well as the size of the household. As personal property holdings were not included in the 1850 census, I did not record them for 1860. I then matched up the households when possible with corresponding entries in the agricultural schedules (Schedule II). I recorded farm value, the amount of improved and unimproved acreage, the numbers of livestock, and the amount of corn and tobacco produced. Finally, I matched the households to the slave schedules (Schedule III) to identify slaveholders. At this stage, I also recorded the size of holdings and the ages and genders of slaves for all slaveowners in the three sample counties, in order to determine median slaveholdings and slave ages.

Using the method described by Frederick A. Bode and Donald E. Ginter in their monograph of farm tenancy and the census in Georgia, I then manipulated the data by further breaking down householders' occupational categories from six to nine, in order to identify the extent of tenancy in Southwest Virginia among self-described "farmers":

Category	Occupation
1	"Farmer": Landowner
2	"Tenant" or "Renter"
3	"Farmer": No Real Property Listed on Schedule I, But Acreage and Farm Value on Schedule II. Probable Tenant.
4	"Farmer": Real Property Listed on Schedule I, Not Appearing on Schedule II. Probable Landowner.
5	"Farmer": No Real Property on Schedule I, Not Appearing on Schedule II. Probable Tenant.
6	Laborer
7	Professional/Businessman
8	Craftsman/Skilled Worker
9	No Occupation/Housekeeper/Matron

Once I collected the data, I processed it using the Statistical Package for the Social Sciences (SPSS) program. The statistics that resulted are not meant to be precise measurements. The skill of census takers varied from county to county, as did their adherence to their instructions. Surely at times they missed households or supplied their own estimates. At other times, householders no doubt misled the census takers with exaggerated or false information. Still, I am confident that if not exact, the statistics nonetheless closely represent the reality of Southwest Virginia.

Notes

AH	*Agricultural History*
AHR	*American Historical Review*
AJ	*Appalachian Journal*
BHU	Baker Library, Harvard Business School, Boston, Mass.
CWH	*Civil War History*
Duke	Special Collections Library, Duke University, Durham, N.C.
Filson	Manuscript Department, The Filson Club, Lexington, Ky.
IHS	Illinois Historical Survey, University of Illinois, Urbana, Ill.
JAH	*Journal of American History*
JNH	*Journal of Negro History*
JSH	*Journal of Southern History*
MVHR	*Mississippi Valley Historical Review*
NA	National Archives and Records Administration, Washington, D.C.
NCHR	*North Carolina Historical Review*
RKHS	*Register of the Kentucky Historical Society*
SHC	Southern Historical Collection, Library of the University of North Carolina, Chapel Hill, N.C.
SHSP	*Southern Historical Society Papers*
THQ	*Tennessee Historical Quarterly*
UVA	Manuscript Division, Special Collections Department, University of Virginia Library, Charlottesville, Va.
VC	*Virginia Cavalcade*
VHS	Virginia Historical Society, Richmond, Va.
VMHB	*Virginia Magazine of History and Biography*
VPI	Special Collections Department, Virginia Polytechnic Institute and State University Libraries, Blacksburg, Va.
VSL	Archives and Records Division, Virginia State Library, Richmond, Va.
WVH	*West Virginia History*
WVU	West Virginia and Regional History Collection, West Virginia University Libraries, Morgantown, W.Va.

Introduction

1. These events can be best followed in Richard Orr Curry, *A House Divided: A Study of Statehood Politics and the Copperhead Movement in West Virginia* (Pittsburgh: University of Pittsburgh Press, 1964).

2. Charles Henry Ambler, *Sectionalism in Virginia from 1776 to 1861* (Chicago: University of Chicago Press, 1910). Ambler repeated his thesis in several works, including "The Cleavage Between Eastern and Western Virginia," *AHR* 15 (July 1910): 762–80; *A History of West Virginia* (New York: Prentice-Hall, 1933); and *Francis H. Pierpont: Civil War Governor of Virginia and Father of West Virginia* (Chapel Hill: University of North Carolina Press, 1937).

3. Curry, *A House Divided;* Henry T. Shanks, "Disloyalty to the Confederacy in Southwestern Virginia, 1861–1865," *NCHR* 21 (Apr. 1944): 118–19; John Alexander Williams, *West Virginia: A Bicentennial History* (New York: W.W. Norton, 1976), esp. 34–94. Philip Morrison Rice, "Internal Improvements in Virginia 1775–1860" (Ph. D. diss., University of Virginia, 1948), 5, and Robert P. Sutton, "The Virginia Constitutional Convention of 1829–30: A Political Analysis of Late-Jeffersonian Virginia" (Ph.D. diss., University of Virginia, 1967), 219–21, also oppose Ambler's model of two Virginias, maintaining that the state instead consisted of several regions whose boundaries and alliances varied over time.

4. Virgil A. Lewis, *How West Virginia Was Made* (Charleston: News-Mail, 1909), 105. This useful volume contains the proceedings of the first two Wheeling conventions as copied from the Wheeling *Intelligencer.*

5. Charles Henry Ambler et al., eds., *Debates and Proceedings of the First Constitutional Convention of West Virginia (1861–1863)* (Huntington, W.Va.: Gentry Brothers, 1939), v.1, p. 315.

6. Lewis, *How West Virginia Was Made,* 237–38.

7. Ibid., 304.

8. Williams, *West Virginia,* 76–86.

9. Richard D. Brown, *Modernization: The Transformation of American Life, 1600–1865* (New York: Hill and Wang, 1976) (quotation from p. 8).

10. Raymond Grew, "Modernization and Its Discontents," *American Behavioral Scientist* 21 (Nov./Dec. 1977): 289–312 (quotation from p. 301). See also another article by Grew, "More on Modernization," *Journal of Social History* 14 (Winter 1980): 179–87, as well as Peter N. Stearns, "Modernization and Social History: Some Suggestions and a Muted Cheer," *Journal of Social History* 14 (Winter 1980): 189–209, and Drew Gilpin Faust, "The Peculiar South Revisited: White Society, Culture, and Politics in the Antebellum Period, 1800–1860," in *Interpreting Southern History: Historiographical Essays in Honor of Sanford W. Higginbotham* ed. John B. Boles and Evelyn Thomas Nolen (Baton Rouge: Louisiana State University Press, 1987), pp. 116–17.

11. See, for example, William L. Barney, "Towards the Civil War: the Dynamics of Change in a Black Belt County," in Orville Vernon Burton and Robert C. McMath, eds., *Class, Conflict, and Consensus: Antebellum Southern Community Studies* (Westport, Conn.: Greenwood, 1982), 146–72; Bill Cecil-Fronsman, *Common Whites: Class and Culture in Antebellum North Carolina* (Lexington: University Press of Kentucky, 1992), esp. 97–132, 163–68; Paul D. Escott, "Yeoman Independence and the Market: Social Status and Economic Development in Antebellum North Carolina," *NCHR* 66 (July 1989): 275–300; Lacy K. Ford,

Origins of Southern Radicalism: The South Carolina Upcountry, 1800–1860 (New York: Oxford University Press, 1988), esp. 215–77; Steven Hahn, *The Roots of Southern Populism: Yeoman Farmers and the Transformation of the Georgia Upcountry, 1850–1890* (New York: Oxford University Press, 1983), esp. 15–85, and "The Yeomanry of the Nonplantation South: Upper Piedmont Georgia, 1850–1860," in Burton and McMath, *Class, Conflict, and Consensus,* 29–56; Ralph Mann, "Mountains, Land, and Kin Networks: Burkes Garden, Virginia, in the 1840s and 1850s," *JSH* 58 (Aug. 1992): 411–34; James Oakes, *Slavery and Freedom: An Interpretation of the Old South* (New York: Alfred A. Knopf, 1990), 42, 97, 104–19; John T. Schlotterbeck, "Plantation and Farm: Social and Economic Change in Orange and Greene Counties, Virginia, 1716 to 1860" (Ph.D. diss., Johns Hopkins University, 1980), esp. 301–15, and "The 'Social Economy' of an Upper South Community: Orange and Greene Counties, Virginia, 1815–1860, in Burton and McMath, *Class, Conflict, and Consensus,* 3–28; and Allen W. Trelease, *The North Carolina Railroad, 1849–1871, and the Modernization of North Carolina* (Chapel Hill: University of North Carolina Press, 1991). I also have learned much from John Mack Faragher, *Sugar Creek: Life on the Illinois Prairie* (New Haven: Yale University Press, 1986), 176–216, and Paul E. Johnson, *A Shopkeeper's Millennium: Society and Revivals in Rochester, New York, 1815–1837* (New York: Hill and Wang, 1978), 15–61, both of which discuss the impact of transportation technology on modernization.

12. William Goodell Frost, "Our Contemporary Ancestors in the Southern Mountains," *Atlantic Monthly* 83 (Mar. 1899): 311–19; Horace Kephart, *Our Southern Highlanders: A Narrative of Adventure in the Southern Appalachians and a Study of Life among the Mountaineers* (New York: Macmillan, 1913), 443–47. John C. Inscoe recently wrote that "if scholars of the South devote almost as much attention to perceptions of the region as they do its realities, the issue of image is even more central to Appalachian scholarship" (Review of Allen W. Batteau, *The Invention of Appalachia, JSH* 58 (Aug. 1992): 540.) While the issue of myth versus reality is an important one in this monograph, I have chosen not to include the usual direct attack on the stereotype that for some years has been *de rigeur.* Frankly, I believe that Appalachian studies have progressed beyond the point of needing to do so. Readers are directed to Batteau's *Invention of Appalachia* (Tucson: University of Arizona Press, 1990) and Henry D. Shapiro, *Appalachia On Our Mind: The Southern Mountains and Mountaineers in the American Consciousness, 1870–1920* (Chapel Hill: University of North Carolina Press, 1978).

13. Ronald D Eller, *Miners, Millhands, and Mountaineers: Industrialization of the Appalachian South, 1870–1930* (Knoxville: University of Tennessee Press, 1982) (The quotation is from p. 13).

14. Dwight Billings, Kathleen Blee, and Louis Swanson, "Culture, Family, and Community in Preindustrial Appalachia," *AJ* 13 (Winter 1986): 154–70; Frederick A. Bode and Donald E. Ginter, *Farm Tenancy and the Census in Antebellum Georgia* (Athens: University of Georgia Press, 1986); Bill Cecil-Fronsman, *Common Whites: Class and Culture in Antebellum North Carolina* (Lexington: University Press of Kentucky, 1992); David Corbin, *Life, Work, and Rebellion in the Coal Fields: The Southern West Virginia Miners* (Urbana: University of Illinois Press, 1981); Durwood Dunn, *Cades Cove: The Life and Death of a Southern Appalachian Community, 1818–1937* (Knoxville: University of Tennessee Press, 1988); several works by John C. Inscoe, notably *Mountain Masters, Slavery, and*

the Sectional Crisis in Western North Carolina (Knoxville: University of Tennessee Press, 1989); Mann, "Mountains"; Gordon B. McKinney, *Southern Mountain Republicans, 1865–1900: Politics and the Appalachian Community* (Chapel Hill: University of North Carolina Press, 1978); Robert D. Mitchell, *Commercialism and Frontier: Perspectives on the Early Shenandoah Valley* (Charlottesville: University Press of Virginia, 1977), and his more recent edited work, *Appalachian Frontiers: Settlement, Society, & Development in the Preindustrial Era* (Lexington: University Press of Kentucky, 1991); James B. Murphy, "Slavery and Freedom in Appalachia: Kentucky as a Demographic Case Study," *RKHS* 80 (Spring 1982); 151–69; Mary Beth Pudup, "The Boundaries of Class in Preindustrial Appalachia," *Journal of Historical Geography* 15 (1989): 139–62, and "The Limits of Subsistence: Agriculture and Industry in Central Appalachia," *AH* 64 (Winter 1990): 61–89; Paul Salstrom, "Appalachia's Path toward Welfare Dependency, 1840–1940" (Ph.D. diss., Brandeis University, 1988); Altina L. Waller, *Feud: Hatfield's, McCoys and Social Change in Appalachia, 1860–1900* (Chapel Hill: University of North Carolina Press, 1988); Paul J. Weingartner, Dwight B. Billings, and Kathleen M. Blee, "Agriculture in Preindustrial Appalachia: Subsistence Farming in Beech Creek, 1850–1880," *Journal of the Appalachian Studies Association* 1 (1989): 70–80; and Gene Wilhelm, Jr., "Appalachian Isolation: Fact or Fiction?" in *An Appalachian Symposium: Essays Written in Honor of Cratis D. Williams*, ed., J. W. Williamson, (Boone, N.C.: Appalachian State University, 1977), 77–91.

15. See John C. Campbell's classic *The Southern Highlander & His Homeland* (New York: Russell Sage Foundation, 1921), 90; Shapiro, *Appalachia on our Minds*, 32–58.

16. Martin Crawford, "Confederate Volunteering and Enlistment in Ashe County, North Carolina, 1861–1862," *CWH* 37 (Mar. 1991): 29–50, and "Political Society in a Southern Mountain Community: Ashe County, North Carolina, 1850–1861," *JSH* 55 (Aug. 1989): 373–90; Paul D. Escott, *After Secession: Jefferson Davis and the Failure of the Confederate Nation* (Baton Rouge: Louisiana State University Press, 1978); W. Todd Groce, "East Tennessee Confederates and the Crisis of the Union" (Paper Presented to the Appalachian Studies Conference, Berea, Ky., Mar. 23, 1991); Ralph Mann, "Family Group, Family Migration, and the Civil War in the Sandy Basin of Virginia," *AJ* 19 (Summer 1992): 374–93; Phillip Shaw Paludan, *Victims: A True Story of the Civil War* (Knoxville: University of Tennessee Press, 1981); Waller, *Feud*. It is safe to say that recent Appalachian scholars have done too little with the war itself, although that is changing too. Many studies go from the 1860 census to that of 1870 with little sense of the conflagration that occurred in between. On the war at least, a few of the much-maligned earlier studies did a better job. See, for example, Harry Caudill's *Night Comes to the Cumberlands: A Biography of a Depressed Area* (Boston: Atlantic Monthly, 1963), 35–51.

17. Needless to say, this paragraph only begins to scratch the surface. A good place to begin is Charles E. Cauthen and Lewis P. Jones, "The Coming of the Civil War," in *Writing Southern History: Essays in Historiography in Honor of Fletcher M. Green*, ed. Arthur S. Link and Rembert W. Patrick (Baton Rouge: Louisiana State University Press, 1965), 224–48.

18. F. N. Boney, *John Letcher of Virginia: The Story of Virginia's Civil War Governor* (University, Ala.: University of Alabama Press, 1966); Daniel W. Crofts, *Reluctant Confederates: Upper South Unionists in the Secession Crisis* (Chapel Hill:

University of North Carolina Press, 1989); William W. Freehling, *The Road to Disunion,* v. 1, *Secessionists at Bay* (New York: Oxford University Press, 1990); Michael P. Johnson, *Towards a Patriarchical Republic: The Secession of Georgia* (Baton Rouge: Louisiana State University Press, 1977); Bertram Wyatt-Brown, *Southern Honor: Ethics and Behavior in the Old South* (New York: Oxford University Press, 1982) and *Yankee Saints and Southern Sinners* (Baton Rouge: Louisiana State University Press, 1985).

19. James M. McPherson, *Battle Cry of Freedom: The Civil War Era* (New York: Oxford University Press, 1988); David R. Goldfield, "The Triumph of Politics Over Society: Virginia, 1851–1861 (Ph.D. diss., University of Maryland, 1970); James M. Woods, *Rebellion and Realignment: Arkansas's Road to Secession* (Fayetteville, Ark.: University of Arkansas Press, 1987); Groce, "East Tennessee"; Inscoe, *Mountain Masters,* Paludan, *Victims* and *"A People's Contest": The Union and the Civil War, 1861–1865* (New York: Harper and Row, 1988). One should also note Gordon McKinney's contention, in *Southern Mountain Republicans,* 19, that Southwest Virginia supported the Confederacy because it was trapped deep within it and thus had no choice. Certainly it was much closer to Union deliverance than unionist East Tennessee or Northern Georgia.

20. See, for example, the tables in *Message of the Governor of Virginia and Accompanying Documents* (Richmond, Va.: William F. Ritchie, 1861).

Chapter 1: "The Railroad Is Completed to Bristol"

1. John E. Gilmer, Emory, Va., to Pa & Ma, Oct. 4, 1856, Gilmer Family Papers, UVA.

2. Ibid.; *Abingdon Democrat,* Oct. 4, 1856.

3. *Abingdon Democrat,* Oct. 4, 1856.

4. Frederick Law Olmsted, *A Journey in the Seaboard States, with Remarks on Their Economy* (1856; reprint, New York: Mason Brothers, 1859), 302–3.

5. Frederick Law Olmsted, *A Journey in the Backcountry in the Winter of 1853–4,* 2d ed. (New York: Mason Brothers, 1863), 281.

6. Brown, *Modernization,* 8–19. For Gilmer's fate, see Thomas M. Rankin, *37th Virginia Infantry* (Lynchburg, Va.: H.E. Howard, 1987), 114.

7. C. R. Boyd, *Resources of Southwest Virginia, Showing the Mineral Deposits of Iron, Coal, Zinc, Copper and Lead....* (New York: John Wiley & Sons, 1881); J. S. Buckingham, *The Slave States of America* (London: Fisher and Son, 1842), 2:530–33; G. W. Featherstonhaugh, *Excursion through the Slave States....* (1844; reprint, New York: Negro Universities Press, 1968), 15; Joseph John Gurney, *A Journey in North America. Described in Familiar Letters to Amelia Opie* (Norwich: Josiah Fletcher, 1841), 54; Joseph Martin, *A New and Comprehensive Gazetteer of Virginia and the District of Columbia....* (Charlottesville, N.C.: Joseph Martin, 1835), 20–30, 298; U.S. Treasury Department, Bureau of Statistics, *Report on the Internal Commerce of the United States....* (Washington: Government Printing Office, 1886), 9; R. Lee Humbert, et al., *Virginia: Economic and Civic* (Richmond, Va.: Whittet and Shepperson, 1933), 48–50, 55–61; Williams, *West Virginia,* 7.

Throughout the book, "Valley" refers to the Valley Grand Division, while "valley" refers to the Southwest Virginia subregion.

8. Thomas Perkins Abernethy, *Three Virginia Frontiers* (University: Louisiana State University Press, 1940), 1–13, 59–90; Robert Beverley, *The History and*

Present State of Virginia: A Selection (Indianapolis: Bobbs-Merrill, 1971), 35–37; Patricia Givens Johnson, *The New River Early Settlement* (Pulaski, Va.: Edmonds, 1983), 115–205; Lewis Preston Summers, *History of Southwest Virginia, 1746–1786; Washington County, 1777–1870* (Richmond, Va.: J. L. Hill, 1903), 53–146; Albert H. Tillson, Jr., "The Localist Roots of Backcountry Loyalism: An Examination of Popular Political Culture in Virginia's New River Valley," *JSH* 54 (Aug. 1988): 389–94. Tillson's *Gentry and Common Folk: Political Culture on a Virginia Frontier, 1740–1789* (Lexington: University Press of Kentucky, 1991) should be consulted for more information on colonial and Revolutionary Southwest Virginia.

9. Goodrich, "Virginia System," 358–59; Morton, *Monroe County,* 211–12; William C. Pendleton, *Political History of Appalachian Virginia* (Dayton, Va.: Shenandoah, 1927), 2–3; Philip Morrison Rice, "Internal Improvements in Virginia, 1775–1860" (Ph.D. diss., University of North Carolina, 1948), 102–32, 384; Walter K. Wood, "Henry Edmundson, the Alleghany Turnpike, and 'Fotheringay' Plantation, 1805–1847: Planting and Trading in Montgomery County, Virginia," *VMHB* 83 (July 1975): 304–9.

10. Goodrich, "Virginia System," 357–61; Rice, "Internal Improvements," 148–49; Charles W. Turner, "The Early Railroad Movement in Virginia," *VMHB* 55 (Oct. 1947): 350.

11. Wayland Fuller Dunaway, *History of the James River and Kanawha Canal* vol. 114, no. 2 (New York: Columbia University Press, 1922), 9–20, 76–84.

12. Dunaway, *James River and Kanawha Canal,* 21–90; Curry, *A House Divided,* 14; Goodrich, "Virginia System," 363–64; Harry C. Handley, "The James River and Kanawha Canal," *WVH* 25 (Jan. 1964): 92–99; Robert F. Hunter, "The Turnpike Movement in Virginia, 1816–1860," *VMHB* 69 (July 1961): 281; Frederick Neely, "The Development of Virginia Taxation: 1775 to 1860" (Ph.D. diss., University of Virginia, 1956), 168–73; Rice, "Internal Improvements," 143–45, 154–65.

13. Ambler, *Sectionalism in Virginia,* 137–74; Dickson D. Bruce, Jr., *The Rhetoric of Conservativism: The Virginia Convention of 1829–30 and the Conservative Tradition in the South* (San Marco, Calif.,: Huntington Library, 1982), esp. 1–69; Alison Goodyear Freehling, *Drift toward Dissolution: The Virginia Slavery Debate of 1831–1832* (Baton Rouge: Louisiana State University Press, 1982), 36–48; Sutton, "Virginia Constitutional Convention," 60–69, 220.

14. Freehling, *Drift toward Dissolution,* 47–81.

15. *Proceedings and Debates of the Virginia State Convention of 1829–30. . . .* (Richmond, Va.: Samuel Shepherd, 1830), 63. The eastern mindset is examined in Avery Odelle Craven, *Soil Exhaustion as a Factor in the Agricultural History of Virginia and Maryland, 1606–1860,* v. 13, no. 1 (Urbana: University of Illinois Press, 1925), the classic account; Schlotterbeck, "Plantation and Farm," 2–4, 255–57, which challenges Craven; David R. Goldfield, *Urban Growth in an Age of Sectionalism: Virginia, 1847–1861* (Baton Rouge: Louisiana State University Press, 1977), 1–4; and most importantly in two works by Robert P. Sutton, "Virginia Constitutional Convention," 2–3, 8–12; and "Nostalgia, Pessimism, and Malaise: the Doomed Aristocrat in Late-Jeffersonian Virginia," *VMHB* 76 (Jan. 1968): 41–55.

16. *Proceedings of 1830,* 3–5, 341–62, 667–90, 881–84, 897–98, 902–3; Edward Hammet, Christiansburg, Va., to John Hammet, May 23, 1830, Hammet-Talbot-Goodell Papers, IHS; Ambler, *Sectionalism in Virginia,* 163–66, 170–72;

Freehling, *Drift toward Dissolution*, 66–70, 76–81, 271; Robert P. Sutton, *Revolution to Secession: Constitution Making in the Old Dominion* (Charlottesville: University Press of Virginia, 1989), 104–5, Curry, *A House Divided*, 20.

17. *Proceedings of 1830*, 148, 692; Neely, "Development of Virginia Taxation," 304; Rice, "Internal Improvements," 180–82; Stephen B. Oates, *The Fires of Jubilee: Nat Turner's Fierce Rebellion* (New York: Mentor, 1975), 70, 73; *Richmond Enquirer*, Nov. 26, 30, 1830, Dec. 7, 11, 1830, Apr. 5, 1831.

18. *Winchester Republican*, Dec. 3, 1830, quoted in Ambler, *Sectionalism in Virginia*, 174.

19. *Richmond Enquirer*, Apr. 2, 5, 8, 1831, Aug. 30, 1831, Jan. 24, 1832, Feb. 4, 14, 1832, Mar. 15, 27, 30, 1832; Ambler, *Sectionalism in Virginia*, 181–85; Robert S. Loving, *Double Destiny: The Story of Bristol, Tennessee-Virginia* 2d ed. (Bristol, Tenn.: King, 1956), 41–42; Rice, "Internal Improvements," 180–91; Striplin, *Norfolk and Western*, 30–31; Turner, "Early Railroad Movement," 357–58. Oates, *Fires of Jubilee*, is the best account of the Turner rebellion. For the debates, see Freehling's *Drift toward Dissolution*, especially 1–10 and 122–228.

20. Robert M. Addington, *History of Scott County, Virginia* (Kingsport, Tenn.: Kingsport, 1932), 141; William C. Pendleton, *History of Tazewell County and Southwest Virginia, 1748–1920* (Richmond, Va.: W. C Hill, 1920), 532; Rice, "Internal Improvements," 321–95; Turner, "Early Railroad Movement," 358.

21. *Richmond Enquirer*, Apr. 1, 5, 8, 1836, Dec. 6, 1836; Ambler, *Sectionalism in Virginia*, 240; Neely, "Virginia Taxation," 307–8; Rice, "Internal Improvements," 321–22; Striplin, *Norfolk and Western*, 32.

22. Neely, "Virginia Taxation," 293–97, 314; Rice, "Internal Improvements," 188–204, 321–23; Striplin, *Norfolk and Western*, 32.

23. Barrett, *Russell County*, 19; Pendleton, *History of Tazewell County*, 532; *Sketch of Western Virginia*, 41–42; Wood, "Henry Edmundson," 313; *Richmond Enquirer*, Jan. 4, 1850.

24. Herbert Wender, *Southern Commercial Conventions, 1837–1859* (Baltimore: Johns Hopkins University Press, 1930), 11–49; Ottis Clark Skipper, *J. D. B. DeBow: Magazinist of the Old South* (Athens: University of Georgia Press, 1958), 220; Charles W. Turner, "Virginia Railroad Development, 1845–1860," *The Historian* (Autumn 1947): 43–45; James E. Vance, Jr., *The Merchant's World: The Geography of Wholesaling* (Englewood Cliffs, N.J.: Prentice-Hall, 1970), 100.

25. Turner, "Virginia Railroad Development," 49–62; Goldfield, *Urban Growth*, 4–27; Striplin, *Norfolk and Western*, 30–33; *Saga of a City*, 25–30; Frank Richardson, *From Sunrise to Sunset: Reminiscence* (Bristol, Tenn.: King, 1910), 190; John Goode, *Recollections of a Lifetime* (New York: Neale, 1906), 29; Obituary Clippings, Burwell Family Papers, UVA; Craig M. Simpson, *A Good Southerner: The Life of Henry A. Wise of Virginia* (Chapel Hill: University of North Carolina Press, 1985), xi.

26. *Journal of the House of Delegates of Virginia. Session of 1844–45* (Richmond, Va.: Samuel Shepherd, 1845), 7–14; *Journal of the House of Delegates of Virginia. Session of 1846–47* (Richmond, Va.: Samuel Shepherd, 1847), 7–19; Neely, "Virginia Taxation," 320–26; John W. Bell, *Memoirs of Governor William Smith of Virginia. His Political, Military, and Personal History* (New York: Moss, 1891), 21–23.

27. The [Abingdon] *Virginian*, Jan. 17, 1846; *Richmond Whig*, Jan. 7, 1848; Thomas Ingles, Ingles Bridge, Va., to the President and Directors of the South Western Turnpike, July 7, 1847, South Western Turnpike Company Papers, UVA; Wilson, *Smyth County*, 224; Wood, "Henry Edmundson," 313.

28. *Richmond Enquirer,* Dec. 3, 1847; *Richmond Whig,* Nov. 19, 23, 30, 1847; Turner, "Virginia Railroad Development," 52–53; Charles W. Turner, "The Virginia Southwestern Railroad System at War, 1861–1865," *NCHR* 24 (Oct. 1947): 468–69; Siegel, *Roots of Southern Distinctiveness,* 52–54.

29. Holman Hamilton, *Prologue to Conflict: The Compromise of 1850* (Lexington: University Press of Kentucky, 1964), 8; McPherson, *Battle Cry of Freedom,* 52–58.

30. *Richmond Enquirer,* Dec. 7, 1847.

31. *Governor's Message and Annual Reports of the Public Officers of the State . . . of Virginia* (Richmond, Va.: Samuel Shepherd, 1847), Document 1, pp. 4–9, Document 16, pp. 1–15; *Richmond Enquirer,* Dec. 7, 1847; *Richmond Whig,* Dec. 10, 1847.

32. Allen T. Caperton, Richmond, Va., to W. Henry Alexander, Dec. 24, 1847, Caperton Family Papers, VHS; *Richmond Whig,* Dec. 10, 1847.

33. John B. Floyd, Richmond, Va., to Leonidas Baugh, Dec. 30, 1847, Leonidas Baugh Papers, UNC.

34. *Richmond Enquirer,* Jan. 7, 11, 18, 1848, Feb. 1, 4, 1848; *Richmond Whig,* Jan. 7, 18, 1848; John M. Belohlavek, "John B. Floyd as Governor of Virginia, 1849–1852," *WVH* 33 (Oct. 1971): 14–15; Summers, *History of Southwest Virginia,* 507.

35. *Acts of the General Assembly of Virginia, Passed at the Session Commencing December 6, 1847, and Ending April 5, 1848. . . .* (Richmond, Va.: Samuel Shepherd, 1848), 185.

36. *Richmond Enquirer,* Jan. 14, 1848, Feb. 22, 1848, Apr. 4, 1848; *Richmond Whig,* Feb. 25, 1848, Mar. 14, 1848.

37. *Richmond Enquirer,* Mar. 10, 17, 1848; *Richmond Whig,* Mar. 14, 17, 1848; Goode, *Recollections,* 28–29.

38. *Richmond Enquirer,* May 5, 16, 1848; *Richmond Whig,* May 5, 1848; Elizabeth Dabney Coleman, "Southwest Virginia's Railroad: Lynchburg Started It; Virginia Built It; the Yankees Wrecked It," *VC* 2 (Spring 1953): 20.

39. *Richmond Enquirer,* Oct. 10, Nov. 24, 28, Dec. 1, 5, 1848.

40. Ibid., Mar. 26, Apr. 30, May 4, 1847, Dec. 5, 12, 1848; *Richmond Whig,* Dec. 15, 1848; Belohlavek, "John B. Floyd," 16–17; Frank Ludwig Klement, "John Buchanan ('Scapegoat') Floyd: A Study of Virginia Politics Through a Biography" (M.Ph. thesis, University of Wisconsin, 1938), 1–30; *Dictionary of American Biography* (New York, 1938), 6:482–83; Pendleton, *Political History,* 160; John Frederick Dorman, *The Prestons of Smithfield and Greenfield in Virginia: Descendants of John and Elizabeth Patton through Five Generations* (Louisville: Filson Club, 1982), 68–69, 289–90; John Goode, *Recollections,* 23. Historians need a modern biography of the controversial Floyd.

41. *Richmond Enquirer,* Nov. 24, 1848, Dec. 1, 1848.

42. Ibid., Dec. 5, 12, 1848; *Richmond Whig,* Dec. 15, 1848; Belohlavek, "John B. Floyd," 16–18.

43. *Richmond Enquirer,* Dec. 15, 22, 1848.

44. *Abingdon Virginian,* Sept. 9, 1849; *Richmond Enquirer,* Dec. 15, 22, 1848; *Richmond Whig,* Dec. 15, 19, 1848; David Campbell, Murfreesboro, Tenn., to William B. Campbell, Dec. 16, 1855. The quote from the Lexington *Valley Star* was taken from the Jan. 5, 1849, edition of the *Whig.*

45. *Journal of the House of Delegates of Virginia. Session of 1848–49* (Richmond, Va.: Samuel Shepherd, 1848), 106.

46. *Journal of the House, 1848–49,* 32, 140.

47. *Lynchburg Patriot,* quoted in the *Richmond Enquirer,* Jan. 30, 1849.

48. *Richmond Whig,* Dec. 29, 1848, Jan. 2, 1849, Feb. 16, 1849. See also the *Richmond Enquirer,* Feb. 9, 1849.

49. *Richmond Whig,* Jan. 23, 1849.

50. *Richmond Enquirer,* Feb. 13, 22, 1849, Mar. 2, 1849, Sept. 4, 1849; *Richmond Whig,* Jan. 30, 1849.

51. *Richmond Enquirer,* Feb. 13, 22, 1849; *Richmond Whig,* Feb. 16, 1849.

52. *Journal of the House of 1848–49,* 314–19, 336, 376, 379–80, 392–93; *Richmond Enquirer,* Feb. 27, 1849, Mar. 2, 6, 1849; *Richmond Whig,* Mar. 2, 6, 1849.

53. John B. Floyd, Richmond, Va., to William Ballard Preston, Mar. 2, 12, 1849, Preston Family Papers, VHS; *Richmond Enquirer,* Mar. 9, 1849; *Journal of the House of 1848–49,* 437.

54. *Abingdon Virginian,* May 19, 1849, June 9, 1849, July 28, 1849; *Richmond Enquirer,* Apr. 24, 1849, June 5, 1849, Aug. 10, 1849, Oct. 13, 1849; *Journal of the House of 1848–49,* 437, 522, 652–53; Summers, *History of Southwest Virginia,* 495.

55. *Richmond Whig,* Dec. 4, 1849; Hamilton, *Prologue to Conflict,* 1–24.

56. *Richmond Whig,* Dec. 4, 1849; Klement, "John Buchanan Floyd," 62.

57. *Richmond Whig,* Dec. 4, 1849.

58. Ibid. See also the *Richmond Whig,* July 19, 1850, Aug. 23, 1850, Oct. 22, 1850.

59. *Richmond Enquirer,* Jan. 15, 1850; *Richmond Whig,* Jan. 4, 15, 1850.

60. *Abingdon Virginian,* Feb. 2, 1850; *Richmond Enquirer,* Jan. 4, 15, 1850.

61. *Richmond Enquirer,* Jan. 4, 1850.

62. *Abingdon Virginian,* Feb. 2, 1850; *Richmond Whig,* Feb. 12, Nov. 15, 1850; Summers, *History of Southwest Virginia,* 507–8; Wilson, *Smyth County,* 224–26.

63. "Minutes, Board of Directors, From Nov. 1, 1853, Va. & Tenn Railroad Co.," 249–50, and June 30, 1856, n.p., Virginia and Tennessee Railroad Collection, VPI. This is the first volume of two, cited hereafter as "V&T Minutes, vol. 1." An especially valuable source, the minutes contain the superintendents's monthly reports and copies of letters as well as minutes. Pagination disappears after 300, so material from latter pages is cited by date. For resistance, see Wayne K. Durrill, "Producing Poverty: Local Government and Economic Development in a New South County, 1874–1884," *JAH* 71 (Mar. 1985): 764, 772–74; and David Thelen, *Paths of Resistance: Tradition and Dignity in Industrializing Missouri* (New York: Oxford University Press, 1986), 11–30, 57–92.

64. Eller, *Miners, Millhands, and Mountaineers,* 65–85, 225–42; Hahn, *Roots of Southern Populism,* 36–40, and "Yeomanry," 41–42; Schlotterbeck, "Plantation and Farm," 211–14; and "Social Economy," 5–21; J. Mills Thornton III, *Politics and Power in a Slave Society: Alabama, 1800–1860* (Baton Rouge: Louisiana State University Press, 1978), xix, 303–11; [Abingdon] *Democrat,* Nov. 29, 1851, Feb. 12, 1853; *Abingdon Virginian,* June 9, 1849, Mar. 12, 1853; *Richmond Whig,* Oct. 1, 1850; Turner, "Virginia Southwestern Railroad System," 467.

65. Turner, "Virginia Southwestern Railroad System," 467; Eller, *Miners, Millhands, and Mountaineers,* 65–85 (quote is from p. 85).

66. Burwell Diary, Oct. 7, 1850, Burwell Family Papers, UVA.

67. *Richmond Enquirer,* Jan. 23, 1850; William Barney, *The Road to Secession: A New Perspective on the Old South* (New York: Praeger, 1972).

68. *Richmond Enquirer,* Jan. 16, 1850.

69. Ibid., May 28, 1850. See also the *Richmond Whig,* Nov. 15, 1850.

70. *Abingdon Virginian,* Feb. 16, 1850, Dec. 25, 1852; Striplin, *Norfolk and Western,* 33; Coleman, "Southwest Virginia's Railroad," 22; *Richmond Whig,* Sept. 3, 1850; *DeBow's Review* 9 (Nov. 1850): 555–56, 14 (Jan. 1853): 87, 88, and 14 (Feb. 1853): 169; "Sixth Annual Meeting of the Stockholders of the Va. & Tenn. RR Co.." (N.p., n.p., 1853?), 16; Robert C. Black, *The Railroads of the Confederacy* (Chapel Hill: University of North Carolina Press, 1952), 30; George Rogers Taylor and Irene D. Neu, *The American Railroad Network, 1861–1890* (Cambridge: Cambridge University Press, 1956), 12, 14, 43, Foldout Maps 1, 2, 3.

71. "Sixth Annual Meeting," 15–16; *DeBow's Review* 14 (Feb. 1853): 169; *Journal of the House of Delegates of the State of Virginia, for the Adjourned Session 1852–3* (Richmond, Va.: William F. Ritchie, 1852), 6, 27, 30–31, 37, 54, 230–31, 280; Turner, "Virginia Railroad Development," 43–62; V&T Minutes, 1:16–17, 46–50, 99, 140–41, Virginia and Tennessee Railroad Collection, VPI; *Abingdon Virginian,* Mar. 12, 1853; *Richmond Whig,* Dec. 16, 1861; David Campbell, Montcalm, to William B. Campbell, Sept. 13, 1853, Campbell Family Papers, Duke.

72. V&T Minutes, 1:48–50; Virginia and Tennessee Railroad Collection, VPI; *Journal of the House for 1852–3,* 217, 301, 373, 377; *Journal of the House of Delegates of the State of Virginia, for the Session 1853–4* (Richmond, Va.: William F. Ritchie, 1853–4), 320, 363; *Journal of the House of Delegates of the State of Virginia for the Session of 1855–56* (Richmond, Va.: William F. Ritchie, 1855–56), 19–20; Rice, *West Virginia,* 100–101; Striplin, *Norfolk and Western,* 34, Summers, *History of Southwest Virginia,* 509–10; Turner, "Virginia Southwestern Railroad System," 468.

73. "Resident Engineers's Report, Virginia and Tennessee Railroad, Document 17, Annual Reports of Internal Improvement Companies to the Board of Public Works, Year Ending Sept. 30, 1860, 68–73, *Message of the Governor of Virginia and Accompanying Documents* (Richmond, Va.: William F. Ritchie, 1861); Black, *Railroads,* 12, 14; Coleman, "Southwest Virginia's Railroad," 22; Angus James Johnston II, *Virginia Railroads in the Civil War* (Chapel Hill: University of North Carolina Press, 1961), 4, 9; Striplin, *Norfolk and Western,* 24, 34–35.

74. Escott, "Yeoman Independence and the Market," 275–300; Trelease, *The North Carolina Railroad;* Schlotterbeck, "Social Economy," 21.

Chapter 2: "The Most Favored Region for Agriculture"

1. Henry Howe, *Historical Collections of Virginia.* . . . (Charleston, S.C.: Babcock, 1845), 152–53. Dorothy Anne Dondore, in the *Dictionary of American Biography,* 9, 288–89, noted that Howe's histories largely were based on firsthand observation or interviews. The "harsh" later literature is discussed expertly in Shapiro, *Appalachia On Our Mind* and Batteau, *Invention of Appalachia.*

2. Eller, *Miners, Millhands, and Mountaineers,* 3–38 (quote is from p. 3).

3. Dunn, *Cades Cove,* 63–89; Inscoe, *Mountain Masters,* 11–58; Mitchell, *Commercialism and Frontier,* x, 1–8; Paul Salstrom, Letter, *Appalachian Journal* 13 (Summer 1986): 340–50. For Hahn, see *Roots of Southern Populism,* 15–85, "The 'Unmaking'of the Southern Yeomanry: The Transformation of the Georgia Upcountry, 1860–1890," in *The Countryside in the Age of Capitalist Transformation: Essays in the Social History of Rural America,* ed. Hahn and Jonathan Prude (Chapel Hill: University of North Carolina Press, 1985), 180–83, and Hahn, "The 'Unmaking' of the Southern Yeomanry," 29–45.

4. U. S. Bureau of the Census, *The Seventh Census of the United States: 1850* (Washington: Robert Armstrong, 1853), 285–96; David Rice McAnally, *Life and Times of Rev. William Patton, and Annals of the Missouri Conference* (St. Louis: Methodist Book Depository, 1858), 113; Donald G. Mathews, *Religion in the Old South* (Chicago: University of Chicago Press, 1977), 28–34, 51–52, 66–75; *The History of American Methodism, in Three Volumes,* (New York: Abingdon, 1964), 2:11–143; Waller, *Feud,* 28.

5. Eller, *Miners, Millhands, and Mountaineers,* 28–38, Schlotterbeck, "Social Economy," 5–15; Robert C. Kenzer, *Kinship and Neighborhood in a Southern Community: Orange County, North Carolina, 1849–1881* (Knoxville: University of Tennessee Press, 1987), esp. 6, 52–70; Mann, "Mountains," 411–13, 418, 428.

6. Howe, *Historical Collections,* 152; George W. L. Bickley, *History of the Settlement and Indian Wars of Tazewell County, Virginia. . . .* (1852; reprint, Parsons, W.V.: McClain, 1974), 124; Dunn, *Cades Cove,* 35; Eller, *Miners, Millhands, and Mountaineers,* 16–18, 23–26; Jackson Turner Main, "The Distribution of Property in Post-Revolutionary Virginia," *MVHR* 41 (Sept. 1954): 241–58; Schlotterbeck, "Social Economy," 5–13.

7. Buckingham, *Slave States,* 285–304, 321; Marianne Finch, *An Englishwoman's Experience in America* (London: Richard Bentley, 1853), 332; Howe, *Historical Collections,* 152–53; Martin, *Gazeteer,* 382, 401, 436, 453, 460–61, 467; Mrs. Anne Royall, *Sketches of History, Life, and Manners in the United States: By a Traveller* (New Haven: The Author, 1826), 39, 69; Eller, *Miners, Millhands, and Mountaineers,* 16–17; Sam Bowers Hilliard, *Hog Meat and Hoecake: Food Supply in the Old South, 1840–1860* (Carbondale: Southern Illinois University Press, 1972), 48–51; Arthur G. Peterson, *Historical Study of Prices Received by Producers of Farm Products in Virginia, 1801–1927* (Blacksburg, Va.: Virginia Polytechnic Institute, 1929), 208–10; *Seventh Census,* 275–82.

8. Buckingham, *Slave States,* 530; Featherstonhaugh, *Excursion,* 39–40.

9. Buckingham, *Slave States,* 285, 301; Howe, *Historical Collections,* 152–53, 284; Martin, *Gazeteer,* 336, 383, 402, 434, 440, 461; Royall, *Sketches,* 71; *Seventh Census,* 273–76; Hilliard, *Hog Meat,* 39–44, 92–97, 112–13; Morton, *Monroe County,* 198; Peterson, *Historical Study of Prices,* 214.

10. John Hammet, Military[?], to James McDowell, Aug. 5, 1827, and John Kelly, Greenfield, Va., to John Hammet, Mar. 20, 1818[?] and May 1, 1819, Hammet-Talbot-Goodell Papers, IHS; Bickley, *Tazewell County,* 103–7; David Campbell, Abingdon, Va., to John B. Floyd, Apr. 17, 1849, Letters Received, Governor's Office, Executive Department, VSL; Howe, *Historical Collections,* 152; Martin, *Gazeteer,* 383; Royall, *Sketches,* 71; *Sketch of Western Virginia,* 7; John B. Radford to William M. Radford, Jan. 18, 1848, Preston-Radford Papers, UVA; *Governor's Message and Annual Reports of the Public Officers of the State,* 49; Hilliard, *Hog Meat,* 115–22; Mann, "Mountains," 416; Mitchell, *Commercialism and Frontier,* 46; Wilhelm, "Appalachian Isolation," 77–91; Wilson, *Smyth County,* 170–71. Forrest McDonald and Grady McWhiney, in two articles, "The Antebellum Southern Herdsmen: A Reinterpretation," *JSH* 41 (May 1975): 147–66, and "The South from Self-Sufficiency to Peonage: An Interpretation," *AHR* 85 (Dec. 1980): 1095–1118, argued that southern herdsmen, men who relied primarily on herding and did very little traditional farming, were a numerous class. Richard K. MacMaster, "The Cattle Trade in Western Virginia, 1760–1830," in Mitchell, *Appalachian Frontiers,* 127–49, argues in contrast that herdsmen were complete capitalists. Certainly, the evidence in Southwest Virginia sup-

ports Macmaster; the manuscript census sample only turned up one individual in 1850 who fit McDonald and McWhiney's criteria.

11. Buckingham, *Slave States,* 298–99.

12. Peterson, *Historical Study of Prices,* 90–99. See also Howe, *Historical Collections,* 152.

13. Inscoe, "Slavery, Sectionalism, and Secession," 11–18, 50; Wilhelm, "Appalachian Isolation," 83. Hilliard, *Hog Meat,* 192–93, generally gives the topic its due, but his study largely excludes Virginia. Imboden's recollections are from the *Report on the Internal Commerce of the United States,* 9.

14. *Report on the Internal Commerce of the United States,* 9–13; Bickley, *Tazewell County,* 107–10; Robley Evans, *A Sailor's Log* (New York: D. Appleton, 1910), 4–5; Howe, *Historical Collections,* 152, 284; Martin, *Gazeteer,* 136–40, 347; Peregrine Prolix [Philip H. Nicklin], *Letters Descriptive of the Virginia Springs. . . .* new annotated ed. (Austin, Tx.: AAR/Tantalus, 1978), 71; Royall, *Sketches,* 56–57, 71; *The Saga of a City: Lynchburg, Virginia, 1786–1936* (Lynchburg: Lynchburg Sesqui-Centennial Association, 1936). 35–30; Amos D. Wood, *Floyd County: A History of Its People and Places* (Radford, Va.: Commonwealth, 1981), 291.

15. Ibid.; *Agriculture of the United States in 1860; Compiled from the Original Returns of the Eight Census. . . .* (Washington: Government Printing Office, 1864), 155–57, 159–61, 163–65, cited hereafter as *Eighth Census: Agriculture;* William Ballard Preston, Speech to the Virginia State Agricultural Society, Preston Family Papers, VHS; Joseph Clarke Robert, *The Tobacco Kingdom: Plantation, Market, and Factory in Virginia and North Carolina, 1800–1860* (1938; reprint, Gloucester, Mass.: Peter Smith, 1965), 154–57. The nine "market counties" were Fayette, Floyd, Giles, Mercer, Monroe, Montgomery, Pulaski, Raleigh, and Washington. See Cecil-Fronsman, *Common Whites,* 99–100, 125–27, 246–47. For similar developments elsewhere, see also Hahn, "Yeomanry," 40–45, and Schlotterbeck, "Social Economy," 21.

16. Manuscript Census, Virginia, Washington County, Schedules I, III, 1860. A useful definition of "household" is provided by Elizabeth Fox-Genovese in *Within the Plantation Household: Black and White Women of the Old South* (Chapel Hill: University of North Carolina Press, 1988), 31: "A basic social unit in which people, whether voluntarily or under compulsion, pool their income and resources. As such, it has no necessary relation to family, although members of households may be related and many households may be coterminous with family membership."

17. Manuscript Census, Virginia, Floyd and Raleigh counties, Schedules I, III, 1860. For comparison, see Ford, *Origins of Southern Radicalism,* 84–85.

18. James M. Johnston, Bristol, to E. C. Johnston, Aug. 31, 1858, Johnston-Railey Papers, UVA.

19. *Seventh Census,* 273–82; *Eighth Census: Agriculture,* 155–59, 163; Peterson, *Prices,* 12, 26–27, 69, 127–30.

20. James M. Johnston, Bristol, Tenn., to E. C. Johnston, Dec. 5, 1860, Johnston-Railey Papers, UVA; *Seventh Census,* 281–82; *Eighth Census: Agriculture,* 155–57, 159, 161, 163–65.

21. Preston, Speech to the Virginia State Agricultural Society, Preston Family Papers, VHS.

22. David Campbell, Abingdon, Va., to John B. Floyd, Apr. 17, 1849, Letters Received, Governor's Office, Executive Department, VSL; Barrett, *Breadbas-*

ket, 10; Peterson, *Prices,* 90–99; Conway Howard Smith, *The Land That Is Pulaski County* (Pulaski, Va.: Edmonds, 1981), 228.

23. [Abingdon] *Democrat,* Sept. 8, 1981; David Campbell, Montcalm, to William B. Campbell, Oct. 4, 1854, Campbell Family Papers, Duke; Pendleton, *Tazewll County,* 534–35; Wilson, *Smyth County,* 171.

24. V&T Minutes, v. 1, p. 186, VPI.

25. Ibid.; E. H. Gill's Report, Nov. 30, 1855, n.p. VPI.

26. Ibid., Dec. 1, 1856, n.p., VPI. See also James M. Johnston, Bristol, Tenn., to E. C. Johnston, Dec. 5. 1860, Johnston-Railey Papers, UVA; Barrett, *Russell County,* 12.

27. V&T Minutes, v. 1, E. H. Gill's Reports of Dec. 1, 1856, Dec. 31, 1856, Minutes of Jan. 15, 1857, n.p., VPI.

28. James M. Johnston, Bristol, Tenn., to E. C. Johnston, Oct. 21, 1858, Johnston-Raily Papers, UVA.

29. *Seventh Census,* 275–76; *Eighth Census: Agriculture,* 155, 159, 163; Salstrom, "Appalachia's Path," 54–55, 71–78.

30. Klaus Wust, *The Virginia Germans* (Charlottesville: University Press of Virginia, 1969), 48–118; Thomas Perkins Abernethy, *Western Lands and the American Revolution* (New York: Russell & Russell, 1959), 4, 79–83, 221–22; Abernethy, *Three Virginia Frontiers,* 58; Albert H. Tillson, Jr., "Political Culture and Social Conflict in the Upper Valley of Virginia, 1740–1789" (Ph.D. diss., University of Texas at Austin, 1986), 2–4, 19–62; and "Localist Roots," 392–97; Summers, *History of Southwest Virginia,* 81–84; David Hackett Fischer, *Albion's Seed: Four British Folkways in America* (New York, 1989), 605–782.

31. Wust, *Virginia Germans,* 93–118, 188–95.

32. Royall, *Sketches,* 26–27.

33. John Hammet to Murty Sullian, May 10, 1818, Hammet-Talbot-Goodell Collection, IHS. See also Hammet, Strouble Creek, Va., to John F. Dabney, June 27, 1823.

34. Royall, *Sketches,* 30–31; Fischer, *Albion's Seed,* 633, 650–51. Anti-German prejudices did not disappear, however, and in fact remained through the Civil War. See Everhard H. Smith, "Chambersburg: Anatomy of a Confederate Reprisal," *AHR* 96 (Apr. 1991): 432:55.

35. David Campbell, Montcalm, Va., to William Campbell, Apr. 22, 1850, and May 19, 1850; David Campbell, n.p., to John M. Patton, Jan. 1850, Campbell Family Papers. Duke.

36. Manuscript Census, Virginia, Washington County, Schedules I, II, 1850.

37. Ibid. Other who have found comparably high rates of tenantry in the southern mountains include Frederick A. Bode and Donald E. Ginter, *Farm Tenantry and the Census in Antebellum Georgia* (Athens: University of Georgia Press, 1986), esp. 1–43, 92–99; Dunn, *Cades Cove,* 72; Charles L. Grant, "An Appalachian Portrait: Black and White in Montgomery County, Virginia, before the Civil War" (M.A. thesis, Virginia Polytechnic Institute and the State University, 1987); and Mann, "Mountains," 415–16, 423–30. For a nonmountain example, see Ford *Origins of Southern Radicalism,* 84–88. In contrast, Pudup, "Limits of Subsistance," 66–67, 86–87, found much lower rates of tenancy in Harlan County and Perry County, Kentucky, ranging from 6.6 percent in Perry to 11 percent in Harlan. Two useful works in addition to Bode and Ginter's on determining rates of tenancy are Jeremy Atack, "Tenants and Yeomen in the Nine-

teenth Century," *AH* 62 (Summer 1988): 6–32; and John T. Houdek and Charles F. Heller, Jr., "Searching for Nineteenth-Century Farm Tenants: An Evaluation of Methods," *Historical Methods* 19 (Spring 1986): 55–61.

It seems safe to count all landowners in the "no occupation" classification as at least yeomen. The 1860 Floyd County manuscripts schedules listed occupations for women as well as for men, contrary to standard practice. Of the twenty-eight women in the sample listed as householders, all the realty owners were identified as "farmers," whereas only 40 percent of the nonlandowners were. I have with trepidation used these percentages as a rule of thumb throughout in calculating the numbers and percentages of yeomen and tenants.

38. Manuscript Census, Virginia, Washington County, Schedules I, II, 1850.

39. Manuscript Census, Virginia, Floyd and Raleigh counties, Schedules I, II, 1850; Bettye-Lou Fields and Jene Hughes, eds., *Grayson County: A History in Words and Pictures* (Independence, Va.: Grayson County Historical Society, 1976), 331.

40. Ibid.; Bode and Ginter, *Farm Tenancy,* 92–99. Mann's study of Burke's Garden, Tazewell County, in "Mountains," 424–26, offers the best look at Southwest Virginia's laborers.

41. *Seventh Census,* 256–57; U.S. Bureau of the Census, *Population of the United States in 1860; Compiled from the Original Returns of the Eighth Census. . . .* (Washington: Government Printing Office, 1864), 516–18.

42. Preston, Speech to the Virginia State Agricultural Society, 1854, Preston Family Paper, VHS.

43. Ibid. For out-migration, see the [Abingdon] *Democrat,* May 1, 1852; *Wytheville Times,* Apr. 25, May 2, May 9, Oct. 3, 1857; James McClaugherty, Mill Creek, Guadalupe County, Texas, to John McClaugherty, Dec. 16, 1859, John McClaugherty Papers, WVU; Ephraim Darter, Columbus, Miss., to Elijah Darter, Aug. 2, 1876 and Jan. 3, 1847, Darter Family Papers, VHS; B. M. Jones, *Rail Roads: Considered in Regard to Their Effects upon the Value of Land. . . .* (Richmond, Va.: Ritchie, Dunnavant, 1860), 10–18, 41–42.

44. Preston, Speech to the Virginia State Agricultural Society, Preston Family Papers, VHS.

45. *Wytheville Times,* May 9, 1857. See also Mann, "Mountains," 427.

46. John Echols, Union, Va., to George Henry Caperton, Mar. 27, 1857, Caperton Family Papers, VHS.

47. Olmsted, *Journey in the Back Country,* 277–79.

48. *Wytheville Times,* May 2, 1857. Jones, *Rail Roads,* 10–18; David Campbell, Montcalm, to William B. Campbell, Mar. 8, 1858, Campbell Family Papers, Duke. See also James Oakes, *Slavery and Freedom: An Interpretation of the Old South* (New York: Alfred A. Knopf), 97, 104–9.

49. Preston, Speech to the Virginia State Agricultural Society, Preston Family Paper, VHS.

50. *Eighth Census, Population,* 516–18; *Journal of the House of Delegates, for the Session of 1857–58* (Richmond, Va.: William F. Ritchie, 1857), 15, 198, 312, 323, 340, 480, 525. Barney, "Towards the Civil War," 148–50, cites increased out-migration as a symptom of the modernization crisis.

51. Manuscript Census, Virginia, Floyd County, Schedules I, II, 1860.

52. Manuscript Census, Virginia, Raleigh and Washington counties, Schedules I, II, 1860. Mann, "Mountains," 425–25, found the same situation in Burke's Garden, Tazewell County.

53. Olmsted, *Journey in the Back Country,* 274–76.

54. Barney, "Towards the Civil War," esp. 148; Oakes, *Slavery and Freedom*, 104–19, 226; Waller, *Feud*, 1, 15, 29.

Chapter 3: "Numerous Interesting Points on the Line"

1. "A Winter in the South," Part 1, *Harper's New Monthly Magazine* 15 (Sept. 1857): 433–43. (Quote is from p. 443.)
2. Ibid., 443.
3. Ibid., 445, 447–51.
4. "A Winter in The South," Part 2, *Harper's New Monthly Magazine* 15 (Oct. 1857): 594.
5. David C. Hsiung, "Local Color Images and Antebellum Realities," Paper Presented to the Appalachian Studies Association Conference, Asheville, N.C., Mar. 21, 1992, argues convincingly that the novella was based on a real trip. I am grateful to him for pointing out the *Harper's* story to me. See also Van Beck Hall, "The Politics of Appalachian Virginia, 1790–1830," in Mitchell, ed., *Appalachian Frontiers*, 166–86. Barney, "Towards the Civil War," 150–52, and Schlotterbeck, "Social Economy," 21, both see urbanization as a direct result of modernization.
6. *Report on the Internal Commerce of the United States*, 9–13; Bickley, *Tazewell County*, 107–10; Evans, *A Sailor's Log*, 4–5; Howe, *Historical Collections*, 152, 284; Martin, *Gazeteer*, 136–40, 347; Prolix, *Letters Descriptive of the Virginia Springs*, 71; Royall, *Sketches*, 56–57, 71; *Saga of a City*, 25–30; Wood, *Floyd County*, 291.
7. Bickley, *Tazewell County*, 109–10; Royall, *Sketches*, 36–38, 71.
8. Pack, Anderson and ——— Vawter? Day Book, 1848–49, Duke; Royall, *Sketches*, 56. Peddlers often remained "foreigners": the Manuscript Census, Virginia, Washington County, Schedule I, 1850, lists peddlers born in Connecticut and New York as well as Virginia.
9. Traugott Bromme, *Reisen durch die Vereingten Staaten und Ober-Canada* (Baltimore: C. Scheid, 1834), 2:149–51; Buckingham, *Slave States*, 273, 283; Featherstonhaugh, *Excursion*, 40; Howe, *Historical Collections*, 498–99; Martin, *Gazeteer*, 273; H. S. Tanner, *A Geographical, Historical and Statistical View of the Central or Middle United States. . . .* (Philadelphia: H. Tanner, 1841), 491.
10. George J. Stevenson, *Increase in Excellence: A History of Emory and Henry College* (New York: Appleton-Century-Crofts, 1963), 6–75.
11. Count Francesco Arese, *A Trip to the Prairies and in the Interior of North America [1837–1838]*, trans. Andrew Evans (New York: Harbor, 1934), 36; Bromme, *Reisen*, 152–53, Buckingham, *Slave States*, 304–5, 326; Featherstonhaugh, *Excursion*, 36–39; Howe, *Historical Collections*, 284–85, 443, 514; Royall, *Sketches*, 36, 53; *South-West Virginia and the Valley* (Roanoke, Va.: A. D. Smith, 1892), 321; Tanner, *Central or Middle United States*, 490–91; Lucile Miller Kincer, *Glimpses of Wythe County; Historic Churches of Wythe County* (Wytheville, Va.: Southwest Virginia Enterprise, 1967), 5–6; Prolix, *Letters*, 86–87.
12. Buckingham, *Slave States*, 273; Featherstonhaugh, *Excursion*, 40; Prolix, *Letters*, 86–87; Royall, *Sketches*, 33–35. Court days and the county court system are discussed in Albert Ogden Porter, *County Government in Virginia: A Legislative History, 1607–1904* (New York: Columbia University Press, 1947), 89–163.
13. Royall, *Sketches*, 33–35.

14. Manuscript Census, Virginia, Floyd, Raleigh, and Washington Counties, Schedules I, II, 1850.

15. Featherstonhaugh, *Excursion,* 39; Howe, *Historical Collections,* 443–44; Royall, *Sketches,* 33–35, 53; Manuscript Census, Virginia, Washington County, Schedule I, 1850.

16. Featherstonhaugh, *Excursion,* 39; Howe, *Historical Collections,* 443–44; Royall, *Sketches,* 33–35, 53. Barney, "Towards the Civil War," 157, views these activities as attempts to recapture the lost kinship ties of the rural community.

17. Samuel M. Keys, Wytheville, Va., to Leonidas Baugh, Jan. 8, 1850, Baugh Family Papers, UVA.

18. William G. Caperton, Rich Creek, Va., to Henry Alexander, 1848, Caperton Family Papers, VHS. Caperton's comments on his "ignorant" neighbors not only reflected his elite biases, but were inaccurate as well. Literacy rates actually were fairly high in the region, though low by northern standards. According to the *Seventh Census,* 270–71, Southwest Virginia in 1850 contained 16,380 illiterates, 10.6 percent of the population. The figure, while no doubt a low estimate, is notable. See also Buckingham, *Slave States,* 275–77; Amanda Jane (Cooley) Robert's Diary, VHS, and Wilhelm, "Appalachian Isolation," 86–87.

19. *Abingdon Virginian,* May 18, 1850.

20. Manuscript Census, Virginia, Floyd, Raleigh, Washington Counties, 1850, 1860, Schedules I, II.

21. *Wytheville Times,* Apr. 24, 1858; James M. Johnston, Bristol, Tenn., to E. C. Johnston, Aug. 31, 1858, Johnston-Railey Papers, UVA; Barrett, *Russell County,* 10–12.

22. Loving, *Double Destiny,* 2, 18–22, 31; *South-West Virginia,* 321; D. Sullins, *Recollections of an Old Man: Seventy Years in Dixie, 1827–1897* (Bristol, Tenn.: King, 1910), 334–36; Summers, *History,* 674–77, 689–90.

23. *Abingdon Democrat,* Oct. 11, 1856.

24. James M. Johnston, Bristol, Tenn., to E. C. Johnston, Aug. 31, 1858, Johnston-Railey Papers, UVA. See also the *Wytheville Times,* May 15 and June 12, 1858.

25. James M. Johnston, Bristol, Tenn., to E. C. Johnston, Aug. 31 and Oct. 21, 1858, Johnston-Railey Papers, UVA. Johnston reported similar encounters in Abingdon.

26. John S. Mosby, *The Memoirs of Colonel John S. Mosby,* ed. by Charles Wells Russell (Boston: Little, Brown, 1917), 11.

27. Howe, *Historical Collections,* 383–84; Martin, *Gazeteer,* 352, 393, 441, 460–61, 467; *Richmond Whig,* Jan. 9, 1849; Robert S. Starobin, *Industrial Slavery in the Old South* (New York: Oxford University Press, 1970), 3–34, 128–37; Dunn, *Cades Cove,* 80–82; Wilhelm, "Appalachian Isolation," 87–88.

28. Manuscript Census, Virginia, Wythe County, Schedule IV, 1850; "Statement Relating to Certain Lead Interests in Virginia," [1853?], Campbell-Preston-Floyd Papers (microfilm), VHS; Howe, *Historical Collections,* 514–15; *Sketch of Western Virginia,* 9; Boyd, *Resources of South-West Virginia,* 71–74; William Kohler, "The Lead Mines," (typescript), Kohler Papers, UVA.

29. Manuscript Census, Virginia, Wythe County, Schedule IV, 1850; "Statement Relating to Certain Coal Lands," [1853?], Campbell-Preston-Floyd papers (microfilm), VHS; Howe, *Historical Collections,* 463; Martin, *Gazeteer,* 24, 30, 43, 467; Humbert, *Virginia,* 16; Boyd, *Resources of South-West Virginia,* 55–71; *Rich-*

mond Whig, Dec. 25, 1849; James T. Laing, "The Early Development of the Coal Industry in the Western Counties of Virginia, 1800–1865," *WVH* (Jan. 1966): 142; Ronald L. Lewis, *Coal, Iron and Slaves: Industrial Slavery in Maryland and Virginia, 1715–1865* (Westport, Conn.: Greenwood, 1979), 11–74; J. A. Whitman, *The Iron Industry of Wythe County from 1792,* rev. ed. (Wytheville, Va.: Southwest Virginia Enterprise, 1942), 3–5, 30.

30. Manuscript Census, Virginia, Smyth and Washington Counties, Schedule IV, 1850; R. G. Dun & Co. Collection, Virginia, v. 52, 35, 86, BHU; "Statement Relating to the Preston Salt-Works in Virginia," Nov. 1, 1853, Campbell-Preston-Floyd Papers (microfilm), VHS; David Campbell, Abingdon, Va., to John B. Floyd, Apr. 17, 1849, Letters Received, Governor's Office, Executive Department, VSL; Buckingham, *Slave States,* 276; Featherstonhaugh, *Excursion,* 40; Howe, *Historical Collections,* 469; E. Meriam, "Great Salt Mines in the Mountains of Virginia," *DeBow's Review* 18 (May 1855): 679–80; Boyd, *Resources of South-west Virginia,* 101–3; *Richmond Whig,* Jan. 9, 1849; Robert, *Tobacco Kingdom,* 31; Stealey, "Slavery and the Salt Industry," 107; Wilson, *Smyth County,* 171.

31. "Statement Relating to Certain Lead Interests in Virginia," [1853?], and "Statement Relating to the Preston Salt–Works in Virginia," Nov. 1, 1853, both in the Campbell-Preston-Floyd Papers (microfilm), VHS; Howe, *Historical Collections,* 514–15; Buckingham, *Slave States,* 291–327; .

32. Manuscript Census, Virginia, Wythe County, Schedule IV, 1860; Kohler, "Lead Mines," 17–21, Kohler Papers (typescript), UVA; "Statement Relating to Lead Interests," Campbell-Preston-Floyd Papers (microfilm), VHS.

33. Kohler, "Lead Mines," 17, Kohler Papers, UVA.

34. Manuscript Census, Virginia, Carroll County, Schedule IV, 1860; V&T Minutes, 1:254, 264–65, VPI; Otis K. Rice, *West Virginia: A History* (Lexington: University Press of Kentucky, 1985), 466.

35. Manuscript Census, Virginia, Wythe County, Schedule IV, 1860; Whitman, *Iron Industry,* 3–5.

36. Manuscript Census, Virginia, Smyth and Wythe Counties, Schedule IV, 1860; V&T Minutes, 1:16–17, 129, 245, VPI; R. G. Dun & Co. Collection, Virginia, v. 52, 35, 63, 70, 86; BHU David Campbell, Murfreesboro, Tenn., to William B. Campbell, Feb. 5 , June 24, 1856, Campbell Family Papers, Duke. Other prorailroad activists, notably William M. Burwell and Samuel Goodson, managed to have the line cross their land as well. See V&T Minutes, v. 1, Sept. 11, 1856, n.p., VPI.

37. U.S. Bureau of the Census, *Manufactures of the United States in 1860.* . . . (Washington: Government Printing Office, 1865), 607, 609, 612–14, 620, 622–23, 627–30, 632–34; Sarah A. B. Look to My Dear Mother and Sisters Olivia and Ellen, Sept. 3, 1854, Jan. 6, 1856, and Sarah A. B. Look, Broad Ford, Smyth County, Va., to Ellen, Oct. 26, 1856, Lincoln-Look Family Papers, VPI; James Hall, Marion, Va., to C. T. Pfohl, July 10, 1860, Christian Thomas Pfohl Papers, SHC; V&T Minutes, 1:256, Dec. 6, 1855, n.p., VPI.

38. Manuscript Census, Virginia, Montgomery County, Schedule IV, 1860; "Statement Relating to Certain Coal Lands," [1853], Campbell-Preston-Floyd Papers, VHS (microfilm); V&T Minutes, 1:111, VPI; Eller, *Miners, Millhands, and Mountaineers,* 69–77; Rice, "Internal Improvements," 465–66; Turner, "Virginia Farmers," 245.

39. Eller, *Miners, Millhands, and Mountaineers,* see especially 13, 65.

40. William Burke, M.D., *Mineral Springs of Western Virginia, with Remarks on their Use, and the Diseases to Which They are Applicable* (New York: Wiley and Putnam, 1842), 21–22; John J. Moorman, M.D., *The Virginia Springs. . . .* (Philadelphia: Lindsay & Blakiston, 1847), 179–203. Burke and Moorman were the resident doctors at Red Sulphur Springs and White Sulphur Springs respectively. A useful secondary account is Percival Reniers, *The Springs of Virginia: Life, Love, and Death at the Waters, 1775–1900,* 3d ed. (Kingsport, Tenn.: Kingsport, 1955), see especially 38–168.

41. Buckingham, *Slave States,* 336–37; Burke, *Mineral Springs,* 25; *DeBow's Review* 12 (Oct. 1852): 425; Featherstonhaugh, *Excursion,* 16; Reniers, *Springs of Virginia,* 67–88.

42. Buckingham, *Slave States,* 335.

43. Ibid., 315–16, 323–24; Burke, *Mineral Springs,* 259; Moorman, *Virginia Springs,* 182–86; Prolix, *Letters,* 26–28, 31, 108.

44. Featherstonhaugh, *Excursion,* 31–33; Gaddis, *Foot-Prints,* 315; Caroline Gilman, *The Poetry of Travelling in the United States. . . .* (New York: S. Colman, 1838), unpaginated preface, 348; Marryat, *Diary,* 233; Prolix, *Letters,* 87–89; Reniers, *Springs of Virginia,* 30–32.

45. Featherstonhaugh, *Excursion,* 23–27.

46. Royall, *Sketches,* 32, 56–57.

47. Buckingham, *Slave States,* 22, 298–99; Finch, *An Englishwoman's Experience,* 329–30; Reniers, *Springs of Virginia,* 31.

48. Arese, *Trip to the Prairies,* 36–37; Featherstonhaugh, *Excursion,* 41–42; Finch, *An Englishwoman's Experience,* 329–30; Frederick Marryat, *A Diary in America, with Remarks on Its Institutions* (New York: Alfred A.Knopf, 1962), 231; Prolix, *Letters,* 21–25, 132; Tanner, *Central or Middle United States,* 472–74; William R. Pepper, Lexington, Va., to John Pepper, Nov. 20, 1847, John Pepper Papers, Duke.

49. Buckingham, *Slave States,* 291–306; Moorman, *Virginia Springs,* 216–18.

50. Buckingham, *Slave States,* 306.

51. Arese, *Trip to the Prairies,* 31–35. See also *DeBow's Review* 12 (Oct. 1852): 425.

52. *DeBow's Review* 12 (Oct. 1852): 425.

53. *Wytheville Times,* June 20, 1857; Turner, "Virginia Farmers," 240, 243.

54. *Wytheville Times,* June 20, 1857; Reniers, *Springs of Virginia,* 183–84; Roderick Lucas, *A Valley and Its People, in Montgomery County, Virginia* (Blacksburg: Southern, 1975), 39–40.

Chapter 4: "A Source of Great Economy"

1. *Documents Containing Statistics of Virginia, Ordered to be Printed by the State Convention Sitting in the City of Richmond, 1850–1851* (Richmond, Va.: William Culley, 1851), Document 13, 1–3; U.S. Bureau of the Census, *The Seventh Census of the United States: 1850* (Washington: Robert Armstrong, 1853), 256–57; U.S. Bureau of the Census, *Heads of Families at the First Census of the United States Taken in the Year 1790, Records of the State Enumerations, 1782 to 1785: Virginia* (Washington: Government Printing Office, 1908), 9; Murphy, "Slavery and Freedom," 151–62.

2. *Richmond Enquirer,* Feb. 7, 1851.

3. See, for example, James W. Taylor, *Alleghania: A Geographical and Statisti-*

cal Memoir (St. Paul: James Davenport, 1862); Campbell, *Southern Highlander;* Frost, "Our Contemporary Ancestors" 311–19; Kephart, *Our Southern Highlanders;* Carter G. Woodson, "Freedom and Slavery in Appalachian America," *Journal of Negro History* 1 (Apr. 1916): 132–50. Brown is discussed in a later chapter.

4. Olmsted, *Journey in the Back Country*. Inscoe, *Mountain Masters,* 107–12, provides a cogent analysis of Olmsted's depictions.

5. Ollinger Crenshaw, "The Knights of the Golden Circle: The Career of George Bickley," *AHR* 47 (Oct. 1941): 24–26. Frank L. Klement, *Dark Lanterns: Secret Political Societies, Conspiracies, and Treason Trials in the Civil War* (Baton Rouge: Louisiana State University Press, 1984), dismisses the KGC as a real threat to the north, but McPherson, *Battle Cry of Freedom,* 116, 599, 763, 878, disagrees.

6. Bickley, *Tazewell County,* x–xi, 45–48, 118–21.

7. Richard B. Drake, "Slavery and Antislavery in Appalachia," *AH* 14 (Winter 1986): 25–33; Robert P. Stuckert, "Black Populations of the Southern Appalachian Mountains," *Phylon* 48 (June 1987): 141–51; Murphy, "Slavery and Freedom," 151–69; Inscoe, *Mountain Masters* and "Mountain Masters: Slaveholding in Western North Carolina," *NCHR* 61 (Apr. 1984): 143–73; Barney, "Towards the Civil War," 146–48; Oakes, *Slavery and Freedom,* 97; Gavin Wright, *The Political Economy of the Cotton South: Households, Markets, and Wealth in the Nineteenth Century* (New York: W. W. Norton, 1978), 62–74.

8. Olmsted, *Journey in the Back Country,* 273.

9. Manuscript Census, Virginia, Floyd, Raleigh, and Washington Counties, Schedules I and III, 1850; Grant, "Appalachian Portrait," 83; Murphy, "Slavery and Freedom," 153–62; *Richmond Enquirer,* Feb. 7, 1851.

10. Olmsted, *Journey in the Back Country,* 253; Inscoe, *Mountain Masters,* 62–68.

11. Ibid.

12. *Seventh Census,* 256–57; *Eight Census: Population,* 516–18; Richard Sutch, "The Breeding of Slaves for Sale and the Westward Expansion of Slavery, 1850–1860," in *Race and Slavery in the Western Hemisphere: Quantitative Studies,* ed. Stanley L. Engerman and Eugene Genovese (Princeton: Princeton University Press, 1975), 177; Freehling. *Secessionists at Bay,* 24, 166–77. The same situation was true in Western North Carolina; see Inscoe, *Mountain Masters,* 85–86.

13. Manuscript Census, Virginia, Floyd County, Schedules I, III, 1850, 1860.

14. *Seventh Census,* 256–57; *Eighth Census: Population,* 508–15; Inscoe, *Mountain Masters,* 85–86.

15. Evans, *A Sailor's Log,* 1–7.

16. Manuscript Census, Virginia, Washington County, Schedules I, III, 1860; *Seventh Census,* 256–57; *Eighth Census: Population,* 508–15; Smith, *Pulaski County,* 217, 241.

17. *Seventh Census,* 256–57; *Eighth Census: Population,* 516–18; Salstrom, "Appalachia's Path," 54–55.

18. *Seventh Census,* 256–57; *Eighth Census: Population,* 508–18.

19. *Seventh Census,* 256–57.

20. Ibid.; *Eighth Census: Population,* 516–18.

21. Manuscript Census, Virginia, Floyd and Raleigh Counties, Schedules I, III, 1860.

22. W. J. Cash, *The Mind of the South* (New York: Alfred A. Knopf, 1941), 219; Gurney, *Journey in North America,* 54; Olmsted, *Journey in the Back Country,* 51–54; Inscoe, *Mountain Masters,* 87–114.

23. G. Wilson, Lewisburg, to Nathaniel Wilson, July 22, 1835, Nathaniel V. Wilson Correspondence, WVU.

24. John Echols, Union, Va., to George Henry Caperton, Jan. 4, 1859, Caperton Family Papers, VHS.

25. Alexander W. Reynolds, Indianola, Texas, to Sallie Preston, Nov. 8, 16, 21, Dec. 8, 20, 1859, Jan. 24, Feb. 4, 1860, Alexander W. Reynolds Letters and Papers, Roy Bird Cook Collection, WVU. (Quote is from the letter of Feb. 4).

26. J. W. Ross, Abingdon, Va., to William B. Campbell, Nov. 5, 1855, and David Campbell, Murfreesboro, Tenn., to William B. Campbell, Nov. 14, 1855, Campbell Family Papers, Duke.

27. *Abingdon Democrat,* Feb. 21, 1857.

28. Featherstonhaugh, *Excursion,* 36–37. Thomas D. Clark identified Armfield in his edited work, *Travels in the Old South: A Bibliography,* vol. 3, *The Antebellum South, 1825–1860: Cotton, Slavery, and Conflict* (Norman, Okla.: University of Oklahoma Press, 1959), 41.

29. Inscoe, *Mountain Masters,* 85–86.

30. Caroline H. Preston, Wythe Court House, Va., to Maria Preston Pope, June 2, 1828, and Fotheringay, Sept. 18, 1828, Preston Family Papers—Joyse Collection, Filson; A. T. Caperton, Richmond, Va., to D'Sir, July 19, 1850, Caperton Family Papers, VHS. Grant, "Appalachian Portrait," 36–37, and Inscoe, *Mountain Masters,* 82–84, assert that owners only sold to slave traders as a last resort.

31. Lewis E. Caperton, Union, Va., to Allen T. Caperton, Dec. 22, 1847, Caperton Family Papers, VHS.

32. John Echols, Union, Va., to George Henry Caperton, Dec. 28, 1857, Caperton Family Papers, VHS; *Abingdon Democrat,* Feb. 6, 1858; Murphy, "Slavery in Appalachia," 158–61.

33. Olmsted, *Journey in the Back Country,* 226.

34. James P. Strother, Marion, Va., to Charles W. Christian, Mar. 9, 1841, James P. Strother Papers, Duke.

35. H. Sanders, Jackson's Ferry, Va., to John P. M. Sanders, Jan. 9, 1851, Richard W. Sanders and John W. Greene Papers and Notebooks, Duke; Inscoe, *Mountain Masters,* 76–81.

36. Richard W. Sanders, Jackson's Ferry, Va., to John P. M. Sanders, May 21, 1851, Richard W. Sanders and John W. Greene Papers and Notebooks, Duke; Lewis E. Caperton, Union, Va., to Allen T. Caperton, Dec. 15, 1847, Caperton Family Papers, VHS; Robley Evans, *A Sailor's Log* (New York: D. Appleton, 1901), 2; Inscoe, *Mountain Masters,* pp. 76–78; John Edmund Stealey III, "Slavery and the Western Virginia Salt Industry," *JNH* 59 (Apr. 1974): 119; Inscoe, *Mountain Masters,* 77–78.

37. Featherstonhaugh, *Excursion,* 16–26; Marryat, *Diary in America,* 236; Olmsted, *Back Country,* 226–28, 273–75; David Campbell, Slave Rental Contract, Nov. 11, 1856, Campbell Family Papers, Duke; *Wytheville Times,* June 20, 1857; Barrett, *Russell County,* 122; Inscoe, *Mountain Masters,* 68–76; Mann, "Mountains," 421; Reniers, *Springs of Virginia,* 184; Schlotterbeck, "Social Economy," 5.

38. Olmsted, *Journey in the Back Country,* 276.

39. V&T Minutes, 1:37, 99–100, 206, Nov. 12, 1856, n.p., Feb. 2, 1857, n.p.; *Board of Directors Minutes, April 8, 1857 to January 11, 1866,* Virginia and Tennessee Railroad Collection, VPI, 2, 82, 87, 192, hereafter cited as V&T Min-

utes, v. 2; *Message of the Governor, 1861,* Document 17, p. 56; David Campbell, Montcalm, to William B. Campbell, May 1, 1854, Campbell Family Papers, Duke; Olmsted, *Journey in the Back Country,* 274; Curry, *A House Divided,* 22–23; W. Harrison Daniel, *Bedford County, Virginia, 1840–1860: The History of an Upper Piedmont County in the Late Antebellum Era* (Bedford, Va.: Print Shop, 1985), 110; McFarland, "Extension of Democracy," 40; Schlotterbeck, "Plantation and Farm," 301–15; Henry T. Shanks, *The Secession Movement in Virginia, 1847–1861* (Richmond, Va.: Garrett and Massie, 1934), 6–7; Simpson, *A Good Southerner,* 142.

Free blacks served the railroad as well as slaves. In 1856, the directors awarded a free black crewman twenty dollars for remaining on a train nearing a collision after the white crewmen jumped off. See V&T Minutes, v. 1, Nov. 12, 1856, n.p., VPI.

40. Olmsted, *Journey in the Back Country,* 271–74.

41. *Sixth Annual Meeting,* 16.

42. V&T Minutes, 2:2., VPI.

43. Ibid., v. 1, Feb. 2, 1857, n.p.; V&T Minutes, 2:82, 87, VPI. The Superintendent's Reports in Volume One of the Minutes constantly note injured or killed workers, several per year. Clearly, constructing and running the line was a dangerous business.

44. Charles W. Turner, "Railroad Service to Virginia Farmers, 1828–1860," *AH* 22 (Oct. 1948): 242.

45. William M. Burwell, "The Commercial Future of the South," *DeBow's Review* 30 (Feb. 1861): 147–49. See also the Notebook of William M. Burwell, Burwell Family Papers, UVA.

46. Notebook of William M. Burwell, Burwell Family Papers, UVA; V&T Minutes, 2:349; *Governor's Message of 1861,* Document 17, pp. 98–99.

Chapter 5: "No Other Chance for Us"

1. The official *Journal Acts and Proceedings of A General Convention of the State of Virginia, Assembled at Richmond on Monday, the Fourteenth Day of October, Eighteen Hundred and Fifty* (Richmond, Va.: William Culley, 1850), is of little use for developments after Mar. 7, 1851, as on that date the official reporter quit in a huff over a salary dispute. Thus, the best sources for information on the convention are the ninety-two four-page Convention Supplements, published as inserts in the Richmond newspapers and generally available on microfilm as constituent sections of those papers. The information on Greenbrier and Monroe is from Convention Supplements No. 21 (Mar. 20–22, 1851), and No. 24 (Mar. 29–Apr. 4, 1851).

The fullest discussion of the convention is Francis Pendleton Gaines, "The Virginia Constitutional Convention of 1850–51: A Study in Sectionalism" (Ph.D. diss., University of Virginia, 1950). It suffers somewhat, however, from both an overreliance on Ambler and from an overly rosy appraisal of the delegates' driving motivations and results. Thus, one also should consult Sutton, *Revolution to Secession,* 121–41, and two works by Craig Simpson, *Good Southerner,* and "Political Compromise and the Protection of Slavery: Henry A. Wise and the Virginia Constitutional Convention of 1850–1851," *VMHB* 83 (Oct. 1975): 387–405. For more detail on southwest Virginia specifically, see chapter 3 of Noe, "Southwest Virginia."

2. William K. Heiskell, Richmond, Va., to Leonidas Baugh, Feb. 20 and 23, 1851, Baugh Family Papers, UVA; David Campbell, Montcalm, to Rev. James P. Carrell, May 8, 1850, Campbell Family Papers, Duke; [Abingdon] *Democrat* Apr. 19, 1850.

3. Convention Supplement No. 41 (May 8–9, 1851).

4. [Abingdon] *Democrat,* Apr. 19, 1851; *Abingdon Virginian,* Mar. 23, 1850; *Richmond Enquirer,* Dec. 14, 1849, Feb. 26, Mar. 20, 22, May 28, 1850; *Richmond Whig,* July 19, Aug. 28, Sept. 3, 1850, May 16, 1851; Harvey Gray, "To the Voters of Russell, Scott, & Lee," July 1, 1850, Baugh Family Papers, UVA; Gaines, "Convention," 79–104; Simpson, "Political Compromise," 388–93.

5. Isaac B. Dunn, Richmond, Va., to Leonidas Baugh, Dec. 8, 1849, Baugh Family Papers, UVA.

6. See especially the unnumbered Convention Supplements of Jan. 27–29 and Feb. 4–16, 1851, as well as No. 9 (Feb. 8–11, 1851) through No. 50 (May 21, 1851); *Journal, Acts and Proceedings,* 84–143, Appendix 11–23; *Abingdon Virginian,* May 3, 1851; *Richmond Enquirer,* Apr. 8, 15, 25, May 13, 16, 20, 1851; *Richmond Whig,* Feb. 4, 11, 28, Apr. 15, May 2, 13, 16, 23, 1851; Gaines, "Convention," 97, 194–226; Simpson, "Political Compromise," 395–400.

7. *New Constitution of the Commonwealth of Virginia Adopted . . . on the 31st Day of July, 1851* (Richmond, Va.: William Culley, 1851), 3–40; *Journal, Acts, and Proceedings,* 419, Appendix 11–23; *Richmond Enquirer,* May 13, 16, 20, July 8, 28, Aug. 1, 1851; *Richmond Whig,* May 13, 16, 23, July 4, Aug. 1, 5, 1851; Gaines, "Convention," 198–278; Appendix IV; Simpson, "Political Compromise," 399–400, 402–5.

8. Thornton, *Politics and Power,* Goldfield, "The Triumph of Politics," 67–95; George M. McFarland, "The Extension of Democracy in Virginia, 1850–1896" (Ph.D. diss., Princeton University, 1934), 9, 15.

9. *Wytheville Republican,* quoted in The [Abingdon] *Democrat,* Nov. 29, 1851; Shanks, "Disloyalty," 118; Fields, *Grayson County,* 83. My use of the "crisis of fear" concept is from Steven A. Channing, *Crisis of Fear: Secession in South Carolina* (New York: Simon and Schuster, 1970), esp. 17–93. For similar developments in western North Carolina, see Crawford, "Political Society," 378–83.

10. McKinney, *Southern Mountain Republicans,* 14–16; James Roger Sharp, *The Jacksonians Versus the Banks: Politics in the States after the Panic of 1837* (New York: Columbia University Press, 1978), 255–57, 264–68, 339–46; Henry Harrison Simms, *The Rise of the Whigs in Virginia, 1824–1840* (Richmond, Va.: William Byrd, 1929), 32, 62, 86–87, 95, 116–17, 139, 158–59; Simpson. *Good Southerner,* 106–14. I also have benefited from two articles by Thomas E. Jeffrey concerning western North Carolina, "Internal Improvements and Political Parties in Antebellum North Carolina, 1836–1860," *NCHR* 55 (Apr. 1978): 111–56, and "National Issues, Local Interests, and the Transformation of Antebellum North Carolina Politics," *JSH* 50 (Feb. 1984): 43–74, as well as from Thornton, *Politics and Power,* xix–xx.

11. Hamilton, *Prologue to Conflict,* 133–208.

12. *Richmond Enquirer,* June 8, 1855, May 27, 1859; David Campbell, Montcalm, to William B. Campbell, Feb. 12, Mar. 20, Apr. 3, June 6, 1855, Campbell Family Papers, Duke; [Abingdon] *Democrat,* May 12, 19, 1855, Apr. 30, 1859; James P. Hambleton, *A Biographical Sketch of Henry A. Wise. . . .* (Richmond, Va.: J. W. Randolph, 1856), esp. 355–58; John Hutchinson, et al., to William Ballard Preston, June 20, 1855, and William Ballard Pre-

ston, Speech to the Virginia State Agricultural Society, 1854, Preston Family Papers, VHS; Olmsted, *Slave States,* 288–303; John S. Wise, *The End of an Era* (Boston: Houghton, Mifflin, 1902), 54–58; Shanks, *Secession Movement,* 61; Simpson, *A Good Southerner,* 106–14.

13. David Donald, *Charles Sumner and the Coming of the Civil War* (New York: Alfred A. Knopf, 1960), 282–94, 308; David Campbell, Montcalm, to William B. Campbell, Aug. 2, Sept. 9, 17, 23 & 24, Oct. 1, 1856, and William B. Campbell, Montcalm, to William H. Macfarland, Oct. 24, 1856, Campbell Family Papers, Duke.

14. *Wytheville Times,* Aug. 1, 1857, May 1, 1858.

15. Boney, *Letcher,* 1–62; William S. Hitchcock, "The Limits of Southern Unionism: Virginia Conservatives and the Gubernatorial Election of 1859," *JSH* 47 (Feb. 1981): 66; Shanks, *Secession Movement,* 57.

16. Henry A. Wise, Richmond, Va., to George A. Booker, Feb. 18, 1857, George Booker Letters, Duke.

17. Alexander Rives, Carlton near Charlottesville, to William Ballard Preston, Dec. 9, 1858, Preston Family Papers, VHS; *Wytheville Times,* July 3, Sept. 24, 1859; Boney, *Letcher,* 37–39, 75–81; Hitchcock, "Limits of Unionism," 60–72; Shanks, *Secession Movement,* 57–59. The *Richmond Enquirer* was very hostile to Letcher until he became the party's nominee. See especially the Nov. 30, 1858 number.

18. *Richmond Enquirer,* June 14, 1859, Nov. 6, 1860; *The Tribune Almanac for the Years 1838 to 1868....* (New York: New York Tribune, 1868), 2:1860; Almanac, 53–54; *Wytheville Times,* Sept. 24, 1859; W. G. Bean, "John Letcher and the Slavery Issue in Virginia's Gubernatorial Contest of 1858–1859," *JSH* 20 (Feb. 1954): 22–49; Boney, *Letcher,* 62, 80–81, 87; Hitchcock, "Limits of Unionism," 70–71; Shanks, *Secession Movement,* 58–61.

19. *Wytheville Times,* Sept. 24, 1859.

20. David Campbell, Montcalm, to William B. Campbell, Nov. 8, 1856, Campbell Family Papers, Duke.

21. Stephen B. Oates, *To Purge This Land with Blood: A Biography of John Brown* (New York: Harper & Row, 1970), 61–64.

22. Ibid., pp. 149–305.

23. *Wytheville Times,* Oct. 22, 29, Nov. 5, 12, 26, 1859, Jan. 28, Feb. 11, 1860; Oates, *To Purge This Land with Blood,* 318–23, 360.

24. James R. Johnston, Goodson, Va., to E. C. Johnston, Nov. 30, 1859, Johnston-Railey Papers, UVA.

25. *Wytheville Times,* Apr. 3, 1858; Oates, *To Purge This Land with Blood,* 322–33.

26. John Caperton, Mossy Creek, Va., to Harriet Caperton, Nov. 21, 1859, Caperton Family Papers, VHS.

27. James N. Bosang, *Memoirs of a Pulaski Veteran* (Pulaski, Va.:N.p., 1912), 3.

28. *Wytheville Times,* Dec. 10, 17, 24, 1859, Jan. 21, 28, Mar. 10, Apr. 14, 1860.

29. Ibid., Mar. 10, 1860.

30. *Wytheville Times,* May 12, 19, 26, June 30, July 7, 21, Aug. 25, Sept. 1, Oct. 13, 20, Nov. 3, 1860; Crofts, *Reluctant Confederates,* 78–88; Shanks, *Secession Movement,* 114–15; Stevenson, *Increase in Excellence,* 85–89.

31. *Abingdon Democrat,* Oct. 12, 1860; Shanks, *Secession Movement,* 123; Rob-

ert W. Johannsen, *Lincoln and the South in 1860* (Fort Wayne, Ind.: Louis A. Warren Lincoln Library and Museum, 1989), 4–21.

32. Alise Caperton to My Dear Mama, Oct. 16, 1860, William Gaston Caperton Family Papers (microfilm), WVU. The significance of women in the secession crisis, both as active participants and influences on the men of their families, is a largely unexplored but vastly significant topic. Anne Firor Scott, *The Southern Lady: From Pedestal to Politics, 1830–1930* (Chicago: University of Chicago Press, 1970), esp. 46–54, 78–79, implied that discontented southern women opposed slavery and, thus, secession. Other recent scholars, however, notably Elizabeth Fox-Genovese, *Within the Plantation Household,* and George Rable, *Civil Wars: Women and the Crisis of Southern Nationalism* (Urbana: University of Illinois Press, 1989), argue that southern women strongly supported secession and slavery, often more enthusiastically than men. Most of the Southwest Virginia women whose papers survive vehemently expressed their support of secession.

33. *Richmond Enquirer,* Nov. 16, 20, Dec. 4, 25, 1861; *Tribune Almanac,* 1861, 50–51; Ambler, "Cleavage," 778; Crofts, *Reluctant Secessionists,* 45–47, 81–86; Maddox, "Presidential Election," 226–27; Shanks, *Secession Movement,* 114–16. William L. Barney, *Road to Secession,* 135–36, 180, maintains that Breckinridge did best in areas where young men were actively using slave labor to raise tobacco, and feared economic collapse if Lincoln were elected. Six of Southwest Virginia's ten leading tobacco producing counties, however, went for Bell.

34. Rev. S. R. Houston Diary, Nov. 16, 30, 1860, in Oren F. Morton, *A History of Monroe County, West Virginia* (1916; reprint, Baltimore: Regional, 1974), 166.

35. *Wytheville Times,* Nov. 17, 24, Dec. 1, 1860.

36. Ibid., Dec. 1, 1860. See Johannsen, *Lincoln,* 1–3, 25–26.

37. Ibid., Dec. 15, 29, 1860.

38. *Journal of the House of Delegates of the State of Virginia, for the Extra Session, 1861* (Richmond, Va.: William F. Ritchie, 1861), xi, xix, xxi–xxii, 3–4; Crofts, *Reluctant Confederates,* 137.

39. *Journal of 1861,* viii–xviii, Crofts, *Reluctant Confederates,* 106–11.

40. *Journal of 1861,* 4, 9–30; George Ellis Moore, *A Banner in the Hills: West Virginia's Statehood* (New York, 1963), 36.

41. *Journal of 1861,* 67.

42. Crofts, *Reluctant Confederates,* 140–41.

43. Johannsen, *Lincoln,* 5–7, 24–25; Crofts, *Reluctant Confederates,* 92–99; William W. Freehling, "The Editorial Revolution, Virginia, and the Coming of the Civil War: A Review Essay," *CWH* 16 (Mar. 1970): 68–72.

44. Crofts, 92–99; Channing, *Crisis of Fear,* 17–57, 141, 231–35, 286; Freehling, "The Editorial Revolution," 68–72; Johannsen, *Lincoln,* 5–7, 24–25; Williams, *West Virginia,* 83–84. Obviously, this argument draws heavily on the work of Bertram Wyatt-Brown. Honor as a factor in secession is analyzed by Wyatt-Brown in his *Yankee Saints and Southern Sinners,* esp. 183–210, and in *Southern Honor.*

45. Henry A. Wise, Rolleston, to George A. Booker, Jan. 20, 1861, George Booker Letters, Duke.

46. John Samuel Apperson Diaries, Jan. 22, 1861, Apperson Family Papers, VPI.

47. William H. Cook, Wytheville, Va., to My Dear Madam, Feb. 5, 1861, William D. Simpson Papers, SHC.

48. Apperson Diaries, Jan. 22, Feb. 4, 9, 1861, Apperson Family Papers, VPI; Gaines, *Biographical Register,* 69.

49. *Abingdon Democrat,* Feb. 22, Mar. 8, 1861.

50. Crofts, *Reluctant Confederates,* 109–11.

51. Sarah H. Preston to Harriet Caperton, Feb. 12, 1861, William Gaston Caperton Family Papers (microfilm), WVU.

52. Crofts, *Reluctant Confederates,* xviii, 106–8, 263; Williams, *West Virginia,* 83–84; Thomas Webster Richey, "The Virginia State Convention of 1861 and Virginia Secession" (Ph.D. diss., University of Georgia, 1990), 14, 57–58.

53. *Abingdon Democrat,* Feb. 8, 1861; Wyatt-Brown, *Yankee Saints,* 202–6; Robert Gray Gunderson, *Old Gentlemen's Convention: The Washington Peace Conference of 1861* (Madison: University of Wisconsin Press, 1961), 1–100; Hitchcock, "Limits of Unionism." 59–60; Shanks, *Secession Movement,* 153–55; Summers, *History,* 512. On the larger issue of the sincerity of Virginia unionism outside the unconditional enclave of the northwestern counties, historians traditionally dismissed the Virginians as hypocrites, as Lincoln himself eventually did. See for example Richard N. Current, *Lincoln and the First Shot* (Philadelphia and New York: J. B. Lippincott, 1963), 30–35, 94–96; and Kenneth M. Stampp, *And the War Came: The North and the Secession Crisis, 1860–1861* (Baton Rouge: Louisiana State University Press, 1950), esp. 129–30, 271–72. Crofts, *Reluctant Confederates,* defends the Virginia unionists as sincere, and argues in effect that only Lincoln's short-sighted policies drove them to secession. On the whole, I believe that the traditional interpretation is more correct, at least in regard to Southwest Virginia. Like Ambler, Crofts tends to see the Northwest as "the" west, although his argument is obviously much more sophisticated.

54. *Abingdon Democrat,* Feb. 8, 1861.

55. *Journal of the Acts and Proceedings of a General Convention of the State of Virginia. . . .* (Richmond, Va.: Wyatt M. Elliott, 1861), 1:117–18; Crofts, *Reluctant Confederates,* 140–41; Gunderson, *Old Gentlemen's Convention,* 100; Shanks, *Secession Movement,* 153–55; Ralph A. Wooster, *The Secession Conventions of the South* (Princeton: Princeton University Press, 1962), 141–42. It should be noted that at least one voter apparently *did* see "wait-a-bits" as outright unionists. See Record Group 233, Records of the U.S. House of Representatives, Barred and Disallowed Case Files of the Southern Claims Commission, Case 12049, NA. This important collection is cited hereafter as RG 233.

56. Gaines, *Register,* 13–83.

57. John B. Floyd, Abingdon, Va., to William M. Burwell, Feb. 7, 1861, Burwell Family Papers, UVA.

58. Apperson Diaries, Feb. 4, 6, 20, 21, 23, Mar. 3, 1861, Apperson Family Papers, VPI.

59. Summers, *History,* 513.

60. Gaines, *Register,* 13–83; Goode, *Recollections of a Lifetime,* 42–50; *Journal of the Acts and Proceedings,* 1:3–12; Wooster, *Secession Conventions,* 142–45. Richey, "Virginia State Convention," is the best secondary account.

61. Shanks, *Secession Movement,* 158–78; Sarah A. Preston to Harriet Caperton, Feb. 12, 1861, William Gaston Caperton Family Papers (microfilm), WVU.

62. *Journal of Acts and Proceedings,* 1:232–38, 245, 240.

63. Ibid., 1:244–45. See Johannsen, *Lincoln,* 22–26.

64. *Journal of Acts and Proceedings,* 1:130–49, 232–33.

65. Ibid., 1:275–76.

66. Roy P. Basler, ed.,*The Collected Works of Abraham Lincoln* (New Brunswick, N.J.: Rutgers University Press, 1953), 4:262–71; McPherson, *Ordeal by Fire,* 262–64.

67. *Journal of Acts and Proceedings,* 1:523–28, 2:32–37; Crofts, *Reluctant Confederates,* 308–13; Shanks, *Secession Movement,* 179–90.

68. *Journal of Acts and Proceedings,* 2:344, 757–61.

69. Quoted in Ibid., 2:761.

70. Ibid., 3:153–64; Shanks, *Secession Movement,* 190, 196.

71. *Journal of Acts and Proceedings,* 3:163; Shanks, *Secession Movement,* 190.

72. Shanks, *Secession Movement,* 183–88; Richey, "Virginia State Convention," 119–20 and generally throughout.

73. *Journal of Acts and Proceedings,* 3:3–7, 50–56, 112–16, 166–70, 507–22, 524–28, 765–67; Curry, *A House Divided,* 32–34. Moore, *Banner in the Hills,* 42–44, argues that reform was a false issue intended to block secession. On the whole, Curry's argument is more convincing.

74. Ibid., 3:170–71, 513–14.

75. Ibid., 3:515–19.

76. Ibid., 3:271–91, 294–369; Abraham Lincoln, Springfield, Ill., to William Ballard Preston, Apr. 20, 1849, May 16, 1849, Preston Family Papers, VHS; Abraham Lincoln to William Ballard Preston, Alexander H. H. Stuart, and George W. Randolph, Apr. 13, 1861, in *Collected Works of Abraham Lincoln,* 4:329–31; Crofts, *Reluctant Confederates,* 308–13; Stampp, *And the War Came,* 283–86; J. G. Randall, *Lincoln the President: Springfield to Gettysburg* (New York: Dodd, Mead, 1945), 1:324–44.

77. Current, *Lincoln and the First Shot,* 131–38; *The* [Christiansburg] *New Star,* Apr. 13, 1861 J. B. Jones, *A Rebel War Clerk's Diary at the Confederate States Capitol,* ed. Howard Swiggett (New York: Old Hickory, 1935), 16–18; R. K. Thompson, Princeton, Va., to John Letcher, Apr. 18, 1861, Letters Received, Governor's Office, Executive Department, VSL.

78. *Journal of Acts and Proceedings,* 3:732.

79. Ibid., 3:676–764; Crofts, *Reluctant Confederates,* 313–34.

80. James C. Taylor, Christiansburg, Va., to John Letcher, Apr., 15, 1861, Letters Received, Governor's Office, Executive Department, VSL.

81. John Apperson Diaries, Apr. 16, 1861, Apperson Family Papers, VPI.

82. Harvy Black to Fellow Citizens, Apr. 17, 1861, Harvy Black Correspondence, VPI.

83. Jones, *Rebel War Clerk's Diary,* 20–22; *Journal of Acts and Proceedings,* 4:3–183; Crofts, *Reluctant Confederates,* 316–22; Current, *Lincoln and the First Shot,* 162; Curry, *House Divided,* 34; Moore, *Banner in the Hills,* 44–46; Shanks, *Secession Movement,* 205–8. See the last three works for more discussion of the creation of West Virginia.

84. S. A. Buckingham, Copper Valley, Floyd County, Va., to John Letcher, Apr. 30, 1861, Letters Received, Governor's Office, Executive Department, VSL. See also the *Richmond Enquirer,* Apr. 30, 1861; and Bosang, *Memoirs,* 3.

85. The best source for gauging secession ardor in Southwest Virginia is the collection of Letters Received, Governor's Office, Executive Department, VSL, for the spring and summer of 1861. Letters written in April that dealt with the valley subregion's support for secession include D. M. Cloyd, Newbern, Va., to John Letcher, Apr. 21, 1861; P. H. Hale, Wytheville, Va., to John Letcher, Apr. 20, 1861; W. K. Heiskell, et al., to John Letcher, Apr. 22, 1861; J. F. Pre-

ston, Christiansburg, Va., to John Echols, Apr. 23, 1861; and J. T. Withers, Newbern, Va., to John Letcher, Apr. 18, 1861. Also consult these telegrams: W. W. Blackford, Abingdon, Va., to William C. Jones, Apr. 23, 1861; W. E. Jones, Abingdon, Va., to John Letcher, Apr. 18, 1861; A. C. Moore, Wytheville, Va., to John Echols, Apr. 23, 1861; A. G. Pendleton, Wytheville, Va., to John Letcher, Apr. 18, 1861; and John F. Terry, Bristol,Tenn., to John Letcher, Apr. 19, 1861. See also the *Richmond Enquirer,* Apr. 27, 1861; Bosang, *Memoirs,* 3; Shanks, *Secession Movement,* 208–9; Stevenson, *Increase in Excellence,* 90; and Summers, *History,* 513.

86. Telegram, R. T. Preston, Christiansburg, Va., to John Letcher, Apr. 19, 1861, Letters Received, Governor's Office, Executive Department, VSL.

87. Bosang, *Memoirs,* 3–4.

88. Marion Mathews, Louisburg (*sic*), Va., to John Letcher, Apr. 19, 1861, Letters Received, Governor's Office, Executive Department, VSL.

89. Henry M. Mathews, Lewisburg, Va., to John Letcher, Apr. 21, 1861, Letters Received, Governor's Office, Executive Department, VSL. For other indications of prosecession sentiment in the plateau, see these letters in the same collection: Charles L. Crockett, Wytheville, Va., to "Dear General," Apr. 22, 1861; R. F. Dennis, Lewisburg, Va., to John Letcher, Apr. 23, 1861; James P. Kelly, Tazewell Court House, Va., to W. H. Richardson, Apr. 28, 1861; L. H. N. Salyer, Wise Court House, Va., to John Letcher, Apr. 23, 1861; A. W. Smith, Wise Court House, Va., to John Letcher, Apr. 22, 1861; W. H. Syme, Lewisburg, Va., to John Letcher, Apr. 25, 1861. See also the *Richmond Enquirer,* May 14, 1861; Luther F. Addington, *The Story of Wise County (Virginia)* (Wise County, Va.: Centennial Committee and School Board of Wise County, Va., 1956), 98, 109; Barrett, *Russell County,* 12; *The Heritage of Russell County, Virginia, 1786–1986,* (Marceline, Mo., 1985), 1:354–55; Kyle McCormick, *The Story of Mercer County* (Charleston, W.Va.: Charleston, 1957), 21–23; Tim McKinney, *The Civil War in Fayette County, West Virginia* (Charleston: Pictorial Histories, W.Va., 1988), 3, 11; Morton, *History of Monroe County,* 151, 156–58, 423–60; Pendleton, *Tazewell County,* 606, 638–54; J. T. Peters and H. B. Carden, *History of Fayette County, West Virginia* (Charleston, W.Va.: Jarrett, 1926), 213–42.

90. Thomas Mathews, Gauley Bridge, Fayette County, Va., to John Letcher, Apr. 30, 1861, Letters Received, Governor's Office, Executive Department, VSL.

91. John A. Campbell, Abingdon, Va., to Col. F. H. Smith, May 5, 1861; J. B. Hamilton, Hawk's Nest, Fayette County, Va., to Col. Tompkins, May 6, 1861; Thomas M. Harris, Blacksburg, Va., to John Letcher, May 4, 1861; James H. Henning, Lafayette, Va., to David Edmundson, May 28, 1861; James L. White, Abingdon, Va., to Col. F. H. Smith, May 4, 1861; James S. White et al., Abingdon, Va., to John Letcher, May 1, 1861, all in Letters Received, Governor's Office, Executive Department, VSL; D. W. L. Charlton, Christiansburg, Va., to Oliver H. P. Carden, May 23, 1861, Charlton Family Papers, VPI; Emma Edie, Christiansburg, to John C. Wade, May 23, 1861, Wade Family of Montgomery County, Virginia, Papers, VHS.

92. RG 233, Case 13473, NA. See also Case 8829.

93. George W. Eakle, White Sulphur Springs, Va., to John Letcher, Apr. 27, 1861, Letters Received, Governor's Office, Executive Department, VSL; Record Group 217, Records of the U.S. General Accounting Office, Third Auditor of the Treasury, Allowed Claims of the Southern Claims Commission, Cases 2434 and 2995, NA, Cited hereafter as RG 217; RG 233, Cases 15019 and 17764;

NA; Barrett, *Russell County,* 20; *Heritage of Russell County,* 354–55; Hila Appleton Richardson, "Raleigh County, West Virginia, in the Civil War," *WVH* 10 (Apr. 1949): 227–29.

94. A. F. Henderson, Wise Court House, Va., to John Letcher, May 7, 1861, Letters Received, Governor's Office, Executive Department, VSL.

95. P. F. Caldwell, Lewisburg, Va., to John Letcher, Apr. 17, 1861, Letters Received, Governor's Office, Executive Department, VSL.

96. United States War Department, *War of the Rebellion, A Compilation of the Official Records of the Union and Confederate Armies* (Washington: Government Printing Office, 1881–1901), ser. 1, 2:955–56, cited hereafter as *OR.*

97. Martha J. Gilmer to Dear Brothers, July 26, 1861, Gilmer Family Papers (microfilm), UVA.

98. Mary Eliza Caperton, White Thorn, to George H. Caperton, May 9, 14, 20, 31, 1861, Caperton Family Papers, VHS. Information on the Price family's unionist sentiments can also be confirmed in RG 233, Case 12049, and in RG 217, Case 19944, NA.

99. C. J. Noel, Wytheville, Va., to John Letcher, May 6, 1861, Letters Received, Governor's Office, Executive Department, VSL; D. W. L Charlton, Christiansburg, Va., to Oliver H. P. Carden, May 23, 1861, Charlton Family Papers, VPI. See also the *Richmond Enquirer,* June 11, 1861; William Ballard Preston to William H. Linkous, May 4, 1861, Preston Family Papers, VHS; and John Echols, Union, Va., to George Henry Caperton, May 10, 1861, Caperton Family Papers, VHS; *OR,* ser. 1, 2:291–93, 981, 1011; ser. 1, 5:152; RG 217, Case 13468 and RG 233, Cases 3491, 5862, 7742, 9127, 14405, NA; Ambler, *History of West Virginia,* 338; and his *Sectionalism in Virginia,* 213–14; Curry, *A House Divided,* 50–52, 141–47; Rable, *Civil Wars,* 43–72.

100. John Echols, Union, Va., to George Henry Caperton, May 10, 1861, Caperton Family Papers, VHS.

101. Mary Eliza Caperton, White Thorn, to George H. Caperton, May 31, 1861, Caperton Family Papers, VHS.

102. S. L. Walton, Camp Lee, Lynchburg, Va., to My Dear Friends, July 14, 1861, S. L. Walton Letters, VPI. For comparison, see Martin Crawford, "Confederate Volunteering and Enlistment in Ashe County, North Carolina, 1861–1862," *CWH* 37 (Mar. 1991): 29–50.

Chapter 6: "Our Land in Every Part Groaning"

1. James I. Robertson, *The Stonewall Brigade* (Baton Rouge: Louisiana State University Press, 1963), 35–45; McPherson, *Battle Cry of Freedom,* 339–46.

2. Robertson, *Stonewall Brigade,* 10–22, 35–45, 248–51.

3. For the later activities of the Stonewall Brigade, see Robertson, *Stonewall Brigade,* 51–241. The Civil War in Southwest Virginia is "forgotten," I argue, in the sense that very little has been written about it in comparison to other aspects of the conflict. Only in 1985 did Gary C. Walker publish the first book on the wider subject, *The War in Southwest Virginia, 1861–1865* (Roanoke, Va.: A&W Enterprise, 1985), and it is concerned largely with military operations in what I have called the valley subregion. Good secondary works that deal with the region's war in part include Howard Rollins McManus, *The Battle of Cloyds Mountain: The Virginia and Tennessee Railroad Raid, April 29–May 19, 1864* (Lynchburg, Va.: H. E. Howard, 1989); George Ellis Moore, *A Banner in the Hills:*

West Virginia's Statehood (New York: Appleton-Century-Crofts, 1963), despite is Amblerian viewpoint, and especially T. Harry Williams, *Hayes of the Twenty-Third: The Civil War Volunteer Officer* (New York: Alfred A. Knopf, 1965). See also Gary W. Gallagher "Home Front and Battlefield: Some Recent Literature Relating to Virginia and the Confederacy," *VMHB* 98 (Apr. 1990): 153–54.

The broad estimate of 15,000 Southwest Virginians in uniform is based on information from the following volumes in H. E. Howard's Virginia Regimental Histories Series: Lee A Wallace, Jr., *A Guide to Virginia Military Organizations, 1861–65*, 2d ed. (Lynchburg, Va., 1986); John Perry Alderman, *29th Virginia Infantry* (Lynchburg, Va., 1989), 60, 75–76; Keith S. Bohannon, *The Giles, Alleghany and Jackson Artillery* (Lynchburg, Va., 1990), 98–99; John D. Chapla, *48th Virginia Infantry* (Lynchburg, Va., 1989), 95; Jack L. Dickinson, *8th Virginia Cavalry* (Lynchburg, Va., 1986), 61–62; Ralph White Gunn, *24th Virginia Infantry* (Lynchburg, Va., 1987), 59, 65–67; Rankin, *37th Virginia Infantry,* 94–95; Susan A. Riggs, *21st Virginia Infantry* (Lynchburg, Va., 1990); James I. Robertson, *4th Virginia Infantry,* 2d ed. (Lynchburg, Va., 1982), 34–35 ; and two volumes by J. L. Scott, *Lowry's, Bryan's and Chapman's Batteries of Virginia Artillery* (Lynchburg, Va., 1988), 23, 61, 95, 98; and *45th Virginia Infantry* (Lynchburg, Va., 1989), 54. Of units composed primarily of Southwest Virginians, only the Fiftieth, Fifty-Fourth, and Sixty-Third Virginia Infantry Regiments currently are unrepresented in the series at this date.

4. Escott, *After Secession,* 94–133. This chapter's debt to Escott should be obvious. In addition to *After Secession,* I also have drawn on Escott's *Many Excellent People: Power and Privilege in North Carolina, 1850–1900* (Chapel Hill: University of North Carolina Press, 1985), and, with Jeffrey J. Crow, "The Social Order and Violent Disorder: An Analysis of North Carolina in the Revolution and the Civil War," *JSH* 52 (Aug. 1986): 373–402. Tillson, "Localist Roots," 387–404, links Escott's ideas to Revolutionary Southwest Virginia. I suspect that Tillson's findings on communities during the Revolution may hold true as well for the Civil War period.

5. *Journal of the House of Delegates of the State of Virginia, For the Adjourned Session, 1863* (Richmond, Va.: William F. Ritchie, 1863), 36; Turner, "Virginia Southwestern Railroad System," 470–79.

6. William Ballard Preston, Smithfield, to William Linkous, May 4, 1861, Preston Family Papers, VHS; Milton W. Humphreys, "Last Days of the Army in Southwest Virginia," *SHSP* (Jan.–Dec. 1905): 345–46; Barrett, *Russell County.*

7. *OR,* ser. 1, 33: 1065–66, 1093, 1112, 1123–24; James H. Gilmore, et al., Marion, Va., to William Smith, Feb. 29, 1864, Letters Received, Governor's Office, Executive Papers, VSL; J. Stoddard Johnson, "Sketches of Operations of General John C. Breckinridge. No. 3—Conclusion," *SHSP* 7 (Aug. 1879): 386.

8. James R. Johnston, Bristol, Tenn., to E. C. Johnston, Dec. 2, 1862, Johnston-Railey Papers, UVA.

9. See for example *OR,* ser. 1, 7:883–85.

10. William Kohler, "The Lead Mines," 21–22 (typescript), Kohler Papers, UVA; Johnston, "Breckinridge," 386; and these letters in the Richard W. Sanders and John W. Greene Papers and Notebooks, Duke: J. R. Anderson & Co., per F. T. Glasgow, Richmond, Va., to J. W. Greene & Co., Dec. 2, 1861; J. W. Green & Co., Richmond, Va., to Josiah Gorgas, Mar. 31, 1862; Josiah Gorgas to J. W. Green & Co., May 31, 1862; Thomas A. Mitchell, Wytheville, Va., to J. W. Green & Co., June 1, 1862; J. M. St.John, Richmond, Va., to J. W. Green

& Co., Jan. 19, 1863; Richard Morton, Richmond, Va., to J. W. Green & Co., Apr. 9, 1863; and "List of Hands Employed by J. W. Green & Co.," 1863. See also Paul D. Escott, "'The Cry of the Sufferers': The Problem of Welfare in the Confederacy," *CWH* 23 (Sept. 1977): 228–40.

11. James R. Johnston, Bristol, Tenn., to E. C. Johnston, Oct. 30, 1861, Jan. 3, Dec. 2, 1862, Johnston-Railey Papers, UVA; Mrs. ——— Gage, Wythe, Va., to Lucy Young, Sept. 15, 1862, William D. Simpson Papers, SHC; Johnston, "Breckinridge," 386; Ella Lonn, *Salt as a Factor in the Confederacy* (New York: Walter Neale, 1933), 26–28, 59, 68, 114, 154; Charles W. Ramsdell, *Behind the Lines in the Southern Confederacy,* ed. Wendell H. Stephenson (Baton Rouge: Louisiana State University Press, 1944), 70–71.

12. Jacob Dolson Cox, *Military Reminiscences of the Civil War,* v. 1, *April 1861–November 1863* (New York: Charles Scribners' Sons, 1900), 144–45; Bruce Catton, *Terrible Swift Sword,* v. 2. *The Centennial History of the Civil War* (Garden City, N.J.: Doubleday, 1963), 46; Striplin, *Norfolk and Western,* 41; Williams, *Hayes,* 104–5.

13. Cox, *Military Reminiscences,* 144.

14. *OR,* ser. 1, 2:2–3, 44–49, 64–73, 193–203, 753, 762, 763, Curry, *House Divided,* 55–68, McPherson, *Battle Cry of Freedom,* 299–302.

15. *OR,* ser. 1, 2:288–93, 908, 986–1011, *OR,* ser. 1, 5:116, 123, 127, 150–58, 605, 766–69, 773–74, 779–81; Leonidas Baugh, Camp Jackson near Wytheville, Va., to Lizzy Baugh, July 10, 13, 1861, Baugh Family Papers, UVA; Charles L. Crockett, Bowlingreen, to William Ballard Preston, Preston Family Papers, VHS; Cox, *Military Reminiscences,* 144; C. A. Fudge, GreenBrier in Lewis County, to Pa, Aug. 8, 1861, Civil War Correspondence, 1861–64 (microfilm), WVU; R. E. Lee, Huntersville, Va., to My Dear Wife, Aug. 4, 1861, and Lee to Misses Annie and Agnes Lee, Aug. 29, 1861, in *The Wartime Papers of Robert E. Lee,* ed. Clifford Dowdey (Boston: Little, Brown, 1961), 61–62, 67, Moore, *Banner in the Hills,* 101–4.

16. Henry Heth, *The Memoirs of Henry Heth,* ed. by James L. Morrison, Jr. (Westport, Conn.: Greenwood, 1974), 152, 155.

17. *OR,* ser. 1, 5:128–29, 146–65, 250–58, 841–45; Heth, *Memoirs,* 154–55; Rutherford Hayes, Gauley River, to Lucy Hayes, Sept. 11, 1861, *Diary and Letters of Rutherford Birchard Hayes. Nineteenth President of the United States,* ed. Charles Richard Williams, v. 2, *1861–1865* (1922; reprint, New York: Kraus, 1971), 90–91. A good secondary source is Terry Lowry, *September Blood: The Battle of Carnifex Ferry* (Charleston, W.Va.: Pictorial Histories, 1985). See also Moore, *Banner in the Hills,* 104–10, and Curry, *A House Divided,* 65–66.

18. *OR,* ser. 1, 5:955, 975, 1009; Gage, Wythe, Va., to Lucy Young, Dec. 25, 1861, William D. Simpson Papers, SHC; J. L. Scott, *36th Virginia Infantry* (Lynchburg, Va.: H. E. Howard, 1987), 9–11. Lee left Southwest Virginia with only two accomplishments, a new beard, which not surprisingly came in gray, and affection for a Greenbrier County gelding he eventually would buy and rename Traveler.

19. Rutherford Hayes to Lucy Hayes, Jan. 12, 1862, *Diary and Letters,* 184.

20. *OR,* ser. 1, 7:40–45, 702, 722, 729–30; *OR,* ser. 1. v. 10, pt. 2, p. 344; F. H. Mason, *The Forty-Second Ohio Infantry: A History of the Organization and Services of that Regiment in the War of the Rebellion. . . .* (Cleveland: Cobb, Andrews, 1876), 84–87; Allan Peskin, *Garfield* (Kent, Ohio: Kent State University Press, 1978), 106–7; Alderman, *29th Virginia,* 1–13.

21. *OR,* ser. 1, 7:47–58, 61; James A. Garfield, Louisville, Ky., to My Dear Harry, Dec. 17, 1861; Garfield, Paintsville, Ky., to My Dear Crete, Jan. 13, 1862; and Garfield, Paintsville, Ky., to Mother, Jan. 26, 1862, in *The Wild Life of the Army: Civil War Letters of James A. Garfield,* Frederick D. Williams (Lansing: Michigan State University Press, 1964), 49, 54–61; Peskin, *Garfield,* 101–3, 108–21.

22. James A. Garfield, Camp Buell, to My Dear Smith, Feb. 15, 1862, in *Wild Life of the Army,* 70.

23. *OR,* ser. 1, 7:53, 57–59, 866, 879, 883–85; James R. Johnston, Bristol, Tenn., to E. C. Johnston, Oct. 30, 1861, Jan. 3, 1862, Johnston-Rainey Papers, UVA.

24. *OR,* ser. 1, 5:674; *OR.,* ser. 1, v. 10, pt. 1, pp. 3, 36–40; *OR,* ser. 1, v. 10, pt. 2, pp. 321–23, 349.

25. *OR,* ser. 1, v. 10, pt. 1, p. 34.

26. *OR,* ser. 1, 5:674; *OR,* ser. 1, 7:34–42; *OR,* ser. 1, v. 10, pt. 2, pp. 360; *OR,* ser. 1, v. 12, pt. 3, p. 58; James W. Sage, Lee County, Va., to Dear Aunt and Cousins, Feb. 7, 1863, in Fields, *Carroll County,* 126–29; Escott, *Many Excellent People,* 52–83; Escott and Crow, "Social Order and Violent Disorder," 376. Marshall characteristically may have been exaggerating.

27. C. A. Fudge, Sweet Springs, Va., to Harriet Fudge, July 26, 1861, Civil War Correspondence, 1861–64 (microfilm), WVU; Scott, *45th Virginia,* 92.

28. Leonidas Baugh, Camp at Meadow Bluff, to Lizzy Baugh, Sept. 23, 1861, Baugh Family Papers, UVA.

29. Rutherford Hayes Diary, Jan. 2, 3, 15, 1862; and Hayes, Camp Union, Fayetteville, Va., to Uncle, Dec. 19, 1861, in *Diary in Letters,* 163, 173–75, 187–88.

30. Rutherford Hayes Diary, Jan. 2, 1862, *Diary and Letters* 173.

31. Rutherford Hayes Diary, Jan. 8, 30, 1862, in *Diary and Letters,* 182, 196–97; Leonidas Baugh to Lizzy Baugh, Oct. 21, 25, 1861, Baugh Family Papers, UVA; Susanna Waddell Diary, Sept. 12, 1863, 20, SHC; Boyd B. Stutler, *West Virginia in the Civil War,* 2d ed. (Charleston, W.Va.: Educational Foundation, 1966), 162–67.

32. Rutherford Hayes, Camp Union, Fayetteville, Va., to Mother Nov. 25, 1861, in *Diary and Letters,* 146–47. Hayes's harsh statements about the region's population elsewhere in his diary and letters, however, suggest that he actually may have been less sympathetic that he implied to his mother. Women's plight in general is discussed in Rable, *Civil Wars,* 74–103.

33. Rutherford Hayes, Birch River Between Summersville and Sutton, Va., to Uncle, Sept. 14, 1861, in *Diaries and Letters,* 92–93.

34. *OR,* ser. 1, v. 12, pt. 3, 194; Chapla, *48th Virginia,* 86; Rutherford Hayes Diary, Dec. 7, 1861, in *Diary and Letters,* 156. See also the diary entry for Jan. 3, 1862, 176.

35. *OR,* ser. 1, 2:1012, 5:771.

36. Ibid., v. 12, pt. 3, 59.

37. Leonidas Baugh, Jones, to Lizzy Baugh, Oct. 25, 1861, Baugh Family Papers, UVA. The best recent source on the guerrilla conflict within the larger Civil War is Michael Fellman, *Inside War: The Guerrilla Conflict in Missouri during the American Civil War* (New York: Oxford University Press, 1989). Fellman's study informs this work's examination of the guerrilla war in Southwest Virginia throughout. See esp. 23–25, 52–65. Other important sources dealing with

the guerrilla conflict in and around the southern mountains are Stephen V. Ash, "Sharks in an Angry Sea: Civilian Resistance and Guerrilla Warfare in Occupied Middle Tennessee, 1862–1865," *THQ* 45 (Fall 1986): 217–29; Dunn, *Cades Cove,* 123–41; James B. Martin, "Black Flag over the Bluegrass: Guerrilla Warfare in Kentucky, 1863–1865," *RKHS* 86 (Autumn 1988): 352–75; Mann, "Family Group," 379–89; and Philip Shaw Paludan, *Victims: A True Story of the Civil War* (Knoxville: University of Tennessee Press, 1981), esp. 62–78.

38. James A. Garfield, Headquarters, Eighteenth Brigade, Camp Buell, to My Dear Harry, Feb. 12, 1862, in *Wild Life of the Army,* 65–66.

39. Ibid., 66.

40. Mason, *Forty-Second Ohio,* 49, 88–89.

41. James D. Fox, *A True Story of the Reign of Terror in Southern Illinois. . . .* (Aurora, Ill.: J. D. Fox, 1884), 19–30.

42. Rutherford Hayes Diary, Jan. 15, 1862, in *Diary and Letters,* 187.

43. *Journal of the House of Delegates of the State of Virginia, For the Extra Session, 1862* (Richmond, Va.: William F. Ritchie, 1862), 33, 40, 44. Cox, *Military Reminiscences,* 421–24; George Crook, *General George Crook: His Autobiography,* ed. Martin F. Schmitt (Norman, Okla.: University of Oklahoma Press, 1986), 87; William Keany, Camp Pierpont, Va., to W. S. Rosecrans, Aug. 20, 1861; L. Ruffner, Kanawha Salines, to Rosecrans, Oct. 26, 1861; and Rosecrans, Gauley Mountain, to George B. McClellan, Nov. 19, 1861, all in RG 393, Letters Received, Mountain Department, NA; W. S. Rosecrans, Wheeling, to F. H. Pierpont, Jan. 28, 1862, RG 393, Letters Sent, Mountain Department, NA; Fellman, *Inside War,* 81–91, 97–101, 115–27. For a preliminary discussion of the relationship between federals' perceptions of mountaineers and the resulting stereotype, see Kenneth W. Noe, "'Appalachia's' Civil War Genesis: Southwest Virginia as Depicted by Northern and European Writers, 1825–1865," *WVH* 50 (1991): 91–108.

44. L. Ruffner, Kanawha Salines, to Genl. Rosecrans, Oct. 26, 1861, RG 393, Letters Received, Mountain Department, NA.

45. William Keany, Camp Pierpont, Va., to W. S. Rosecrans, Aug. 25, 1861, RG 393, Letters Received, Mountain Department, NA.

46. Fellman, *Inside War,* 81–115, 123–27.

47. Crook, *General George Crook,* 87–88; Reid Mitchell. *Civil War Soldiers* (New York: Viking, 1988), 134–35.

48. Ibid. See also Oliver Parker, Camp Summersville, to Brother, Apr. 22, 1862, v. 1, Civil War Bound Notebook Series, Roy Bird Cook Collection, WVU; Fellman, *Inside War,* 29–38, 158, 167; and Williams, *West Virginia,* 64–67.

49. Sarah A. Preston, White [?], to Harriet Caperton, Dec. 10, 1861, William Gaston Caperton Family Papers (microfilm), WVU.

Chapter 7: "What Will Become of the Poor and Widows?"

1. Henry Kyd Douglas, *I Rode with Stonewall* (1940; reprint, New York: Fawcett, 1961), 144.

2. *OR,* ser. 1, v. 10, pt. 2, p. 345; Peskin, *Garfield,* 129.

3. *OR,* ser. 1. v. 10, pt. 2, pp. 345, 347.

4. Ibid., ser. 1, v. 10, pt. 1, pp. 3, 33–35; *OR,* ser. 1, v. 10, pt. 2, pp. 345–47, 374, 444–49, 504, 521–22, 603–4; *OR,* ser. 1, v. 12, pt. 3, pp. 921–22, 927, 938; *OR,* ser. 1, v. 16, pt. 1, pp. 958, 991, 1012, 1020, 1089, 1145; *OR,* ser. 1, v. 16,

pt. 2, pp. 535, 633, 650, 742–935; Peskin, *Garfield,* 129–31; Charles H. Gilmer, Castlewood, Russell County, Va., to Cummings Gilbert, Sept. 2, 1862, Gilmer Family Papers (microfilm), UVA.

5. *OR,* ser. 1, v. 12, pt. 3, pp. 8, 10–11, 24, 34–35, 829–39, 855, 861, 868–70, 873; Edwin Attarman, Camp Bloody Run, to Harriet Fudge, Mar. 23, 1862, Civil War Correspondence, 1861–64 (microfilm), WVU.

6. *OR,* ser. 1, v. 12, pt. 3, p. 97.

7. Ibid., v. 12, pt. 3, pp. 53–57, 110–14, 128, 132, 137; Rutherford Hayes Diary, Apr. 24, May 1, 3, 1862, in *Diary and Letters,* 235, 238–40, 247–48.

8. Rutherford Hayes, Princeton, Va., to E. P. Scammon, May 5, 1862, in *Diary and Letters,* 251; *OR,* ser. 1, v. 12, pt. 3, pp. 137–40.

9. *OR,* ser. 1, v. 12, pt. 3, pp. 157–58, 176–77, 182–83, 193, 198–206.

10. Ibid., 193, 204–5, 209, 228, 242, 255, 901–3; Rutherford Hayes Diary, May 24, 1862, in *Diary and Letters,* 277; Edwin A. Harman, Salt Sulphur Springs, Va., to Harriet Fudge, May 25, 1862, Civil War Correspondence, 1861–64 (microfilm), WVU; Oliver Parker, Lewisburg, Va., to Brother, May 26, [1862], vol. 1, Civil War Bound Notebooks Series, Roy Bird Cook Collection, WVU; A. S. to Sallie Patton, May 23, 1862, Sallie Patton Papers, also in the Roy Bird Cook Collection, WVU.

11. *OR,* ser. 1, v. 12, pt. 3, pp. 228, 288, 320, 442, 460, 551.

12. Rutherford Hayes, Flat Top Mountain, to Lucy Hayes, June 3, 1862, in *Diary and Letters,* 285.

13. *OR,* ser. 1, v. 27, pt. 2, pp. 941–50.

14. Ibid., 941.

15. Rutherford Hayes, Camp White, to Lucy Hayes, July 24, 1863, in *Diary and Letters,* 422.

16. Crook, *General George Crook,* 90; G. C. Forsinger, Abingdon, Va., to Albert Ball, Sept. 17, 1864, Letters Received, Governor's Office, Executive Department, VSL; Fox, *True History,* 20–24, 28–29; Rutherford Hayes Diary, May 7, 1862, in *Diary and Letters,* 254; S. B. Hern, Camp near Pisgah Church, Va., to Sallie Patton, Feb. 24, 1864, Sallie Patton Papers, Roy Bird Cook Collection, WVU; James S. Peery, Camp Delusion, to Maria Witten, Jan. 1, 1863, in Robert Leroy Hilldrup, "The Romance of the Man in Gray—Including the Love Letters of Captain James S. Peery, Forty Fifth Virginia Regiment, C.S.A.," *WVH* 22 (July 1961): 229–30; Oliver Parker, Meadow Bluff, Greenbrier County, Va., to Father, July 29, 1862, v. 1, Civil War Bound Notebook Series, Roy Bird Cook Collection, WVU; C. B. Thomas, Marion Magnetic Furnace, to C. F. Pfohl, Aug. 10, 1863, Christian Thomas Pfohl Papers (microfilm), SHC; Susanna Waddell Diary, v. 1, Aug. 28–Sept. 2, Sept. 11, 16–17, 1863, Dec. 16, 1863; 2:6, SHC; J. V. Young, Meadow Bluff, to Wife, May 21, 1864, and Young, Munger's Mills, to Emma, May 24, 1864, Young Civil War Papers, Bound Notebook Series, Roy Bird Cook Collection, WVU; *OR,* ser. 1, v. 10, pt. 2, p. 448; Ibid., ser. 1, v. 12, pt. 3, pp. 3, 34, 38, 59, 140, 194, 830; Patricia Givens Johnson, *The United States Army Invades the New River Valley, May 1864* (Christiansburg, Va.: Walpa, 1986), 58, 87–88; Shanks, "Disloyalty," 118–26.

17. *Journal for the Extra Session, 1862,* 26.

18. Ginger Wade to John C. Wade, May 13, 1863, Wade Family of Montgomery County, Virginia, Papers, VHS.

19. Mollie Black, Blacksburg, Va., to Harvy Black, Nov. 29, 1863, Harvy Black Correspondence, Black Family Papers, VPI. See also Edwin A. Harman, Camp

Near Saltville, Va., to Harriet Fudge, Nov. 11, 1863, Civil War Correspondence, 1861–64 (microfilm), WVU.

20. *OR*, ser. 1, v. 12, pt. 3, 862; *Journal of the House of Delegates of the State of Virginia, for the Session of 1861–62* (Richmond, Va.: William F. Ritchie, 1861), 85, 94, 96, 104, 128, 161, 175; "Choctaw", Saltville, Va., to Little Nannie, June 7, 1863, and Mar. 6, 1864, Anne Leftwich and William King Correspondence, UVA; Fox, *True History,* 29; Mrs. —— Gage, Wythe, Va., to Lucy Young, Sept. 15, 1862, William D. Simpson Papers, SHC; Nancy Hunt, Mountain Cove, Va., to Mr. and Mrs. J. H. Hoppings, Dec. 7, 1862, v. 1, Civil War Bound Notebooks Series, Roy Bird Cook Collection, WVU; James R. Johnston, Bristol, Tenn., to E. C. Johnston, Dec. 2, 1862, Johnston-Railey Papers, UVA; Kohler, "The Lead Mines," 21–22; Susanna Waddell Diary, v. 1, Oct. 2, 1862, 12; Escott, *Many Excellent People,* 52; Paludan, *Victims,* 81–82; Ramsdell, *Behind the Lines,* 43, 64; Shanks, "Disloyalty," 122–23.

21. Mrs. —— Gage, Wythe Va., to Dear Cousin, Sept. 15, 1862, William D. Simpson Papers, SHC.

22. *Journal of the House of Delegates of the State of Virginia, for the Called Session of 1863* (Richmond, Va.: William F. Ritchie, 1863), iii, xii–xiii, 5, 11, 15, 17, 22–26, 36, 39, 45, 49; *Journal of 1861–62,* 15, 204, 312–13; *Journal for the Extra Session 1862,* 11, 13, 18–19, 21–25; Boney, *John Letcher,* 169–70; Lonn, *Salt,* 68, 78, 114, 139–40. The quote is from Charles C. Campbell, Bristol, Tenn., to the Southern Claims Commission, June 2, 1879, Record Group 56, General Records of the Department of the Treasury, Records of the Commissioners of Claims (Southern Claims Commission) 1871–80, Microfilm 87, National Archives, Washington, D.C., hereafter cited as RG 56.

23. *Journal of 1863,* ix–xii; Boney, *Letcher,* 170–73; Lonn, *Salt,* 38–40, 115–16, 140–45, 154–55; Ramsdell, *Behind the Lines,* 105.

24. *Journal of 1863,* 32, 39, 50–51, 171, 183, 187, 213; Order of County Court of Russell County, Virginia, Sept. 12, 1863; and Henry J. Fisher, Independence, Va., to G. W. Mumford, [Jan. 6, 1864?], in Letters Received, Governor's Office, Executive Papers, VSL; William E. Swear, Salt Sulphur Springs, Va., to Mr. Alexander, Apr. 3, 1863, William Gaston Caperton Papers (microfilm), WVU; *OR*, ser. 1, 33:1289; RG 233, Case 9127, NA; E. Merton Coulter, *The Confederate States of America, 1861–1865* (Baton Rouge: Louisiana State University Press, 1950), 7:178–80; Stephen E. Ambrose, "Yeoman Discontent in the Confederacy," *CWH* 8 (Sept. 1962): 262.

25. Henry J. Fisher, Independence, Va., to G. W. Mumford, Jan. 6, 1864[?]. Letters Received, Governor's Office, Executive Department, VSL.

26. The Letters Received, Governor's Office, Executive Department collection at the Virginia State Library contains many county court orders regarding their opposition to slave impressment. The collection includes "Virginia, At a Special Court, Continued and Held for the County of Giles, at the Court House, Thereof, on Monday the 13th Day of February 1864"; Montgomery County Court to William Smith, Feb. 6, 1864; "Order of County Court of Russell County," Sept. 12, 1863; "Order of County Court of Russell County Relative to Slaves to Work on Fortifications, Feb. 20, 1864; James H. Gilmore, et al., Marion, Va., to William Smith, Feb. 29, 1864; "At a Special Court at the County of Tazewell, Convened at the Court House on Friday, the 26th Day of February 1864"; William P. Cecil to William Smith, Mar. 21, 1864; "At a Court Held for Washington County the 6th Day of February 1864"; "Wythe County

Court Memorial," Feb. 23, 1864; F. H. Shores, Wythe County, Va., to William Smith, Apr. 4, 1864.

27. G. P. Cowan to ———, Feb. 11, 1864, Letters Received, Governor's Office, Executive Papers, VSL.

28. William P. Cecil to William Smith, Mar. 21, 1864, Letters Received, Governor's Office, Executive Department, VSL. The quotation was used by both Lovenia Wills and Owen Jones, two former Washington County slaves, in RG 217, cases 13467 and 13472, NA.

29. S. B. Hern, Camp Near Pisgah Church, Va., to Sallie Patton, Feb. 24, 1864, Sallie Patton Papers, Roy Bird Cook Collection, WVU.

30. G. C. Forsinger, Abingdon, Va., to Albert, Sept. 17, 1864, Letters Received, Governor's Office, Executive Department, VSL.

31. *Journal of the House of Delegates of the State of Virginia, For the Session of 1863–64* (Richmond, Va.: William F. Ritchie, 1863), 172; G. C. Forsinger, Abingdon, Va., to Albert, Sept. 17, 1864, and John Shannon, Saltville, Va., to William Smith, Jan. 6, 1864, both in Letters Received, Governor's Office, Executive Department, VSL; Charlie E. McCluer, Richmond, Va., to John C. Wade, Oct. 14, 1864, Wade Family of Montgomery County, Virginia, Papers, VHS; Oliver Parker, Carthage, Smyth County, Va., to Father, Feb. 6, 1863, v. 1, Civil War Bound Notebook Series, Roy Bird Cook Collection, WVU; S. A. Walton to Sefrins L. Walton, Nancy A. Walton, and Scenin A. Walton, Apr. 10, 1864, S. L. Walton Letters, VPI; RG 217, Cases 2993, 3453, and 3687; National Archives, Washington, D.C.; RG 233, Cases 4509 and 13891, NA; Frederick W. B. Hassler, "The Campaign in West Virginia, 1861 and 1862," *Historical Magazine* 6 (Dec. 1869): 355–56; Coulter, *Confederate States of America*, pp. 314–28; Escott, *After Secession*, 116–17; McKinney, *Southern Mountain Republicans*, 24–25; Shanks, "Disloyalty," 125–26.

32. *Journal For the Called Session, 1862,* viii–ix; *Journal for the Extra Session, 1862,* 15–19, 26–27; *OR,* ser. 1, v. 10, pt. 2, 411–12, 433, 765–66; *OR,* ser. 1, v. 12, pt. 3, pp. 910–11; C. M. Clarke, Camp Lyon, Mo., to Edwin C. Hewett, Feb. 19, 1862, Edwin C. Hewett Correspondence, IHS; Edwin A. Harman, Camp Bloody Run, to Harriet Fudge, Mar. 23, 1862, Civil War Correspondence, 1861–64 (microfilm), WVU; William H. Richardson, Richmond, Va., to David Edmundson, June 1862, Edmundson Family Papers, VHS; Boney, *Letcher*, 157, 164–65; Ramsdell, *Behind the Lines*, p. 54; Shanks, "Disloyalty," 119–20. Benjamin Franklin Cooling, *Forts Henry and Donelson: The Key to the Confederate Heartland* (Knoxville: University of Tennessee Press, 1987), is the best secondary account of that important campaign, although Cooling incorrectly refers to Floyd as John *Bell* Floyd throughout.

33. *OR,* ser. 1, v. 12, pt. 3, pp. 75, 83–85, 165–67; RG 393, General Orders #11, Mountain Department, Apr. 7, 1862, NA; Charles A. Fudge, Camp Dixie, to Harriet Fudge, Apr. 6, 1862, Civil War Correspondence, 1861–64 (microfilm), WVU; Rutherford Hayes Diary, Mar. 28, 1863, in *Diary and Letters*, 398; Nancy Hunt, Mountain Cove, Va., to Mr. and Mrs. J. H. Hoppings, Dec. 7, 1862; and Hunt to ———, Sept. 28, 1863, v. 1, Civil War Bound Notebooks Series, Roy Bird Cook Collection, WVU; RG 217, Case 2990, NA; Mason, *Forty-Second Ohio*, 81; William Davis Slease, *The Fourteenth Pennsylvania Cavalry in the Civil War: A History of the Fourteenth Pennsylvania Volunteer Cavalry from Its Organization until the Close of the Civil War, 1861–1865* (Pittsburgh: Art Engraving and Printing, 1915), 114; Waller, *Feud*, 2, 31; William E. Cox. "The Civil War Letters of

Laban Gwinn: A Union Refugee," *WVH* 43 (Spring 1982): 227–37; Johnson, *United States Army,* 81–82.

34. Nancy Hunt to ———, Sept. 28, 1863, vol. 1, Civil War Bound Notebook Series, Roy Bird Cook Collection, WVU. William C. Quantrill's Confederate raiders sacked Lawrence, Kansas, a month before Hunt's letter.

35. Milton Charlton, Rocky Gap, to Oliver H. P. Charlton, July 29, [1862?], Charlton Family Papers, VPI.

36. Milton Charlton, Rocky Gap, to Oliver H. P. Carden, July 29, [1862?], Charlton Family Papers, VPI; A. J. Hoback, Flathead, Floyd County, Va., to G. W. Mumford, Apr. 26, 1864, Letters Received, Governor's Office, Executive Department, VSL; R. E. Lee, Headquarters, Army of Northern Virginia, to Jefferson Davis, Aug. 17, 1863, in *Wartime Papers of R. E. Lee,* p. 591; Wise, *End of an Era,* 385–86; Edward A. Pollard, "The Virginia Tourist," *Lippincott's Monthly Magazine* 5 (May 1870), 494; Shanks, "Disloyalty," 124–25. The classic study of Civil War desertion is Ella Lonn, *Desertion during the Civil War* (New York: Century, 1928), see esp. 26, 62–64, as well as the map located on the flyleaf.

37. RG 217, Case 14402, NA.

38. *OR,* ser. 1, 33:1269–70; G. W. Cornest, Elk Creek, Va., to William Smith, Feb. 24, 1864, Letters Received, Governor's Office, Executive Department, VSL; Edwin A. Harman, Camp, 45th Regt., to Harriet Fudge, Jan. 4, 1863, Civil War Correspondence, 1861–64 (microfilm), WVU; Escott, *After Secession,* 132–33; Shanks, "Disloyalty," 124–25; Summers, *History of Southwest Virginia,* 529.

39. See Thomas B. Alexander and Richard E. Baringer, *The Anatomy of the Confederate Congress: A Study of the Influences of Member Characteristics on Legislative Voting Behavior, 1861–1865* (Nashville: Vanderbilt University Press, 1972), 141, 202, 285; and Wilfred Buck Yearns, *The Confederate Congress* (Athens: University of Georgia Press, 1960), 133, 211, 242, 244, for information on Southwest Virginia's Confederate legislators.

40. Nancy Hunt, Mountain Cove, Va., to ———, Sept. 28, 1863, v. 1, Civil War Bound Notebooks Series, Roy Bird Cook Collection, WVU.

41. *OR,* ser. 1, v. 32, pt. 3, pp. 245–46; *OR,* ser. 1, 33:758, 765–66, 827–29, 893, 911, 986, 1027–28; *OR,* ser. 1, 37:368–69; Crook, *General George Crook,* 114–15.

42. *OR,* ser. 1, 33:1107–10, 1124, 1130, 1136–38, 1141, 1155, 1172, 1210–11, 1296–97, 1302, 1305–11, 1317, 1319, 1322–24, 1334; *OR,* ser. 1, v. 37, pt. 1, pp. 712, 716, 718–19, 722.

43. Ibid., 8, 11–13, 16, 20, 44–46, 49, 68; E. C. Arthur, Springfield, Ohio, to D. M. Cloyd, Nov. 26, 1887, Cloyd Family Papers, VHS; J. W. Cracraft Journal, May 9–11, 1864, v. 1, Civil War Bound Notebooks Series, Roy Bird Cook Collection, WVU; Michael Egan, *The Flying Gray-Haired Yank; or, The Adventures of a Volunteer. . . .* (Philadelphia: Hubbard Brothers, 1888), 159–64; Rutherford Hayes Diary, May 9, 1864, in *Diary and Letters,* 456; Francis W. Obenchain, Chicago, Ill., to James W. Obenchain, Apr. 28, 1904, and n.d., Francis W. Obenchain Collection, IHS. The best secondary source is McManus, *Battle of Cloyd's Mountain,* see esp. 50–56. See also Johnson, *United States Army,* 4, 32, 39–43, 61–63, 84–85, and Williams, *Hayes,* 183.

44. *OR,* ser. 1, v. 37, pt. 1, pp. 10, 41–42.

45. Ibid., 42.

46. *OR,* ser. 1, v. 37, pt. 1, pp. 12–13, 18, 27–28, 42; Nancy Hunt, Mountain Cove, Va., to ———, May 29, 1864, Civil War Bound Notebooks Series,

and, J. V. Young, Meadow Bluff, Va., to Pauline Young, May 20, 1864, Young Civil War Papers, Roy Bird Cook Collection, WVU; Susanna Waddell Diary, 2:11–14, 19, 24, SHC; RG 233, Case 14616, NA; Johnson, *United States Army,* 57, 60, 87–88.

47. J. W. Cracraft Journal, June 1, 1864, v. 1, Civil War Bound Notebooks Series, Roy Bird Cook Collection, WVU.

48. Walker, *Eighteenth Regiment,* 271.

49. J. V. Young, Mungers Mills, Va., to Emma Young, May 24, 1864, Young Civil War Papers, Roy Bird Cook Collection, WVU.

50. *OR,* ser. 1, v. 39, pt. 1, pp. 234, 351, 552–67; Walker, *War in Southwest Virginia,* 160, 163; William C. Davis, "The Massacre at Saltville," *CWTI* 9 (Feb. 1971): 4–11, 43–48. Davis blames Ferguson's superior, Brigadier General Felix H. Robertson, for the massacre. Ferguson was executed in Oct., 1865.

51. *OR,* ser. 1, v. 39, pt. 1, pp. 885–93; *OR,* ser. 1, v. 40, pt. 1, pp. 808–9, 823, 876, 884, 896, 933, 951, 967–68, 992, 1073–74, 1083, 1104, 1129, 1164; *OR,* ser. 1, v. 41, pt. 1, p. 40; Summers, *History of Southwest Virginia,* 542–43.

52. *OR,* ser. 1, v. 40, pt. 1, pp. 808, 814. Most claims in RG 217 and RG 233, NA, involve horses and foodstuffs taken by Stoneman.

53. Samuel Clarke Farrar, *The Twenty-Second Pennsylvania Cavalry and the Ringgold Battalion 1861–1865* (Pittsburgh: Twenty-Second Pennsylvania Ringgold Cavalry Association, 1911), 246–51; Harriet Fudge, Green Meadows, Va., to Charles A. Fudge, Nov. 27, 1864, Civil War Correspondence 1861–64 (microfilm), WVU; Martha J. Gilmer, Cedar Grove, Va., to Brother, Jan. 15, 1865, Gilmer Family Papers (microfilm), UVA; Nathan Look to Parents, June 8, 1864, copied in Laura Look, Wyoming, N.Y., to Laura Lincoln, July 14, 1864, and Nathan Look, Wyoming, N.Y., to Laura Lincoln, Aug. 23, 1864, Lincoln-Look Family Papers, VPI; S. A. Walton to Sefrins L. Walton, Nancy A. Walton, and Scenin A. Walton, Apr. 10, 1864, S. L. Walton Letters, VPI; *OR,* ser. 1, v. 37, pt. 1, pp. 42, 740.

54. ——— to John Caperton, Apr. 9, 1865, William Gaston Caperton Family Papers (microfilm), WVU; William Smith, Jr., Richmond, Va. to Honorable Courts of the Counties, Cities, &c., Mar. 4, 1865, Letters Received, Governor's Office, Executive Department, VSL; RG 233, Case 13470, NA.

55. Susanna Waddell Diary, v. 2, June 30, 1864, p. 19, SHC.

56. [?] to My Dear John, "At Home," Apr. 9, 1865, William Gaston Caperton Family Papers (microfilm), WVU.

57. *OR,* ser. 1, v. 40, pt. 1, p. 824; James W. Walton to S. A. Walton, [Aug. 5?], 1864, and S.A, Walton to Sefrins L. Walton, Nancy A. Walton, Scenin A. Walton, Apr. 10, 1864, S. L. Walton Letters, VPI; Wise, *End of an Era,* 385–90; Johnson, *United States Army,* 103; Shanks, "Disloyalty," 134–35.

58. Joseph H. Wilson to Son, Mar. 17, 1865, S. L. Walton Letters, VPI.

59. RG 217, Case 14402, and RG 233, Cases 2001 and 14406, NA; William T. Auman and David D. Scarboro, "The Heroes of America in Civil War North Carolina," *NCHR* 58 (Autumn 1981): 327–63; "Virginia" to William Smith, Apr. 6, 1864, and A. J. Hoback, Flat Head, Floyd County, Va., to G. W. Mumford, Apr. 26, 1864, Letters Received, Governors Office, Executive Department, VSL; Kenneth W. Noe, "Red String Scare: Civil War Southwest Virginia and the Heroes of America," *NCHR* 69 (July 1992): 301–22. The quotation is from RG 233, Case 14406.

60. *OR,* ser. 4, 3:802–16; Barney, *Road to Secession,* 179–80.

61. *OR,* ser. 4, v.3, 804, 814–15.

62. Shanks, "Disloyalty," 134.

63. Frank L. Klement, *Dark Lanterns: Secret Political Societies, Conspiracies, and Treason Trials in the Civil War* (Baton Rouge: Louisiana State University Press, 1984).

64. *OR,* ser. 1, v.4, 805–6.

65. Ibid., 807–8.

66. Ibid., 808.

67. Auman and Scarboro, "Heroes of America," 363; McKinney, *Southern Mountain Republicans,* 28–29; Fields, *Grayson County,* 139, 142; Richard Lowe, *Republicans and Reconstruction in Virginia, 1856–70* (Charlottesville: University Press of Virginia, 1991), 74, 89, 127–28, 132.

68. Charles C. Campbell, Bristol, to Southern Claims Commission, Jan. 27, 1875, and Apr. 22, 1879; James L. Tompkins, Floyd Court House, Va., to Southern Claims Commission, Oct. 26, 1874; Frank Findlay, Abingdon, Va., to William H. beck, Feb. 7, 1873; "Special Commissioners, List of Those Notified This Day of Discontinuance of Their Authority and Functions From and After March 10, 1877," all in Record Group 56, General Records of the Department of the Treasury, Records of the Commissioners of Claims (Southern Claims Commission) 1871–80, Microfilm M87, National Archives, Washington, D.C.; Frank W. Klingberg, *The Southern Claims Commission* (Berkeley: University of California Press, 1955), 50:vii, 17–18, 55–57, 72, 157; Gary B. Mills, *Civil War Claims in the South: An Index of Damage Claims Filed before the Southern Claims Commission, 1871–1880* (Laguna Hills, Ca.: Aegean Park, 1980).

69. RG 233, Case 16144, NA; Klingberg, *Southern Claims Commission,* vii, 17–18, 55–57, 72, 157; *OR,* ser. 4, v.3, 806–9, 816; Mills, *Civil War Claims.*

70. RG 233, Case 2001, NA; Auman and Scarboro, "Heroes of America," 363; Klingberg, *Southern Claims Commission,* 157.

71. S. A. Walton to Sefrins L. Walton, Nancy A. Walton, Scenin A. Walton, Apr. 10, 1864, S. L. Walton Letters, VPI.

Epilogue

1. Bosang, *Memoirs,* 24.

2. Ibid., 24–25.

3. John Echols, Staunton, Va., to George Henry Caperton, July 12, 1866, Caperton Family Papers, VHS.

4. *Greenbrier Independent,* July 31, 1875, and "Roll of Chapman's Battery," and "Company B—Edgar's Battalion," Andrew N. Campbell Papers, WVU. Bosang, *Memoirs,* 25.

5. John L. Andriot, compiler and ed., *Population Abstract of the United States,* v. 1. Tables (McClean, Va.: Andriot, 1983), 821–26, 855–57. Dunn, *Cades Cove,* 140, discusses a similar situation, but the phenomenon overall remains unexplored.

6. Johnson, *United States Army,* 104–5.

7. Curry, *House Divided,* 149–52.

8. Ambler, *History of West Virginia,* 357–77.

9. Eller, *Miners, Millhands, and Mountaineers,* 65–85, 132–40.

10. Ibid., 242.

11. Ibid., 96–98, 149–53.

12. Jack P. Maddex, Jr., *The Virginia Conservatives, 1867–1879: A Study in Reconstruction Politics* (Chapel Hill: University of North Carolina Press, 1970), 175, 276–90; Allen W. Moger, *Virginia: Bourbonism to Byrd, 1870–1925* (Charlottesville: University Press of Virginia, 1969), 5–37.

13. Moger, *Virginia*, 8–37, 54–56, 93–108, 133–41, 431–34; McKinney, *Southern Mountain Republicans*, 99–101; James Tice Moore, *Two Paths to the Old South: The Virginia Debt Controversy, 1870–1883* (Lexington: University Press of Kentucky, 1974), 10–11, 19–28, 83–84; Raymond H. Pulley, *Old Virginia Restored: An Interpretation of the Progressive Impulse, 1870–1930* (Charlottesville: University Press of Virginia, 1968), 27–36.

14. McKinney, *Southern Mountain Republicans*, 101–8, 199, 219; Moger, *Virginia*, 37–68, 82–108, 144–45, 192–221; Moore, *Two Paths*, 57; Pulley, *Old Virginia Restored*, 37–87; Michael Barone and Grant Ujifusa, *The Almanac of American Politics 1986* (Washington: National Journal, 1986), 1398–99.

Bibliography

Primary Sources

Manuscripts

    Baugh Family Papers (#9308)
    Burwell Family Papers (#4400-B)
    Gilmer Family Papers (#5194)
    Johnston-Railey Papers (#4254)
    William Kohler, "The Lead Mines," Typescript (#38-494)
    Anne Leftwich and William King Correspondence (#2798)
    Preston Family Papers (#6353)
    South Western Turnpike Company Papers (#4826)
Baker Library, Harvard Business School, Boston, Mass.
    R. G. Dun & Company Collection, Virginia
Special Collections Library, Duke University Library, Durham, N.C.
    George Booker Letters
    Campbell Family Papers
    Pack, Anderson and ———— Vawter? Day Book
    Caleb D. Parker Papers
    John Pepper Papers
    Richard W. Sanders and John W. Greene Papers and Notebooks
    J. B. Shelor Papers
    James P. Strother Papers
    Henry Alexander Wise Papers
Manuscript Department, Filson Club, Louisville, Ky.
    Preston Family Papers—Joyes Collection
Illinois Historical Survey, University of Illinois at Urbana-Champaign, Urbana, Ill.
    Hammet-Talbot-Goodell Family Papers
    Francis W. Obenchain Collection
National Archives and Records Administration, Washington, D.C.
    Manuscript Censuses, Virginia, Floyd, Montgomery, Raleigh, Smyth, Washington, Wythe Counties, Schedules I, II, III, IV, 1850, 1860
    Record Group 56, General Records of the Department of the Treasury, Records of the Commissioners of Claims (Southern Claims Commission), 1871–80, Microfilm Publication 87
    Record Group 217, Records of the U.S. General Accounting Office, Allowed Case Files of the Southern Claims Commission
    Record Group 233, Records of the U.S. House of Representatives, Barred and Disallowed Claims of the Southern Claims Commission

Record Group 393, Records of the U.S. Army Continental Commands, 1821–1920, Mountain Department, 1861–62

Southern Historical Collection, Library of the University of North Carolina at Chapel Hill, Chapel Hill, N.C.

Manuscripts Division, Special Collections Department, University of Virginia Library, Charlottesville, Va.

Special Collections Department, Virginia Polytechnic Institute and State University Libraries, Blacksburg, Va.

   Apperson Family Papers
   Black Family Papers
   Charlton Family Papers
   Lincoln-Look Family Papers
   Virginia and Tennessee Railroad Collection
   S. L. Walton Letters

Virginia Historical Society, Richmond, Va.

   Caperton Family Papers
   Cloyd Family Papers
   Campbell-Preston-Floyd Papers (microfilm)
   Darter Family Papers
   Edmundson Family Papers
   Preston Family Papers
   Amanda Jane (Cooley) Roberts Diary
   Wade Family of Montgomery County, Virginia Papers
   Leonidas Baugh Papers (photostats) #1813
   Christian Thomas Pfohl Papers (microfilm) M-3331
   William D. Simpson Papers #3344
   Susanna Waddell Diary #2383

Archives and Records Division Virginia State Library and Archives, Richmond, Va.

   Letters Received, Governor's Office, Executive Department

West Virginia and Regional History Collection, West Virginia University Libraries, Morgantown, W.Va.

   Andrew N. Campbell Papers
   William Gaston Caperton Family Papers
   Civil War Correspondence, 1861–64 (microfilm)
   Roy Bird Cook Collection
   Civil War Bound Notebook Series
   Sallie Patton Papers
   Alexander W. Reynolds Letters and Papers
   Young Civil War Papers
   John McClaugherty Papers
   R. S. Rudd Diaries (microfilm)
   Nathaniel V. Wilson Correspondence

Newspapers and Periodicals

Abingdon Democrat
[Abingdon] *Democrat*
Abingdon Virginian

[[Abingdon] *Virginian*
[Christiansburg] *New Star*
DeBow's Review of the Southern and Western States
Greenbrier Independent
Richmond Enquirer [semi-weekly]
Richmond Whig and Public Advertiser
Supplement to the Enquirer, Whig, Examiner Times, Republican Advocate
[Washington] *National Intelligencer*
Wytheville Times

Government Publications

Acts of the General Assembly, Passed at the Session Commencing December 6, 1847, and Ending April 5, 1848. . . . Richmond, Va.: Samuel Shepherd, 1848.
Ambler, Charles H., et al. *Debates and Proceedings of the First Constitutional Convention of West Virginia (1861–1863).* 3 v. Huntington, W.Va.: Gentry Brothers, 1939.
Documents Containing Statistics of Virginia, Ordered to be Printed by the State Convention Sitting in the City of Richmond, 1850–1851. Richmond, Va.: William Culley, 1851.
Governor's Message and Annual Reports of the Public Officers of the State . . . of Virginia. 1847. Reprint. Richmond, Va.: William F. Ritchie, 1851, 1852.
Journal, Acts, and Proceedings of a General Convention of the State of Virginia. Assembled at Richmond on Monday, the Fourteenth Day of October, Eighteen Hundred and Fifty. Richmond, Va.: William Culley, 1850.
Journal of the Acts and Proceedings of a General Convention of the State of Virginia. . . . Richmond, Va.: Wyatt M. Elliott, 1861.
Journal of the House of Delegates of Virginia. 1848–64. Richmond, Va.: Samuel Shepherd, 1844–48; Richmond, Va.: William F. Ritchie, 1849–64.
Journal of the Senate of the Commonwealth of Virginia: Begun and Held at the Capitol in the City of Richmond, on Monday, the Fifth Day of December. . . . Richmond, Va.: James E. Goode, 1859.
Message of the Governor of Virginia and Accompanying Documents. Richmond, Va.: William F. Ritchie, 1861.
New Constitution of the Commonwealth of Virginia Adopted . . . on the 31st Day of July, 1851. Richmond, Va.: William Culley, 1851.
Proceedings and Debates of the Virginia State Convention of 1829–30. . . . Richmond, Va.: Samuel Shepherd, 1830.
Proceedings of the Virginia State Convention of 1861. 4 vols. Richmond, Va.: Virginia State Library, 1965.
U.S. Bureau of the Census. *Agriculture of the United States in 1860; Compiled From the Original Returns of the Eighth Census.* . . . Washington: Government Printing Office, 1864.
———. *Heads of Families at the First Census of the United States Taken in the Year 1790, Records of the State Enumerations: 1782 to 1785: Virginia.* Washington: Government Printing Office, 1908.
———. *Manufactures of the United States in 1860; Compiled from the Original Returns of the Eighth Census.* . . . Washington: Government Printing Office, 1865.

————. *Population of the United States in 1860; Compiled From the Original Returns of the Eighth Census.* . . . Washington: Government Printing Office, 1864.

————. *The Seventh Census of the United States: 1850.* Washington: Robert Armstrong, 1853.

U.S. Bureau of Statistics, Treasury Department. *Report on the Internal Commerce of the United States.* . . . Washington: Government Printing Office, 1886.

The War of the Rebellion: A Compilation of the Official Records of the Union and Confederate Armies. 70 vols. Washington: Government Printing Office, 1880–1901.

Books and Articles

Arese, Count Francesco. *A Trip to the Prairies and in the Interior of America [1837–1838].* Trans. Andrew Evans. New York: Harbor, 1934.

Bell, John W. *Memoirs of Governor William Smith of Virginia: His Political, Military, and Personal History.* New York: Moss, 1891.

Beverley, Robert. *The History and Present State of Virginia: A Selection.* Indianapolis: Bobbs-Merrill, 1971.

Bickley, George W. L. *History of the Settlement and Indian Wars of Tazewell County, Virginia.* . . . Added Materials Compiled by J. Allen Neal. 1852. Reprint. Parsons, W.Va.: McClain, 1974.

Boles, John B., and Evelyn Thomas Nolen, eds. *Interpreting Southern History: Historiographical Essays in Honor of Sanford W. Higginbotham* Baton Rouge: Louisiana State University Press, 1987.

Bosang, James N. *Memoirs of a Pulaski Veteran.* Pulaski, Va.: N.p., 1912.

Bromme, Traugott. *Reisen durch die Vereinigten Staaten und Ober-Canada.* 3 vols. Baltimore: C. Scheid, 1834.

Buckingham, J. S. *The Slave States of America.* 2 vols. London: Fisher, Son, 1842.

Burke, William. *Mineral Springs of Virginia: With Remarks on Their Use, and the Diseases to Which They Are Applicable.* New York: Wiley and Putnam, 1842.

Caddall, J. B. "The Pulaski Guards, Company C, 4th Virginia Infantry, at the First Battle of Manassas, July 18, 1861: The Original Rebel Yell." *Southern Historical Society Papers* 32 (January–December 1904): 174–178.

Cox, Jacob Dolson. *Military Reminiscences of the Civil War.* 2 vols. New York: Charles Scribner's Sons, 1900.

Crook, George. *General George Crook: His Autobiography.* Edited and Annotated by Martin F. Schmitt. Foreword by Joseph C. Porter. Norman, Okla.: University of Oklahoma Press, 1986.

Douglas, Henry Kyd. *I Rode with Stonewall.* 1940. Reprint. New York: Fawcett, 1961.

Egan, Michael. *The Flying, Gray-Haired Yank; or, The Adventures of a Volunteer.* . . . Philadelphia: Hubbard Brothers, 1888.

Evans, Robley. *A Sailor's Log.* New York: D. Appleton, 1901.

Farrar, Samuel Clarke. *The Twenty-Second Pennsylvania Cavalry and the Ringgold Battalion, 1861–1865.* Pittsburgh: Twenty-Second Pennsylvania Ringgold Cavalry Association, 1911.

Featherstonhaugh, G. W. *Excursion through the Slave States.* . . . 1844. Reprint. New York: Negro Universities Press, 1968.

Finch, Marianne. *An Englishwoman's Experience in America.* London: Richard Bentley, 1853.

Fox, James D. *A True History of the Reign of Terror in Southern Illinois.* . . . Aurora, Ill.: J. D. Fox, 1884.

Frost, William Goodell. "Our Contemporary Ancestors in the Southern Mountains." *Atlantic Monthly* 83 (Mar. 1899): 311–19.

Gilman, Caroline. *The Poetry of Travelling in the United States.* . . . New York: S. Colman, 1838.

Goode, John. *Recollections of a Lifetime.* New York: Neale, 1906.

Gurney, Joseph John. *A Journey in North America Described in Familiar Letters to Amelia Opie.* Norwich: Josiah Fletcher, 1841.

Hambleton, James P. *A Biographical Sketch of Henry A. Wise.* . . . Richmond, Va.: J. W. Randolph, 1856.

Hassler, Frederick W. B. "The Campaign in West Virginia, 1861 and 1863." *Historical Magazine* 6 (Dec. 1869): 355–58.

Heth, Henry. *The Memoirs of Henry Heth.* Edited by James L. Morrison. Westport, Conn.: Greenwood, 1974.

Howe, Henry. *Historical Collections of Virginia.* . . . Charleston, S.C.: Babcock, 1845.

Humphreys, Milton W. "Last Days of the Army in Southwest Virginia." *Southern Historical Society Papers* 33 (Jan.–Dec. 1905): 344–50.

Johnston, J. Stoddard. "Sketches of Operations of General John C. Breckinridge. No. 3—Conclusion." *Southern Historical Society Papers* 7 (August 1879): 385–392.

Jones, B. M. *Rail Roads: Considered in Regard to Their Effects upon the Value of Land.* . . . Richmond, Va.: Ritchie and Dunnavant, 1860.

Jones, J. B. *A Rebel War Clerk's Diary at the Confederate States Capital.* Ed. Howard Swigget. New York: Old Hickory Bookshop, 1935.

Lewis, Virgil A. *How West Virginia Was Made.* Charleston: News-Mail, 1909.

Lynch, Charles H. *The Civil War Diary, 1862–1865, of Charles H. Lynch, 18th Conn. Vol's.* Hartford: Case, Lockwood & Brainard, 1915.

Marryat, Frederick. *A Diary in America, with Remarks on Its Institutions.* Ed. Sydney Jackson. New York: Alfred A. Knopf, 1962.

Martin, Joseph. *A New and Comprehensive Gazetter of Virginia and the District of Columbia.* . . . Charlottesville: Joseph Martin, 1835.

Mason, F. H. *The Forty-Second Infantry: A History of the Organization and Services of That Regiment in the War of the Rebellion.* . . . Cleveland: Cobb, Andrews, 1876.

McAnally, David Rice. *Life and Times of Rev. William Patton, and Annals of the Missouri Conference.* St Louis: Methodist Book Depository, 1858.

Moormann, John J., M.D. *The Virginia Springs.* . . . Philadelphia: Lindsay and Blakiston, 1847.

Mosby, John S. *The Memoirs of John S. Mosby.* Ed. Charles Wells Russell. Boston: Little, Brown 1917.

Olmsted, Frederick Law. *A Journey in the Back Country in the Winter of 1853–54.* 2d ed. New York: Mason Brothers, 1863.

———. *Journey in the Seaboard Slave States: With Remarks on Their Economy.* 1856. Reprint. New York: Mason Brothers, 1859.

Pollard, Edward. "The Virginia Tourist." *Lippincott's Monthly Magazine* 5 (May 1870): 487–97.

Prolix, Peregrine. *Letters Descriptive of the Virginia Springs. . . .* 1837. Reprint. Austin, Tex.: AAR/Tanalus, 1978.

Richardson, Frank. *From Sunrise to Sunset: Reminiscence.* Bristol, Tenn.: King, 1910.

[Royall, Anne]. *Sketches of History, Life, and Manners in the United States: By a Traveller.* New Haven: The Author, 1826.

Sixth Annual Meeting of the Stockholders of the Va. & Tenn. Railroad Company. N.p.: N.p., 1853.

Sketch of Western Virginia: For the Use of British Settlers in That Country. London: Edward Bull, 1837.

Slease, William Davis. *The Fourteenth Pennsylvania Cavalry in the Civil War: A History of the Fourteenth Pennsylvania Volunteer Cavalry from Its Organization Until the Close of the Civil War, 1861–1865.* Pittsburgh: Art Engraving & Printing, 1915.

Sullins, D. *Recollections of an Old Man: Seventy Years in Dixie, 1827–1897.* Bristol, Tenn.: King, 1915.

Tanner, H. S. *A Geographical, Historical, and Statistical View of the Central or Middle United States. . . .* Philadelphia: H. Tanner, 1841.

Taylor, James W. *Alleghania: A Geographical and Statistical Memoir.* St. Paul: James Davenport, 1862.

Temple, Oliver P. *East Tennessee and the Civil War.* Cincinnati: Robert Clarke, 1899.

The Tribune Almanac for the Years 1838 to 1868. . . . 2 vols. New York: New York Tribune, 1868.

Walker, William C. *History of the Eighteenth Regiment Conn: Volunteers in the War for the Union.* Norwich, Conn.: Gordon Wilcox, 1885.

"A Winter in the South," Parts 1 and 2. *Harper's New Monthly Magazine* 15 (Sept., Oct. 1857): 433–51, 594–606

Wise, John S. *The End of an Era.* Boston: Houghton, Mifflin, 1902.

Secondary Sources

Books and Articles

Abernethy, Thomas Perkins. *Three Virginia Frontiers.* University: Louisiana State University Press, 1940.

———. *Western Lands and the American Revolution.* New York: Russell & Russell, 1959.

Addington, Luther F. *The Story of Wise County (Virginia).* Wise County, Va.: Centennial Committee and School Board of Wise County, Va., 1956.

Addington, Robert M. *History of Scott County, Virginia.* Kingsport, Tenn.: Kingsport, 1932.

Alderman, John Perry. *29th Virginia Infantry.* Lynchburg, Va.: H. E. Howard, 1989.

Alexander, Thomas B., and Richard E. Beringer. *The Anatomy of the Con-*

federate Congress: A Study of the Influence of Member Characteristics on Legislative Voting Behavior, 1861–1865. Nashville: Vanderbilt University Press, 1972.

Ambler, Charles H. "The Cleavage Between Eastern and Western Virginia." *American Historical Review* 15 (July 1910): 762–80.

———. *A History of West Virginia.* Prentice-Hall History Series. New York: Prentice-Hall, 1933.

———. *Francis H. Pierpont: Union War Governor of Virginia and Father of West Virginia.* Chapel Hill: University of North Carolina Press, 1937.

———. *Sectionalism in Virginia from 1776 to 1861.* 1910. Reprint. New York: Russell & Russell, 1964.

Ambrose, Stephen E. "Yeoman Discontent in the Confederacy." *Civil War History* 8 (Sept. 1962): 259–68.

Andriot, John L., compiler and editor. *Population Abstract of the United States.* McLean, Va.: Andriot, 1983.

Ash, Stephen V. "Sharks in an Angry Sea: Civilian Resistance and Guerrilla Warfare in Occupied Middle Tennessee, 1862–1865." *Tennessee Historical Quarterly* 45 (Fall 1986): 217–29.

Auman, William T., and David Scarboro. "The Heroes of America in Civil War North Carolina." *North Carolina Historical Review* 58 (Autumn 1981): 327–63.

Bailey, Fred Arthur. *Class and Tennessee's Confederate Generation.* Chapel Hill: University of North Carolina Press, 1987.

Barney, William L. *The Road to Secession: A New Perspective on the Old South.* New York: Praeger, 1972.

———. "Towards the Civil War: The Dynamics of Change in a Black Belt County." In *Class, Conflict, and Consensus: Antebellum Southern Community Studies.* Ed. Orville Vernon Burton and Robert C. McMath, Jr. Westport, Conn.: Greenwood, 1982, 146–72.

Barone, William, and Grant Ujifusa. *The Almanac of American Politics, 1986.* Washington: National Journal, 1986.

Barrett, Theodosia Wells. *Russell County: A Confederate Breadbasket.* N.p.: N.p., 1981.

Basler, Roy P., ed. *The Collected Works of Abraham Lincoln.* 8 vols. New Brunswick, N.J.: Rutgers University Press, 1953.

Bateman, Fred, and Thomas Weiss. *A Deplorable Scarcity: The Failure of Industrialization in the Slave Economy.* Chapel Hill: University of North Carolina Press, 1981.

Bean, W. G. "John Letcher and the Slavery Issue in Virginia's Gubernatorial Contest of 1858–1859." *Journal of Southern History* 20 (Febr. 1954): 22–49.

Belohlavek, John M. "John B. Floyd as Governor of Virginia, 1849–1852." *West Virginia History* 33 (Oct. 1971): 14–26.

Billings, Dwight, Kathleen Blee, and Louis Swanson. "Culture, Family, and Community in Preindustrial Appalachia." *Appalachian Journal* 13 (Winter 1986): 154–70.

Black, Robert C., III. *The Railroads of the Confederacy.* Chapel Hill: University of North Carolina Press, 1952.

Bode, Frederick A., and Donald E. Ginter. *Farm Tenancy and the Census in Antebellum Georgia.* Athens: University of Georgia Press, 1986.

Bohannon, Keith S. *The Giles, Alleghany, and Jackson Artillery.* Lynchburg, Va.: H. E. Howard, 1990.

Boney, F. N. *John Letcher of Virginia: The Story of Virginia's Civil War Governor.* University: University of Alabama Press, 1966.

Boyd, C. R. *Resources of South-West Virginia, Showing the Mineral Deposits of Iron, Coal, Zinc, Copper, and Lead. . . .* New York: John Wiley & Sons, 1881.

Brown, Richard D. *Modernization: The Transformation of American Life, 1600–1865.* New York: Hill and Wang, 1976.

Bruce, Dickson D., Jr. *The Rhetoric of Conservatism: The Virginia Convention of 1829–30 and the Conservative Tradition in the South.* San Marino, Calif.: Huntington Library, 1982.

Burton, Orville Vernon, and Robert C. McMath, Jr., eds. *Class, Conflict, and Consensus: Antebellum Southern Community Studies.* Westport, Conn.: Greenwood, 1982.

Campbell, John C. *The Southern Highlander & His Homeland.* 1921. Reprint. Lexington: University Press of Kentucky, 1969.

Cash, W. J. *The Mind of the South.* 1941. Reprint. New York: Vintage, 1961.

Catton, Bruce. *The Centennial History of the Civil War.* 3 vols. Garden City, N.Y.: Doubleday, 1961–65.

Caudill, Harry M. *Night Comes to the Cumberlands: A Biography of a Depressed Area.* Boston: Atlantic Monthly, 1963.

Cauthen, Charles E., and Lewis P. Jones. "The Coming of the Civil War." In *Writing Southern History: Essays in Historiography in Honor of Fletcher M. Green.* Ed. Arthur S. Link and Rembert W. Patrick. Baton Rouge: Louisiana State University Press, 1965.

Cecil-Fronsman, Bill. *Common Whites: Class and Culture in Antebellum North Carolina.* Lexington: University Press of Kentucky, 1992.

Channing, Steven A. *Crisis of Fear: Secession in South Carolina.* New York: Simon and Schuster, 1970.

Chapla, John D. *48th Virginia Infantry.* Lynchburg, Va.: H. E. Howard, 1989.

Clark, Thomas D., ed. *Travels in the Old South: A Bibliography.* 3 vols. Norman: University of Oklahoma Press, 1959.

Coleman, Elizabeth Dabney. "Southwest Virginia's Railroad: Lynchburg Started It; Virginia Built It; The Yankees Wrecked It." *Virginia Cavalcade* 2 (Spring 1953): 20–27.

Cooling, Benjamin Franklin. *Forts Henry and Donelson: The Key to the Confederate Heartland.* Knoxville: University of Tennessee Press, 1987.

Corbin, David. *Life, Work, and Rebellion in the Coal Fields: The Southern West Virginia Miners, 1880–1922.* Urbana: University of Illinois Press, 1981.

Coulter, E. Merton. *The Confederate States of America, 1861–1865.* Baton Rouge: Louisiana State University Press, 1950.

Cox, William E. "The Civil War Letters of Laban Gwinn: A Union Refugee." *West Virginia History* 43 (Spring 1982): 227–45.

Craven, Avery Odelle. *Soil Exhaustion as a Factor in the Agricultural History of Virginia and Maryland, 1606–1860.* Urbana: University of Illinois Press, 1925.

Crawford, Martin. "Confederate Volunteering and Enlistment in Ashe County, North Carolina, 1861–1862." *Civil War History* 37 (Mar. 1991): 29–50.

———. "Political Society in a Southern Mountain Community: Ashe County, North Carolina, 1850–1861." *Journal of Southern History* 55 (Aug. 1989): 373–90.

Crenshaw, Olinger. "The Knights of the Golden Circle: The Career of George Bickley." *American Historical Review* 47 (Oct. 1941): 23–50.

Crofts, Daniel W. *Reluctant Confederates: Upper South Unionists in the Secession Crisis.* Chapel Hill: University of Illinois Press, 1989.

Current, Richard N. *Lincoln and the First Shot.* Philadelphia: J. B. Lippincott, 1963.

Curry, Richard Orr. *A House Divided: A Study of Statehood Politics and the Copperhead Movement in West Virginia.* Pittsburgh: University of Pittsburgh Press, 1964.

———. "Crisis Politics in West Virginia, 1861–1870." In *Radicalism, Racism, and Party Realignment: The Border States During Reconstruction.* Ed. Richard O. Curry. Baltimore: Johns Hopkins University Press, 1969, 80–104.

———, ed. *Radicalism, Racism, and Party Realignment: The Border States During Reconstruction.* Baltimore: Johns Hopkins University Press, 1969.

Daniel, W. Harrison. *Bedford County, Virginia, 1840–1860: The History of an Upper Piedmont County in the Late Antebellum Era.* Bedford, Va.: Print Shop, 1985.

Dawson, John Harper. *Wildcat Cavalry: A Synoptic History of the Seventeenth Virginia Cavalry Regiment of the Jenkins-McCausland Brigade in the War Between the States.* Dayton, Ohio: Morningside, 1982.

Dickinson, Jack L. *8th Virginia Cavalry.* Lynchburg, Va.: H. E. Howard, 1986.

Donald, David. *Charles Sumner and the Coming of the Civil War.* New York: Alfred A. Knopf, 1960.

Dorman, John Frederick. *The Prestons of Smithfield and Greenfield in Virginia: Descendants of John and Elizabeth (Patton) Preston through Five Generations.* Louisville: Filson Club, 1982.

Dowdey, Clifford, ed. *The Wartime Papers of Robert E. Lee.* Boston: Little, Brown, 1961.

Drake, Richard B. "Slavery and Antislavery in Appalachia." *Appalachian Heritage* 14 (Winter 1986): 25–33.

Dunaway, Wayland Fuller. *History of the James River and Kanawha Company.* New York: Columbia University Press, 1922.

Dunn, Durwood. *Cades Cove: The Life and Death of a Southern Appalachian Community, 1818–1937.* Knoxville: University of Tennessee Press, 1988.

Durrill, Wayne K. "Producing Poverty: Local Government and Economic Development in a New South County, 1874–1884." *Journal of American History* 71 (Mar. 1985): 764–81.

Eller Ronald D. *Miners, Millhands, and Mountaineers: Industrialization of the Appalachian South, 1880–1930.* Knoxville: University of Tennessee Press, 1982.

Escott, Paul D. *After Secession: Jefferson Davis and the Failure of the Confederate Nation.* Baton Rouge: Louisiana State University Press, 1978.

———. "'The Cry of the Sufferers': The Problem of Welfare in The Confederacy." *Civil War History* 23 (Sept. 1977): 228–40.

———. *Many Excellent People: Power and Privilege in North Carolina, 1850–1900.* Chapel Hill: University of North Carolina Press, 1985.

———. "Yeoman Independence and the Market: Social Status and Economic Development in Antebellum North Carolina." *North Carolina Historical Review* 66 (July 1989): 275–300.

Escott, Paul D., and Jeffrey J. Crow. "The Social Order and Violent Disorder: An Analysis of North Carolina in the Revolution and the Civil War." *Journal of Southern History* 52 (Aug. 1986): 373–402.

Faragher, John Mack. *Sugar Creek: Life on the Illinois Prairie.* New Haven: Yale University Press, 1986.

Fellman, Michael. *Inside War: The Guerrilla Conflict in Missouri during the American Civil War.* New York: Oxford University Press, 1989.

Fields, Bettye-Lou, and Jene Hughes, eds. *Grayson County: A History in Words and Pictures.* Independence, Va.: Grayson County Historical Society, 1976.

Fischer, David Hackett. *Albion's Seed: Four British Folkways in America.* New York: Oxford University Press, 1989.

Ford, Lacy K., Jr. *Origins of Southern Radicalism: The South Carolina Upcountry, 1800–1860.* New York: Oxford University Press, 1988.

———. "Rednecks and Merchants: Economic Development and Social Tensions in the South Carolina Upcountry, 1865–1900." *Journal of American History* 71 (Sept. 1984): 294–318.

Fox-Genovese, Elizabeth. *Within the Plantation Household: Black and White Women of the Old South.* Chapel Hill: University of Noth Carolina Press, 1988.

Freehling, Alison Goodyear. *Drift toward Dissolution: The Virginia Slavery Debate of 1831–1832.* Baton Rouge: Louisiana State University Press, 1982.

Freehling, William W. *The Road to Disunion.* 2 vols. New York: Oxford University Press, 1990– .

Gaines, William H., Jr. *Biographical Register of Members, Virginia State Convention of 1861, First Session.* Richmond, Va.: Virginia State Library, 1969.

Gallagher, Gary W. "Home Front and Battlefield: Some Recent Literature Relating to Virginia and to the Confederacy." *Virginia Magazine of History and Biography* 98 (Apr. 1990): 135–68.

Goldfield, David R. *Urban Growth in the Age of Sectionalism: Virginia, 1847–1861.* Baton Rouge: Louisiana State University Press, 1977.

Goodrich, Carter. "The Virginia System of Mixed Enterprise: A Study of State Planning of Internal Improvements." *Political Science Quarterly* 64 (Sept. 1949): 355–87.

Grew, Raymond. "Modernization and Its Discontents." *American Behavioral Scientist* 21 (Nov./Dec. 1977): 289–312.

———. "More on Modernization." *Journal of Social History* 14 (Winter 1980): 179–87.

Groce, W. Todd. "East Tennessee Confederates and the Crisis of the Union."

Paper Presented to the Appalachian Studies Conference, Berea, Ky., Mar. 22, 1991.

Gunderson, Robert Gray. *Old Gentleman's Convention: the Washington Peace Conference of 1861.* Madison: University of Wisconsin Press, 1961.

Gunn, Ralph White. *24th Virginia Infantry.* Lynchburg, Va.: H. E. Howard, 1987.

Hahn, Steven. *The Roots of Southern Populism: Yeoman Farmers and the Transformation of the Georgia Upcountry, 1850–1890.* New York: Oxford University Press, 1983.

———. "The 'Unmaking' of the Southern Yeomanry: The Transformation of the Georgia Upcountry, 1860–1890." In *The Countryside in the Age of Capitalist Transformation: Essays in the Social History of Rural America.* Ed. Steven Hahn and Jonathan Prude. Chapel Hill: University of North Carolina Press, 1985.

———. "The Yeomanry of the Nonplantation South: Upper Piedmont Georgia, 1850–1860." In *Class, Conflict, and Consensus: Antebellum Southern Community Studies.* Ed. Orville Vernon Burton and Robert C. McMath, Jr. Westport, Conn.: Greenwood, 1982, 29–56.

Hahn, Steven, and Jonathan Prude, eds. *The Countryside in the Age of Capitalist Transformation: Essays in the Social History of Rural America.* Chapel Hill: University of North

Hall, Van Beck. "The Politics of Appalachian Virginia, 1790–1830." In *Appalachian Frontiers: Settlement, Society, & Development in the Preinsdustrial Era.* Ed. Robert D. Mitchell Lexington: University Press of Kentucky, 1991, 166–86.

Hamilton, Holman. *Prologue to Conflict: The Crisis and Compromise of 1850.* Lexington: University Press of Kentucky, 1964.

Handley, Harry E. "The James River and Kanawha Canal." *West Virginia History* 25 (Jan. 1964): 92–101.

The Heritage of Russell County, Virginia, 1786–1986. 2 vols. Marceline, Mo.: N.p., 1985.

Hilldrup, Robert Leroy. "The Romance of a Man in Gray—Including the Love Letters of Captain James S. Peery, Forty Fifth Virginia Infantry Regiment, C.S.A." *West Virginia History* 22 (Jan., Apr., July 1961): 83–116, 166–83, 217–39.

Hilliard, Sam Bowers. *Hog Meat and Hoecake: Food Supply in the Old South.* Carbondale: Southern Illinois University Press, 1972.

The History of American Methodism, in Three Volumes. New York: Abingdon, 1964.

Hitchcock, William S. "The Limits of Southern Unionism: Virginia Conservatives and the Gubernatorial Election of 1859." *Journal of Southern History* (Feb. 1981): 57–72.

Hsiung, David C. "Local Color Images and Appalachian Realities." Paper Presented to the Appalachian Studies Conference, Asheville, N.C., Mar. 21, 1992.

Humbert, R. Lee, et al. *Virginia: Economic and Civic.* Richmond, Va.: Whittet & Shepperson, 1933.

Hunter, Robert F. "The Turnpike Movement in Virginia, 1816–1860." *Virginia Magazine of History and Biography* 69 (July 1961): 278–89.

Inscoe, John C. "Mountain Masters: Slaveholding in Western North Carolina." *North Carolina Historical Review* 61 (Apr. 1984): 143–73.

——. *Mountain Masters, Slavery, and the Sectional Crisis in Western North Carolina*. Knoxville: University of Tennessee Press, 1989.

——. "Review of Allen W. Batteau, *The Invention of Appalachia*" *Journal of Southern History* 58 (Aug. 1992): 540

——. "Thomas Clingman, Mountain Whiggery, and the Southern Cause." *Civil War History* 33 (Mar. 1987): 42–62.

Jeffrey, Thomas E. "Internal Improvements and Political Parties in Antebellum North Carolina, 1836–1860." *North Carolina Historical Review* 55 (Apr. 1978): 111–56.

——. "National Issues, Local Interests, and the Transformation of Antebellum North Carolina Politics." *Journal of Southern History* 50 (Feb. 1984): 43–74.

Johannsen, Robert W. *Lincoln and the South*. Fort Wayne, Ind.: Louis A. Warren Lincoln Library and Museum, 1989.

——. *Stephen A. Douglas*. New York: Oxford University Press, 1973.

Johnson, Michael P. *Toward a Patriarchical Republic: The Secession of Georgia*. Baton Rouge: Louisiana State University Press, 1977.

Johnson, Patricia Givens. *The New River Early Settlement*. Pulaski, Va.: Edmonds, 1983.

——. *The United States Army Invades the New River Valley, May 1864*. Christiansburg, Va.: Walpa, 1986.

Johnson, Paul E. *A Shopkeeper's Millennium: Society and Revivals in Rochester, New York, 1815–1837*. New York: Hill and Wang, 1978.

Johnston, Angus James, II. *Virginia Railroads in the Civil War*. Chapel Hill: University of North Carolina Press, 1961.

Kenzer, Robert C. *Kinship and Neighborhoods in a Southern Community: Orange County, North Carolina, 1849–1881*. Knoxville: University of Tennessee Press, 1987.

Kephart, Horace. *Our Southern Highlanders: A Narrative of Adventure in the Southern Appalachians and a Study of Life among the Mountaineers*. New York: Macmillan, 1913.

Kincer, Lucile Miller. *Glimpses of Wythe County: Historic Churches of Wythe County*. Wytheville: Southwest Virginia Enterprise, 1967.

Klement, Frank L. *Dark Lanterns: Secret Political Societies, Conspiracies, and Treason Trials in the Civil War*. Baton Rouge: Louisiana State University Press, 1984.

Klingberg, Frank L. *The Southern Claims Commission*. Berkeley: University of California Press, 1955.

Laing, James T. "The Early Development of the Coal Industry in the Western Counties of Virginia, 1800–1865." *West Virginia History* 27 (Jan. 1966): 144–55.

Lewis, Ronald L. *Coal, Iron, and Slaves: Industrial Slavery in Maryland and Virginia, 1715–1865*. Westport, Conn.: Grenwood, 1979.

Lonn, Ella. *Desertion During the Civil War*. New York: Century, 1928.

——. *Salt as a Factor in the Confederacy*. New York: Walter Neale, 1933.

Loving, Robert S. *Double Destiny: The Story of Bristol, Tennessee-Virginia*. 2d ed. Bristol, Tenn.: King, 1956.

Lowe, Richard. *Republicans and Reconstruction in Virginia, 1856–70*. Charlottesville: University Press of Virginia, 1991.

Lowry, Terry. *September Blood: The Battle of Carnifex Ferry*. Charleston, W.Va.: Pictorial Histories, 1985.

Lucas, Roderick. *A Valley and Its People, in Montgomery County, Virginia*. Blacksburg, Va.: Southern, 1975.

Macmaster, Richard K. "The Cattle Trade in Western Virginia, 1760–1830." In *Appalachian Frontiers: Settlement, Society, & Development in the Preindustrial Era*. Ed. Robert D. Mitchell. Lexington: University Press of Kentucky, 1991, 127–49.

Maddex, Jack P. Jr. *The Virginia Conservatives, 1867–1879: A Study in Reconstruction Politics*. Chapel Hill: University of North Carolina Press, 1970.

Maddox, Robert Franklin. "The Presidential Election of 1860 in Western Virginia." *West Virginia History* 25 (Apr. 1964): 211–27.

Main, Jackson Turner. "The Distribution of Property in Revolutionary Virginia." *Mississippi Valley Historical Review* 41 (Sept. 1954): 241–58.

Mann, Ralph. "Family Group, Family Migration, and the Civil War in the Sandy Basin of Virginia." *Appalachian Journal* 19 (Summer 1992): 374–93.

———. "Mountains, Land, and Kin Networks: Burkes Garden, Virginia, in the 1840s and 1850s." *Journal of Southern History* 58 (Aug. 1992): 411–34.

Martin, James B. "Black Flag over the Bluegrass: Guerrilla Warfare in Kentucky, 1863–1865." *Register of the Kentucky Historical Society* 86 (Autumn 1988): 352–75.

Mathews, Donald G. *Religion in the Old South*. Chicago: University of Chicago Press, 1977.

McCormick, Kyle. *The Story of Mercer County*. Charleston, W.Va.: Charleston, 1957.

McDonald, Forrest, and Grady McWhiney. "The Antebellum Southern Herdsman: An Reinterpretation." *Journal of Southern History* 41 (May 1975): 147–66.

———. "The South from Self-Sufficiency to Peonage: An Interpretation." *American Historical Review* 85 (Dec. 1980): 1095–1118.

McFeely, William S. *Grant: A Biography*. New York: Norton, 1981.

McKinney, Gordon B. *Southern Mountain Republicans, 1865–1900: Politics and the Appalachian Community*. Chapel Hill: University of North Carolina Press, 1978.

McKinney, Tim. *The Civil War in Fayette County, West Virginia*. Charleston, W.Va.: Pictorial Histories, 1988.

McManus, Howard Rollins. *The Battle of Cloyd's Mountain: The Virginia and Tennessee Railroad Raid, April 29–May 19, 1864*. Lynchburg, Va.: H. E. Howard, 1989.

McPherson, James B. *Battle Cry of Freedom: The Civil War Era*. New York: Oxford University Press, 1988.

Mills, Gary B. *Civil War Claims in the South: An Index of Civil War Damage Claims Filed before the Southern Claims Commission, 1871–1880*. Laguna Hills, Calif.: Aegean Park, 1980.

Mitchell, Reid. *Civil War Soldiers*. New York: Viking, 1988.

Mitchell, Robert D. *Commercialism and Frontier: Perspectives on the Early Shenandoah Valley*. Charlottesville: University Press of Virginia, 1977.

———, ed. *Appalachian Frontiers: Settlement, Society, & Development in the Preindustrial Era*. Lexington: University Press of Kentucky, 1991.

Moger, Allan W. *Virginia: Bourbonism to Byrd, 1870–1925*. Charlottesville: University Press of Virginia, 1968.

Moore, George Ellis. *A Banner in the Hills: West Virginia's Statehood*. New York: Appleton-Century-Crofts, 1963.

Moore, James Tice. *Two Paths to the Old South: The Virginia Debt Controversy, 1870–1883*. Lexington: University Press of Kentucky, 1974.

Morton, Oren F. *A History of Monroe County, West Virginia*. 1916. Reprint. Baltimore: Regional Publishing, 1974.

Murphy, James B. "Slavery and Freedom in Appalachia: Kentucky as a Demographic Case Study." *Register of the Kentucky Historical Society* 80 (Spring 1982): 151–69.

Noe, Kenneth W. "'Appalachia's' Civil War Genesis: Southwest Virginia as Depicted by Northern and European Writers, 1825–1865." *West Virginia History* 50 (1991): 91–108.

———. "Red String Scare: Civil War Southwest Virginia and the Heroes of America." *North Carolina Historical Review* 69 (July 1992): 301–22.

Oakes, James. *Slavery and Freedom: An Interpretation of the Old South*. New York: Alfred A. Knopf, 1990.

Oates, Stephen B. *The Fires of Jubilee: Nat Turner's Fierce Rebellion*. New York: Mentor, 1975.

———. *To Purge This Land with Blood: A Biography of John Brown*. New York: Harper & Row, 1970.

Paludan, Phillip Shaw. *"A People's Contest": The Union and the Civil War*. New York: Harper & Row, 1988.

———. *Victims: A True Story of the Civil War*. Knoxville: University of Tennessee, 1981.

Pendleton, William C. *History of Tazewell County and Southwest Virginia, 1748–1920*. Richmond, Va.: W. C. Hill, 1920.

———. *Political History of Appalachian Virginia*. Dayton, Va.: Shenandoah, 1927.

Peskin, Allan. *Garfield*. Kent, Ohio: Kent State University Press, 1978.

Peters, J. T., and H. B. Carden. *History of Fayette County, West Virginia*. Charleston, W.Va.: Jarrett, 1926.

Peterson, Arthur G. *Historical Study of Prices Received by Producers of Farm Products in Virginia, 1801–1927*. Blacksburg: Virginia Polytechnic Institute, 1929.

Porter, Albert Ogden. *County Government in Virginia: A Leglslative History, 1607–1904*. New York: Columbia University Press, 1947.

Pudup, Mary Beth. "The Boundaries of Class in Preindustrial Appalachia." *Journal of Historical Geography* 15 (1989): 139–62.

————. "The Limits of Subsistence: Agriculture and Industry in Central Appalachia." *Agricultural History* 64 (Winter 1990): 61–89.

Pulley, Raymond H. *Old Virginia Restored: An Interpretation of the Progressive Impulse, 1870–1930.* Charlottesville: University Press of Virginia, 1968.

Pulliam, David Loyd. *The Constitutional Conventions of Virginia: From the Foundation of the Commonwealth to the Present Times.* Richmond, Va.: John T. West, 1901.

Rable, George C. *Civil Wars: Women and the Crisis of Southern Nationalism.* Urbana: University of Illinois Press, 1989.

Ramsdell, Charles W. *Behind the Lines in the Southern Confederacy.* Ed. Wendell H. Stephenson. Baton Rouge: Louisiana State University Press, 1944.

Randall, J. G. *Lincoln, the President.* 4 vols. New York: Dodd, Mead, 1945–55.

Rankin, Thomas M. *37th Virginia Infantry.* Lynchburg, Va.: H. E. Howard, 1987.

Reniers, Perceval. *The Springs of Virginia: Life, Love, and Death at the Waters, 1775–1900.* 3d ed. Kingsport, Tenn.: Kingsport, 1955.

Rice, Otis K. *West Virginia: A History.* Lexington: University Press of Kentucky, 1985.

Richardson, Hila Appleton. "Raleigh County, West Virginia, in the Civil War." *West Virginia History* 10 (April 1949): 213–98.

Riggs, Susan A. *21st Virginia Infantry.* Lynchburg, Va.: H. E. Howard, 1990.

Robert, Joseph Clarke. *The Tobacco Kingdom: Plantation, Market, and Factory in Virginia and North Carolina, 1800–1860.* 1938. Reprint. Gloucester, Mass.: Peter Smith, 1965.

Robertson, James I. *4th Virginia Infantry.* 2d ed. Lynchburg, Va.: H. E. Howard, 1982.

————. *The Stonewall Brigade.* Baton Rouge: Louisiana State University Press, 1963.

The Saga of a City: Lynchburg, Virginia, 1786–1936. Lynchburg, Va.: Lynchburg Sesqui-Centennial Association, 1936.

Salstrom, Paul. Letter to the Editor. *Appalachian Journal* 13 (Summer 1986): 340–50.

Schlotterbeck, John T. "The 'Social Economy' of an Upper South Community: Orange and Greene Counties, Virginia, 1815–1860." In *Class, Conflict, and Consensus: Antebellum Southern Community Studies.* Ed. Orville Vernon Burton and Robert C. McMath, Jr. Contributions in American History Number 96. Westport, Conn.: Greenwood, 1982, 3–28.

Scott, Anne Firor. *The Southern Lady: From Pedestal to Politics 1830–1930.* Chicago: University of Chicago Press, 1970.

Scott, J. L. *45th Virginia Infantry.* Lynchburg, Va.: H. E. Howard, 1989.

————. *Lowry's, Bryan's and Chapman's Batteries of Virginia Artillery.* Lynchburg, Va.: H. E. Howard, 1988.

————. *36th Virginia Infantry.* Lynchburg, Va.: H. E. Howard, 1987.

Shanks, Henry T. "Disloyalty to the Confederacy in Southwestern Virginia, 1861–1865." *North Carolina Historical Review* 21 (Apr. 1944): 118–35.

———. *The Secession Movement in Virginia, 1847–1861.* Richmond, Va.: Garrett & Massie, 1934.

Shapiro, Henry D. *Appalachia on Our Minds: The Southern Mountains and Mountaineers in the American Consciousness, 1870–1920.* Chapel Hill: University of North Carolina Press, 1978.

Sharp, James Roger. *The Jacksonians Versus the Banks: Politics in the States after the Panic of 1837.* New York: Columbia University Press, 1978.

Siegel, Frederick F. *The Roots of Southern Distinctiveness: Tobacco and Society in Danville, Virginia, 1780–1865.* Chapel Hill: University of North Carolina Press, 1987.

Simms, Henry Harrison. *The Rise of the Whigs in Virginia, 1824–1840.* Richmond, Va.: William Byrd, 1929.

Simon, John Y., ed. *The Papers of Ulysses S. Grant.* 16 vol. Carbondale: Southern Illinois University Press, 1967– .

Simpson, Craig M. *A Good Southerner: The Life of Henry A. Wise of Virginia.* Chapel Hill: University of North Carolina Press, 1985.

———. "Political Compromise and the Protection of Slavery: Henry A. Wise and the Virginia Constitutional Convention of 1850–1851." *Virginia Magazine of History and Biography* 83 (Oct. 1975): 387–405.

Skipper, Ottis Clark. *J. D. B. DeBow: Magazinist of the Old South.* Athens: University of Georgia Press, 1958.

Smith, Conway Howard. *The Land That Is Pulaski County.* Pulaski, Va.: Edmonds, 1981.

Smith, Everhard H. "Chambersburg: Anatomy of a Confederate Reprisal." *American Historical Review* 96 (Apr. 1991): 432–55.

South-West Virginia and the Valley. Roanoke, Va.: A. D. Smith, 1892.

Stampp, Kenneth M. *And the War Came: The North and the Secession Crisis, 1860–1861.* Baton Rouge: Louisiana State University Press, 1950.

Starobin, Robert S. *Industrial Slavery in the Old South.* New York: Oxford University Press, 1970.

Stealey, John Edmund, III. "Slavery and the Western Virginia Salt Industry." *Journal of Negro History* 59 (Apr. 1974): 105–31.

Stearns, Peter N. "Modernization and Social History: Some Suggestions and a Muted Cheer." *Journal of Social History* 14 (Winter 1980): 189–209.

Stevenson, George J. *Increase in Excellence: A History of Emory and Henry College.* New York: Appleton-Century-Crofts, 1963.

Stover, John F. *The Railroads of the South, 1865–1900: A Study in Finance and Control.* Chapel Hill: University of North Carolina Press, 1955.

Striplin, E. F. Pat. *The Norfolk and Western: A History.* Roanoke, Va.: Norfolk and Western, 1981.

Stuckert, Robert P. "Black Populations of the Southern Appalachian Mountains." *Phylon* 48 (June 1987): 141–51.

Stutler, Boyd B. *West Virginia in the Civil War.* 2d ed. Charleston, W.Va.: Educational Foundation, 1966.

Summers, Lewis Preston. *History of Southwest Virginia, 1746–1786; Washington County, 1777–1870.* Richmond, Va.: J. L. Hill, 1903.

Sutch, Richard. "The Breeding of Slaves for Sale and the Westward Expansion of Slavery, 1850–1860." In *Race and Slavery in the Western Hemisphere: Quantitative Studies.* Ed. Stanley L. Engerman and Eugene D. Genovese. Princeton: Princeton University Press, 1975, 173–210.

Sutton, Robert P. "Nostalgia, Pessimism, and Malaise: The Doomed Aristocrat in Late-Jeffersonian Virginia." *Virginia Magazine of History and Biography* 76 (Jan. 1968): 41–55.

———. *Revolution to Secession: Constitution Making in the Old Dominion.* Charlottesville: University Press of Virginia, 1989.

———. "Sectionalism and Social Structure: A Case Study of Jeffersonian Democracy." *Virginia Magazine of History and Biography* 80 (Jan. 1972): 70–84.

Tatum, Georgia Lee. *Disloyalty in the Confederacy.* Chapel Hill: University of North Carolina Press, 1934.

Taylor, George Rogers, and Irene D. Neu. *The American Railroad Network, 1861–1890.* Cambridge: Harvard University Press, 1956.

Thelen, David. *Paths of Resistance: Tradition and Dignity in Industrializing Missouri.* New York: Oxford University Press, 1986.

Thornton, J. Mills, III. *Politics and Power in a Slave Society: Alabama, 1800–1860.* Baton Rouge: Louisiana State University Press, 1978.

Tillson, Albert H., Jr. *Gentry and Common Folk: Political Culture on a Virginia Frontier, 1740–1789.* Lexington: University Press of Kentucky, 1991.

———. "The Localist Roots of Backcountry Loyalism: An Examination of Popular Political Culture in Virginia's New River Valley." *Journal of Southern History* 54 (Aug. 1988): 387–404.

Trelease, Allen W. *The North Carolina Railroad, 1849–1871, and the Modernization of North Carolina.* Chapel Hill: University of North Carolina Press, 1991.

Turner, Charles W. "The Early Railroad Movement in Virginia." *Virginia Magazine of History and Biography* 55 (Oct. 1947): 350–71.

———. "Railroad Service to Virginia Farmers, 1828–1860." *Agricultural History* 22 (Oct. 1948): 239–48.

———. "Virginia Railroad Development, 1845–1860." *The Historian* 10 (Autumn 1947): 43–62.

———. "The Virginia Southwestern Railroad System at War, 1861–1865." *North Carolina Historical Review* 24 (Oct. 1947): 467–84.

Vance, James E., Jr. *The Merchant's World: The Geography of Wholesaling.* Englewood Cliffs, N.J.: Prentice-Hall, 1970.

Walker, Gary C. *The War in Southwest Virginia, 1861–1865.* Roanoke, Va.: A&W Enterprise, 1985.

Wallace, Lee A., Jr. *A Guide to Virginia Military Organizations 1861–1865.* Revised 2d ed. Lynchburg, Va.: H.E. Howard, 1986.

Waller, Altina L. *Feud: Hatfields, McCoys and Social Change in Appalachia, 1860–1900.* Chapel Hill: University of North Carolina Press, 1988.

Weingartner, Paul J., Dwight B. Billings, and Kathleen M. Blee. "Agriculture in Preindustrial Agriculture: Subsistence Farming in Beech Creek, 1850–1880." *Journal of the Appalachian Studies Association* 1 (1989): 70–80.

Wender, Herbert. *Southern Commercial Conventions, 1837–1859*. Baltimore: Johns Hopkins University Press, 1930.

Whitman, J. A. *The Iron Industry in Wythe County from 1792*. Revised ed. Wytheville, Va.: Southwest Virginia Enterprise, 1942.

Wilhelm, Gene, Jr. "Appalachian Isolation: Fact or Fiction?" In *An Appalachian Symposium: Essays Written in Honor of Cratis D. Williams*. Ed. J. W. Williamson. Boone, N.C.: Appalachian State University Press, 1977, 71–91.

Williams, Charles Richard, ed. *Diary and Letters of Rutherford Birchard Hayes, Nineteenth President of the United States*. 5 vol. 1922. Reprint. New York: Kraus, 1971.

Williams, Frederick D., ed. *The Wild Life of the Army: Civil War Letters of James A. Garfield*. Lansing: Michigan State University Press, 1964.

Williams, John Alexander. *West Virginia: A Bicentennial History*. New York: W. W. Norton, 1976.

Williams, T. Harry. *Hayes of the Twenty-Third: The Civil War Volunteer Officer*. New York: Alfred A. Knopf, 1965.

Wilson, Goodridge. *Smyth County History and Traditions*. Kingsport, Tenn.: Kingsport, 1932.

Wise, Barton H. *The Life of Henry A. Wise of Virginia, 1806–1876, by His Grandson, the Late Barton A. Wise*. New York: Macmillan, 1899.

Wood, Amos D. *Floyd County: A History of Its People and Places*. Radford, Va.: Commonwealth, 1981.

Wood, Walter K. "Henry Edmundson, the Alleghany Turnpike, and 'Fotheringay' Plantation, 1805–1847: Planting and Trading in Montgomery County, Virginia." *Virginia Magazine of History and Biography* 83 (July 1975): 304–20.

Woods, James M. *Rebellion and Realignment: Arkansas's Road to Secession*. Fayetteville: University of Arkansas Press, 1987.

Woodson, Carter G. "Freedom and Slavery in Appalachian America." *Journal of Negro History* 1 (Apr. 1916): 132–50.

Wooster, Ralph A. *The Secession Conventions of the South*. Princeton: Princeton University Press, 1962.

Wright, Gavin. *The Political Economy of the Cotton South: Households, Markets, and Wealth in the Nineteenth Century*. New York: W. W. Norton, 1978.

Wust, Klaus. *The Virginia Germans*. Charlottesville: University Press of Virginia, 1969.

Wyatt-Brown, Bertram. *Southern Honor: Ethics and Behavior in the Old South*. New York: Oxford University Press, 1982.

Wyatt-Brown, Bertram. *Yankee Saints and Southern Sinners*. Baton Rouge: Louisiana State University Press, 1985.

Yearns, Wilfred Buck. *The Confederate Congress*. Athens: University of Georgia Press, 1960.

Dissertations and Theses

Eller, Ronald D. "Mountain Road: A Study of the Construction of the Chesapeake and Ohio Railroad in Southern West Virginia, 1867–1873." M.A. thesis, University of North Carolina at Chapel Hill, 1973.

Gaines, Francis Pendleton, Jr. "The Virginia Constitutional Convention of 1850–51: A Study in Sectionalism." Ph.D. diss., University of Virginia, 1950.

Goldfield, David R. "The Triumph of Politics Over Society: Virginia, 1851–1861." Ph.D. diss., University of Maryland, 1970.

Grant, Charles L. "An Appalachian Portrait: Black and White in Montgomery County, Virginia, before the Civil War." M.A. thesis, Virginia Polytechnic Institute and State University, 1987.

Inscoe, John Cunningham. "Slavery, Sectionalism, and Secession in Western North Carolina." Ph.D. diss., University of North Carolina at Chapel Hill, 1985.

Klement, Frank Ludwig. "John Buchanan ('Scapegoat') Floyd: A Study in Virginia Politics through a Biography." M.Ph. thesis, University of Wisconsin, 1938.

McFarland, George M. "The Extension of Democracy in Virginia, 1850–1896." Ph.D. diss., Princeton University, 1934.

Musser, Carl Wilson. "Economic and Social Aspects of Negro Slavery in Wythe County, Virginia, 1790–1861." M.A. thesis, George Washington University, 1958.

Neely, Frederick Tilden. "The Development of Virginia Taxation: 1775 to 1860." Ph.D. diss., University of Virginia, 1956.

Noe, Kenneth William. "Southwest Virginia, the Virginia and Tennessee Railroad, and the Union, 1816–1865." Ph.D. diss., University of Illinois at Urbana-Champaign, 1990.

Rice, Philip Morrison. "Internal Improvements in Virginia 1775–1860." Ph.D. diss., University of North Carolina at Chapel Hill, 1948.

Richey, Thomas Webster. "The Virginia State Convention of 1861 and Virginia Secession." Ph.D. diss., University of Georgia, 1990.

Salstrom, Paul. "Appalachia's Path toward Welfare Dependency, 1840–1940." Ph.D. diss., Brandeis University, 1988.

Schlotterbeck, John Thomas. "Plantation and Farm: Social and Economic Change in Orange and Greene Counties, Virginia, 1716 to 1860." Ph.D. diss., Johns Hopkins University, 1980.

Sutton, Robert P. "The Virginia Constitutional Convention of 1829–30: A Profile Analysis of Late-Jeffersonian Virginia." Ph.D. diss., University of Virginia, 1967.

Tillson, Albert Holmes, Jr. "Political Culture and Social Conflict in the Upper Valley of Virginia, 1740–1789." Ph.D. diss., University of Texas at Austin, 1986.

Index

KENNETH W. NOE, a native of Southwest Virginia, received his Ph.D. from the University of Illinois. He is currently assistant professor of history at West Georgia College, Carrollton.